CLASSIC, ROMANTIC AND MODERN

CLASSIC, ROMANTIC
AND
MODERN

by Jacques Barzun

The University of Chicago Press

Chicago and London

The University of Chicago Press, Chicago 60637
The University of Chicago Press, Ltd., London

81   80   9876543

International Standard Book Number: 0-226-03852-1
Library of Congress Catalog Card Number: 61-14543

Few things are more benighting than the condescension of one age for another. . . . The historian needs something more than sympathy, for sympathy may be . . . pitying, contemptuous . . . it must be the sympathy of the man who stands in the midst and sees like one within, not like one without, like a native, not like an alien. He must not sit like a judge exercising extra-territorial jurisdiction.

—WOODROW WILSON, 1904

Contents

Contents

Preface to the Second Edition

If he is to be of use—and I have no use for any that is not usable—the cultural historian must lead a double life. He must see the strivings of past epochs with generous fellow feeling, and he must feel as well the needs—which include the lacks—of his own time. Out of the contrasts come, one hopes, the critical judgments that lead to truth.

This double exercise of the sympathies and of the mind's eye is perhaps harder to sustain in discussions of art, thought, and emotion than in those of past politics and social life, where the things discussed seem rather objects offered to our choice than parts of our intimate self, qualities of our being. In these privities the contrast of past and present may be uncommonly harsh and emotional accuracy correspondingly difficult. Such was the contrast between the cultural reality of 1830 and the mind of 1930. That is why, when I first wrote this book, I gave it the title *Romanticism and the Modern Ego*. It did not seem to me possible at that time to describe Romanticism truthfully without also characterizing the twentieth-century outlook which was its enemy.

In those two decades before the second world war, the nineteenth century was considered a regrettable interlude with but a few isolated figures to redeem it. The early, or Romantic part of that century was held in particular detestation and contempt: it was naïve, silly, wrongheaded, stupidly passionate, criminally hopeful, and intolerably rhetorical. The word "romantic" in fact stood for these defects wherever they might

be found, as well as for anything else suggestive of that remote generation which had either not lived in the world we
knew, or lived in it with all its senses stopped, including its
common sense.

These were the opinions, unchallenged by any of my friends
and mentors, that I found prevailing in the books and conversations of my early manhood, in the late 1920s and early
1930s. This was the teaching alike of the university and of the
literary journals. As for the artists to whom I listened on the
subject, they believed that the beginning of a return to sane
tradition came late in the past century, with the Impressionists.
The poets believed that the revolution in poetry had occurred
but a short time back, with Baudelaire and Rimbaud. The
musicians agreed: they found Beethoven portentous; they
despised Verdi and Berlioz, tolerated Wagner only as a comprehensive dictionary of chords, and based their own music
upon either the classic solidity of Brahms or the pure sensibility of Debussy. Sensibility, nuance, suggestiveness, and subtlety were the marks of true art, and this was enough to
disqualify Romanticism and its sequel Realism, which was
looked upon as an unsuccessful reaction against the original
error.

In the domain of abstract ideas, the state of mind was if
possible even more hardened. Professor Irving Babbitt of Harvard was only one of numerous publicists who demonstrated
the folly of Romantic thought in art and life. Rousseau, being
well known by name as well as a central influence upon the
Romantics, was the chief scapegoat. But it was also convenient
to attack the ideas of Coleridge and Shelley, the sexual adventures of Byron and Victor Hugo, the sentiments of Keats
and Leopardi, the autobiographical errors of Chateaubriand
and Berlioz, the religious vacillations of Schlegel and Newman.
When the centenary of Goethe's death occurred in 1932 he
received more abuse than conventional praise—an extraordinary reversal of custom. This was because scholarship, too,
was of the party. From its deliverances one learned that the
Romantics had bungled every opportunity: they could not
write scientific history; they misunderstood Greece, Rome, and
the Middle Ages; they lacked proper principles of archaeology,

philology, sociology, and psychology. Indeed, they spoiled whatever they touched. While they ruined religion and morals by their introspection and positivism, they endangered true science by espousing vitalism and pantheism. There was nothing to be said for Romanticism—or so very little that it seemed odd so much had to be said, over and over again, against it.

For autobiographical reasons that I have detailed elsewhere, I could not concur in this orgy of denunciation. As a student of history, and particularly of cultural history, which was not then a popular field, I thought I saw clear evidence that the twentieth-century notion of Romanticism was an illusion. I could sympathize with the need of my own time to break away from sentiments and techniques that had been well exploited for a full century. I could understand the irritation modern artists felt at the vocabulary and attitudes expressed in romanticist work. I was as readily sickened as they by the fifth-hand imitations of romanticism still found in cheap popular art, and I could appreciate the criticisms leveled by contemporary philosophers and scientists at the imperfections of their Romantic predecessors. But none of this seemed to me to justify the anti-Romantic animus everywhere encountered, and even less the distortion of historical facts to bolster it up.

As for a change of direction in our culture, I would have welcomed it, whatever its form—classical, primitive, or archaic. It struck me, however, that a true change would require a break, not with what had happened a century earlier or with its lifeless imitations, but with what had happened only thirty years before; that is, the break should be not with Romanticism, which was certainly of the past, but with Impressionism and Symbolism, which had done their work and could be deemed new and fresh only by virtue of a cultural lag. It is fortunately not the duty of the cultural historian to ordain cultural change. It is enough if he tells what he sees, and this I determined to do, waiting only for enough reflection and a suitable occasion.

A first, casual opportunity came in 1939, when I wrote for *The American Scholar* a short essay entitled "To the Rescue of Romanticism." The editorial obstacles I ran into, and the correspondence that followed publication, showed that I had hold of an explosive subject. I therefore looked for the chance to express my dissent at greater length. This occurred when I was invited to give the Lowell Lectures in the winter of 1941. I had just published a study called *Darwin, Marx, Wagner,* which undertook to trace our connections with the Age of Realism, and which had led me to study anew its Romantic antecedents, to give them, indeed, their due place behind the achievements of my three titular heroes. Having satisfied myself that the great revolution in thought, art, and feeling came at the beginning of the nineteenth century, not toward the end as everybody assumed, I resolved to set forth as clearly as I could what in essence the Romanticism of 1790–1830 was about, and how the succession of other -isms, down to and including Modernism, stood in relation to the first.

This attempt to give in short compass and against prevailing opinion a general view of a large subject was beset with difficulties. Looking back on my undertaking after twenty years, I am more than ever convinced of the desirability for the student or general reader of an "apperceptive mass"—in common terms, a large dose of information with which to fill out the abstractions he is so ready to accept or reject on their mere congeniality or the reverse. The trouble is, if one instructs and harangues at the same time, one's books grow large and forbidding. The innocence that kept me from making such a monster of persuasion was partly due to the circumstances of my teaching in Columbia College at that time. Beginning in 1934 I had been entrusted with a course in the thought and culture of the nineteenth century, and I was at the same time assigned to give with Lionel Trilling a colloquium on certain great books from Bacon to William James. Every Wednesday evening for two and a half hours we beat the contents out of some representative work with the aid of a dozen or so advanced students of literature, philosophy, history, and the arts. Six years of this exercise had accustomed us to every form of conventional belief in the public mind and to every tenable position in face of the facts. I not unnaturally came to think of these facts as common property. I thus left my book what it still is, a study, not a treatise.

When the work was ready for the press, after another three

years of our "colloquial" discipline, productive in us both of scholarly and polemical writing, I dedicated *Romanticism* to Lionel Trilling, not suspecting that our Wednesday sessions were acquiring the force of a lifelong habit and the ill fame of an institution. The fact remains that soon after our studies began to appear and our students to scatter, rumors began to be heard of the "neo-Romantic school at Columbia." This was of course absurd. "Schools" are not made by criticism but by new art, and Romanticism was old—else we could not have studied it as we did, for our pleasure and the instruction of those who cared to listen. As far as I can see, that intention was exactly fulfilled. For although Romanticism has become respectable again and most attacks now deal legitimately with its substance and not a phantom, no systematic review of the case has been conducted by opinion at large. The tone of textbooks has changed, gradually, and with it that of people concerned with art and ideas.

The demand for the present book (which I warmly rededicate to its Wednesday godfather) and its continued life here and abroad have been due to the teachers who have found it convenient to assign, sometimes in conjunction with one of Irving Babbitt's. This is done, I presume, so that the Romanticist mind and the rectangular may be seen side by side. But this unequal dialogue does not warrant the conjuring up of a rival school, even if to the present book is added Lionel Trilling's famous critique of Parrington's *Main Currents in American Thought*.

The gradual reconsideration of Romanticism was aided by causes more diffuse and hence more ubiquitous than books. The second world war *as war* was one such cause. It swept away "sophistication" and brought back the vividness of terror, love, and death: I remember certain people's sudden discovery after an exhibition of Gros, Géricault, and Delacroix that when these men painted massacres it was not make-believe, it was not "romantic," it was Romanticist reality.

In those twenty years also, the idea of cultural history, which was still a novelty ten years earlier, became acclimated. It bred an interest in the comparison of styles, and I had the satisfaction of seeing a main hypothesis of the present book—

namely, that cultural periods are united by their questions, not their answers—taken for granted as common knowledge. Since that time, historical revisionism and the diagnosis of periods have become a lively game, at once useful and entertaining.

What most concerns the man of today is, of course, where this abundance of historical explanation leads. If he is in truth the remote offspring of Romanticism, how does this help him find his way among the products of contemporary art and thought? Taste was a sure instrument when style was single. Only quality had to be sought. But in our esthetic jungle the intellect has a preliminary task which it can carry out only if it is historically informed, and this in a manner that links past and present.

That is why I have added to the chapters of the first edition an Epilogue that tells what seems to me to have happened in the arts since 1940, and what I am sure has changed in my own view of the meaning of the contemporary scene. For the rest, I have left the text substantially as it was, only removing a number of topical allusions and recasting sentences for greater brevity and clarity. I wish it were practicable for me to rework the whole and modify the statement of each subject in the light of an inevitably changed perspective. I would then give more space and a very different interpretation to nineteenth-century architecture. Carroll V. Meeks's superb book, *The Railroad Station*, has opened my eyes to many neglected facts and ideas, and I recommend the work as an antidote to my mistaken and inadequate remarks.

The main burden of my study, however, I find no cause to change. I still see the difference between the neo-classic Enlightenment and its successor, Romanticism, as fundamentally social and political. This may seem a double paradox, first because Romanticism is generally believed to pose an esthetic, not a political, question; and second, because "Romanticism in politics" is variously taken to mean the excessive individualism that leads to anarchy and the excessive authority that leads to tyranny. Rousseau is made to bear the guilt for both. When originally published, my thesis had to meet the plausible arguments of those who believed that German and Italian fascism were Romanticism resurgent. Others thought that Russian communism was the logical consequence of Romantic socialism and nationalism. Today, when threats to a passable life are found severally in mass culture, in the conservative revolution, and in the revolt of the beat generation, the temptation is again strong to explain and damn them all by reference to a new wave of romanticism.

These imputations are all correct insofar as they assert the reality of the political issue. But if we distinguish between historic and perennial romanticism as I try to do in Chapter I, it becomes clear that the tendency of historic Romanticism was away from authority and toward liberty, away from the acceptance of caked wisdom and toward the exploratory development of the individual, away from the secure fixities and toward the drama of the unforeseeable, away from monarchy and toward the sovereignty of the people. The classical Age of Reason has in mind an aristocracy even when the new enlightenment reaches down to the lower middle class, as it did in the French Revolution. Romanticism is populist (not to use the ambiguous word "democratic") even when the Romanticist, like Scott or Carlyle, preaches a feudal order. This divergence of Classic and Romantic corresponds to that which obtains in the conception of the individual: the eighteenth century entrusts everything to the intellect and loves Man abstractly, as an archetype, whereas Romanticism studies sensation and emotion and embraces man as he is actually found—diverse, mysterious, and irregular, which is to say, in the form of particular men and peoples.

It is accordingly not hard to understand why the systematic assaults against Romanticism most often come from the extreme right. It was logic and not accident that Irving Babbitt should see in Mussolini the hope of undoing Rousseau's work, even though the dictator's appeals to heroism might superficially suggest the Romantics' love of risk and daring. Today, the outcry against industrial civilization comes from those who feel threatened by the extent of the liberation begun in the French Revolution and acknowledged in Romanticism—the recognition of the people and all their vulgar works. Individualism, in short, leads to populism and thereby creates obstacles to its own survival. To put it differently, Romantic diversity ends by making men desire classical order, just as in the beginning Romanticism showed that the only possible life lay outside the classical trammels.

Such are the reasons why the many-faceted art and philosophy of Romanticism must be understood otherwise than through clichés and must be regarded first as responses to a political desire. If the movement also proposes to answer the psychological riddle—what is the nature of man?—that, too, is a way of stating the political issue. All political theories begin with a psychology, explicit or assumed, for the same reason that all revolutions want to control the mind. Romanticism has this merit over later revolutions that it was never an ideology. If it had been, it would long ago have been classified, put away, and forgotten, and I should never have had to write this book.

J. B.

August 1, 1960

I

Romanticism—Dead or Alive?

I

Romanticism is supposed to have died over a century ago. The French date its demise with false precision from the failure of Victor Hugo's last produced play in 1843. Others make the knell sound earlier or later, but the fact of death is rather complacently taken for granted.

And yet if one opens other books, equally reputable, and if one looks at the periodical press devoted to politics and letters, one finds that romanticism is considered still a living threat. It is held plausible to say that the "romantic view of life" is the enemy of reason, science, and democracy. The Romantic writers from Byron, Carlyle, and Goethe to their so-called neo-Romantic disciples, Nietzsche and William James, are quoted and rebuked as inspirers of the various totalitarian movements of this century. Rousseau is mauled from time to time by intemperate journalists and Hegel credited with the feat of having turned Germany into a militarist people. Romanticism, though "outgrown" and repudiated, seems still to be a force in the battle of ideas.

We are thus faced at the outset with a flat contradiction, which does not disappear but deepens and spreads as we go farther into the subject. Is romanticism really dead? How can totalitarianism be a "romantic" phenomenon when what we most deplore (and try to imitate) is its so-called political "realism"? How can the supposedly dreamy romantic individualists of early nineteenth-century Germany be the creators of the modern anti-individualistic state? And, more particularly, what have the romantic philosophers in common with James and Nietzsche, who spent a good part of their lives in combating them?

These are questions for the historian of ideas. But Romanticism, as we just saw, is not merely a topic for historians. It is a live subject for this age of social and cultural revolution and it poses practical questions: Is Romanticism native to the human mind or is it an aberration? If an aberration, what are its symptoms and how can it be dealt with? What likeness and difference are there between Romanticism a hundred years ago and Romanticism today? And if neo-romanticism has been the enemy at the gate since the nineties, what is the opposing view or tradition to adopt and fight for as our own?

All these questions take one thing for granted—namely, that everybody knows what romanticism is. The words "great romantics" or "German romantics" are used as if their meaning were perfectly clear and agreed upon by everybody. That is the impression infallibly gathered from reading books. The truth is that at least half the contradictions come from the tolerated looseness in this use of the term "Romanticism."

Somebody has said that it is a great convenience to have a number of words that will answer the purpose of ridicule or reprobation without having any precise meaning. "Romantic" is such a word. Others have served their turn: such words as "Puritan," "Jacobin," "Gothic." It is only lately that "Baroque" has been rescued from the vocabulary of abuse and returned to the uses of description. To attempt a similar rescue of "Romantic" may be unkind as well as foolhardy; it must seem like robbing the common vocabulary of a necessary word-of-all-work, a word which perhaps we cannot define, though when we use it "we all know what we mean." The answer to this objection is that when a password leads to our confusing friends with enemies it had better be changed.

To find a core of fixed sense in "romantic" and "romanticism" requires that we consider certain common aspects of a great many subjects. The quest takes us from political and social history to critical facts about poetry, the arts, and philosophy; and thence to matters of psychology, religion, and common belief. The reader may be bewildered at first to find in various contexts the names of men whose work and lives do not commonly come to his mind. There is indeed no reason why anyone who is not a specialist in the history of the Romantic period should know more than a few, but since these few may be different for different persons, according to their special interests, it is necessary to name whole battalions. My purpose is to illustrate general conclusions with historical examples and to make the conclusions of the survey testable by anyone familiar with at least some of the facts.

The necessities of the case will also compel me to use common critical words, such as "sentimental" or "rational" or "realistic," in a more precise and limited way than is usual; I shall of course indicate for each word the limits I mean to observe, and if at first this upsets the usual associations raised by these terms, I can promise that the context will make my meaning clearer and clearer as I proceed.

The excuse for this preliminary warning is that the subject of this book is not simply Romanticism, but the relations of Romanticism, Classicism, and what has come to be called the Modern. What I am about to discuss is not some vague literary and emotional outlook known as Romantic, but the meaning of a whole age as seen against the background of its close predecessor by yet a third age—our own. That is why the reader will not find here a chronological account of romantic music, or politics, or landscape gardening, as such. Rather, he will find an essay in cultural history and criticism linking past and present. Treated thus, Romanticism appears as something more than an isolated poetic movement in one country or another. It is a European phenomenon, occurring within certain historic dates and possessing certain characteristics.

If we wish to disinfect a word or an idea from casual and false associations, we begin by trying to define it. Unfortunately, definitions of romanticism already exist by the dozen and have remained without effect. One reason is that definition is not enough. We must also have a clear conception of the many proper uses to which a comprehensive term of this sort can be put. Because in the past many different things have been called romantic, some scholars have denied the possibility of giving a definition that will hold in all cases; or they have denied that romanticism stood for anything clear or solid. This is to play into the hands of the woolly-minded by suggesting that unless a word means one thing and one only, it can mean anything or nothing. Our daily conversation proves the opposite. A concrete word like "chair" can mean an article of furniture, a professorship, or the person who presides at a meeting: the context prevents confusion. An abstract word like "American" can refer to North America, to the United States, to the three Americas, and to all the conceivable things contained in any of these, from aboriginal Indians to a form of the English language: again, the context prevents confusion.

Now "romantic" has two distinct fields of application. In one sense, it refers to human traits which may be exhibited at any time or place. In the second sense, it is a name given to a period in history because of the notable figures that gave it its peculiar character. These two meanings are obviously related. A period has a given character simply because at that time a human tendency is dominant. A Romantic, a Puritan, a Rationalist, a Pietist, are not separate zoological species, but recurring varieties of human beings, distinguished from one another by the relative value they place on certain attitudes. But this differentiation by means of dominant traits does not exclude the presence of others. The Rationalist is not the only man possessed of reason, nor are the Puritan and the Pietist devoid of it—any more than the Realist or the Romantic. When we call the eighteenth century the Age of Reason, we only mean an age when men talked a great deal about reason and hoped that its conscious use would bring about a marked improvement in human affairs. Only a hardened literalist supposes the name to imply that the eighteenth century had a monopoly of rationality and that before and after men were unreasoning or unreasonable.

With the word "romantic" it is this kind of false implication that gets in the way of its descriptive use. Few speakers or writers stop to check the applicability of the term by seeing how well it will cover other cases that deserve the name equally with the one they have chosen. Take a familiar criticism of Byron. Here is a romantic, it has been said, who glories in the kinship between the energies of men and the wild forces of Nature. This is to legitimize wild passion; it is the mood of the lawless despot. Accepting this inference for the sake of argument, one may well ask, what does it establish about Romanticism as a whole? Suppose we take another poet who has an equal right to the title "romantic"—Wordsworth or Pushkin. Shall we then be able to forge the same link binding their views with those of a Hitler? And what about the "great romantics" in the other arts—in painting, in music, in dancing? Were they early totalitarians also? The difficulty of showing clear connections increases with each step that we take towards a more inclusive view. What actual relation is there between Keats's *Ode to a Nightingale* and *Mein Kampf*, or between Goya's etchings of the War of Liberation in Spain and the exploits of modern dictators in the same peninsula?

Usually, two ways are taken to evade this difficulty. One is to pick and choose among the romanticists those who are fancied to be "wholly" or "essentially" romantic—to choose a passage from Byron and drop out of sight all of Keats, Wordsworth, Shelley, Coleridge, and a hundred others. This is an admission of failure for any generality. Nor is it essentially different to say that only the German romantics are to blame for the new lawlessness. For, on that assumption, how did the dictators in other countries achieve *their* synthesis with no German tradition to aid them? And further, how is German romanticism different from the French, English, and Spanish kinds? The difference, if any, must be the source of the evil, and not the romanticism itself.

In other words, if we are committed to the view that an objectionable development in society is a new expression of historic romanticism, we must be able to show that most of the great men who lived a hundred and twenty-five years ago advocated or worked for that particular result. We must show that Goethe, Byron, Kant, Schiller, Carlyle, Emerson, Beethoven, Mickiewicz, Blake, Delacroix, Shelley, Schopenhauer, Heine, Berlioz, Pushkin, Scott, Dumas, Manzoni, Chopin, Lamb, Hazlitt, Thoreau, and perhaps a hundred other representative figures of the early nineteenth century, were pioneers of the totalitarian or welfare or other unwelcome kind of state. We can perhaps tolerate a few exceptions to the proposed generality, but obviously we cannot have more exceptions than cases in which the generality holds true.

The second way out of the impasse consists in saying that it is not in the romantics' expressed opinions or outward acts that we find the roots of militant tyranny. It is in the spirit underlying all romanticist work—whether it be a poem or a political theory. At this rate, Wordsworth's love of nature and Delacroix's love of a divided palette are equally dangerous to the future of democracy. On this same view, the liberal Byron and the conservative Sir Walter Scott were in the same party preparing the way for dictatorship. It was in them some secret but powerful germ which time has brought to full growth in the form of persecution and military imperialism.

This second hypothesis is no better than the first. It deals too much in abstraction, both when it talks about romanticism and when it reduces the transformations of modern societies to an advocacy of force and conquest. Indeed, the slightest acquaintance with the mere bulk of the subject matter involved in this comparison shows the frivolity of the supposition. But before examining romanticism historically and pragmatically, we must recognize one more ambiguity in the supposed relation between romanticism and the police state.

If one consults the accepted sources of information about romanticism, one is likely to be told that its outstanding feature is individualism. Romanticism places a high value upon the individual. According to some, it exaggerates the worth and powers of individual man. I am not questioning here whether this is true or not. This is what is *said*. Now then, how does mass tyranny embody romanticism? What do we find in the literature of both the extreme right and the extreme left but the condemnation of individualism as a disintegrating force? Where, in the present day do you find the romantic individual —the rebel, the eccentric, the egotist whom we so readily conjure up when we think of historic romanticism? If romanticism regards the individual as valuable, then we must find elsewhere the theory that glorifies the single-minded group, and produces the oppressed, collectivized, regimented nation.

II

By this time the reader should be thoroughly confused, for there is, of course, a genuine connection between romanticism and the politics of today. I have deliberately tried to reproduce the existing confusion in order to break up the casual and one-sided, yet persistent, association between the notion of romanticism and the various imperialisms, internal and external, which are fathered upon it. Neither the gifted men of a century ago nor a hidden something in their make-up will directly account for our bad world. Leaving till later the question of a link between romanticism and modern collectivism, I go on now with the questions that this linkage has raised: Who are the romanticists and what is the common bond that makes them bear a common name?

In English, the noun "Romanticism" gives two adjectives— romantic and romanticist. They are not commonly differentiated, but it is to be desired that they should be. We should then be able to tell apart the two distinct fields of application I have begun to distinguish: romanticism as an historical movement and romanticism as a characteristic of human beings. We should then say: "My friend X is a romantic" and "the poet Byron is a romantic*ist*." When we say *the romanticists* at large we should mean a number of men who lived at a particular time and place, and who did certain things that fixed them in the mind of posterity. However much they differ ideally or fought among themselves, Byron, Wordsworth, Shelley, Victor Hugo, Leopardi, Mickiewicz, and Schiller were romanticists. They received the name whether they liked it or not. Indeed, many romanticists vigorously disclaimed the title, like Delacroix, or accepted it for only half their work, like Goethe. In this sense, romanticism is a mere tag and not an adequate description. You cannot infer a man's personal characteristics, much less his opinions, from his correct labeling as a romanticist. What you can infer, we shall shortly see. Meantime, think of romanticist as a term comparable to "Man of the Renaissance." If someone had addressed the living Leonardo da Vinci and asked him: "Are you a typical *Renaissance-*

mensch?" he would have said, "What nonsense are you talking about?" Nevertheless, in any survey of the period, there is Leonardo, "typical of his age," and there is also the very different Michelangelo, his antagonist, but no less typical. They have been caught in the chronological net and historiography has stamped them with a convenient label.

With romanticism, the problem is complicated by the fact that during the romantic period small groups of writers or thinkers appropriated the general name to themselves. In Germany, for instance, scholars distinguish between Early and Late Romantic. But in neither of these groups will you find Schiller and Goethe. They stand apart, and yet Goethe's *Faust* is a bible of Romanticism. If you wish to find another German romanticist, Heine, you must look for him among the "Young Germany" group. This is the petty politics of cultural history. In French romanticism likewise, you will at one time find Victor Hugo and Stendhal on opposite sides, each representing a different shade of literary policy. In England, no one was called a Romanticist while living. All this is of great interest to the biographer or the historian of the several arts. But to use these temporary distinctions, as some have done, in order to blur the outlines of an era is to be guilty of obscurantism through pedantry. When the educated man has a true general conception of romanticism, it will be time to refine upon its details. For our present purpose, historic romanticism can be defined as comprising those Europeans whose birth falls between 1770 and 1815, and who achieved distinction in philosophy, statecraft, and the arts during the first half of the nineteenth century.

Some of course were born outside these arbitrary limits of time, like Goethe. There are others whose fame came after the terminal date, like Blake. A few more resist classification with the main body. So long as they are few these irregularities will not disturb anyone who remembers that we are dealing with an historical grouping. History does not arrange its products in bunches; it is man who seeks to put order into the disarray of history. Hence the ragged edges, but they are the edges of something central and solid.

We have then a group of men known as romanticists and

living as contemporaries between 1770 and 1850. What, besides time, binds them together? It is at this point that we pass
from *historic* romanticism to what may be called *intrinsic* romanticism. I have suggested that if an attitude becomes noticeable or dominant in a given period, its elements must be
latent in human beings, or in certain human beings, all the
time. In individual instances we call it this or that kind of
temperament. For example, it is probable that there are Puri-
tans at all times and places; but when a great many occur at
the same time and place, then we have a Puritan period. In
the same manner there are heroic ages and ages of luxury,
ages of classicism, of rationalism, of renaissance, of decadence
—and of romanticism. Not that each of these represents a fixed
type; rather it is a combination of human traits which for one
reason or another happens to be stressed, valued, cultivated
at a given historical moment. Why one attitude is preferred to
another is something for the cultural historian to explain after
the event, but *that* it is preferred is the reason for our being
able to speak of a romantic period.

This distinction between *permanent* elements in human nature and their periodic emphasis in history is the first of the
devices by which we can make more exact and serviceable
our use of the name "romantic." If, for instance, we hear William James called a romantic, we are entitled to say: "James
was not contemporary with Byron; what precisely have you
in mind when you classify them under the same head?" If, as
is likely, the answer given is: "I call him romantic because
of his irrationalism," the field is then open to argument over
the correctness of the description and over the propriety of
making one belief or opinion taken at random symptomatic of a
whole temperament or philosophy. The libraries are full of
books, usually written in wartime, and which show that from
Luther to Hitler, or from Fichte to Mussolini, or from Rousseau to Stalin "one increasing purpose runs." The demonstration is made by stringing together on one line of development
all thinkers who "believe in the will" or "believe in hero worship" or "believe in the divine right of the people." In these
works the intention of human ideas is disregarded for the sake
of finding a collection of scapegoats.

The history of ideas cannot be written so, like an invoice of standardized goods. It is a subject requiring infinite tact. On the one hand, diversity must be reduced to clear patterns for the sake of intelligibility; on the other, the meaning of each idea must be preserved from falsification by constant reference to its place and purport in history. It is strictly meaningless to speak of someone as "a believer in a strong state"—strong for what, for whom, by what means, against whom?

The same is true of irrationalism, which is only one of the alleged symptoms of the romantic temper. Granting that the connection between romanticism and irrationalism exists, in what direction does it point? And, to begin with, what is the meaning of irrational? To hear critics wax indignant over irrationalism in such highly organized persons as James, Nietzsche, Bergson, and Freud, one would suppose that they repudiated reason and behaved like maenads. One almost expects that their writings will be ungrammatical and demented. Instead of which one finds an extraordinary concentration of thought, a great skill in raising and meeting objections, and a solicitous care for order and form.

What is true of these four moderns who are supposed to be the fountainheads of neo-romanticism is true of their predecessors of over a century ago. They were not men of one book or one idea. Hence any reduction of their thoughts or accomplishments to a single notion is inevitably belied by the facts. It is an explanation doomed to swift and complete refutation at the hands of anyone possessing even a fragment of firsthand knowledge about the subject.

At this point I may state dogmatically what I shall show in the sequel, that romanticism is not equivalent to irrationalism, nor sentimentality, nor individualism, nor collectivism, nor utopian aspirations, nor love, nor hate, nor indolence, nor feeble-mindedness. Consequently if any of these human traits particularly excite one's disapproval one must call them by their proper names, and not shirk responsibility for the judgment by terming their manifestations "romantic."

If anyone should doubt that these attributes have been made the distinguishing marks of romanticism, let him simply turn to the sampling of usage given in Chapter X, or else consult any of a dozen popular biographies of the so-called "romantic figures." For pleasure and instruction one could do far worse than to go to the conscientious work by L. and R. Stebbins on the romantic composer Carl Maria von Weber. It is the best, most scholarly, and most intelligent book on the subject; but dealing as it does with a figure from the romantic period, it accurately betrays the prevailing idea of that movement. On the jacket of the book we find the unthinking echo of what is said within: "Weber was no romantic composer, but a serious hard-working musician." In other words, a romantic composer is one who does no work, and it is a wonder how the romantic school of music managed to produce what it did.

Dip into the book itself and you come across equally bewildering generalizations, such as this concerning a German duke of obviously unbalanced mind: "He . . . was either insane or the embodiment of the nth degree of early German romanticism—which, indeed, amounts to much the same thing." Here romanticism is insanity, but in the next sentence this sweeping condemnation is mitigated: "Certainly, he exemplified the school both in aversion to effort and in a behavior which followed the impulses of his subconscious without curb." In other words, the noble duke was a rake and an idler, like thousands of other men before and since the romantic period. What was specifically romantic about him? We are never told, and an earlier definition seems to describe the movement very differently. "There was a time," we are informed, when "a man could say, godlike, 'life is thus; but thus I will not have it. Standing on the intolerable reality I recreate.' This is the essence of romanticism."

Not satisfied with this essence, however, the biographers look for another in the possible "causes" of their romantic subject, in this case, Weber: "Was he a romanticist because of his convictions, or because he was dragged about by an unpredictable father, had no proper education and was nurtured on his mother's stories of the Catholic church?" There being no reasonable answer to such questions, another, equally plausible, is put: "Schelling's romanticized teachings exerted a strong influence upon him. Would a different philosophy have shaped a classicist instead of a romantic composer?" This is followed by a still deeper muddle: Schelling and Weber have each been philosophizing, but "it was impossible to write or speak openly of liberty . . . the contemplation of eternal problems was postponed for a freer age, and romanticism provided the usual escape." Schelling, I may mention in passing, was the famed author of a work on Human Freedom.

Now for a few comments on romanticism and the affections: "Their friendship was of a romantic nature and lasted until death. . . ." "He fell in love many times," [but] "not with the easy sentimentality of his fellow romantics. . . ." And to conclude, some judgments of value about a man who is admitted on all hands to be an ornament of the romantic school: "The German romanticist proscribed labor, but there never was a man who worked harder than Weber; the German romanticist was an introvert with a subjective mind, but Weber liked society and saw his creations with an objective eye." And lastly: "One cannot lightly disregard the judgments of the great romantics, Meyerbeer and von Weber."

The juxtaposition of these sentences gives them, of course, a ludicrous air, though this is not intended, nor do I mean to discredit the biography. If the book were mere journeyman work, the authors' treatment of romanticism might matter less. But their opinions are educated opinions, and the point of singling out sentences is that they faithfully represent the usual view. Not one reader in a thousand would dwell skeptically upon them as they occur in the midst of interesting and well-documented paragraphs. These pronouncements seem to state the accepted fact; which only means that their mutual inconsistency and inherent falsity have been so often repeated that we no longer notice anything wrong.

According to this so-called educated opinion, romanticism is insanity, escape, introversion, sentimentality, and laziness; but a given romantic is objective, hard-working, steadfast in friendship, a creator of lasting works and one whose judgment is not lightly to be disregarded. I pass over the superficial psychology that makes of a shiftless father, a Roman Catholic mother, or the German philosopher Schelling the decisive factor in the production of a romanticist musician. The belief here seems to be that a man's outlook is picked up by chance or put on casually like hat and gloves. This is part and parcel of that other belief that somehow a romantic is a creature wholly different from other men, the men we know and see at work. Which makes it a matter for surprise to the biographer when his romantic subject behaves rationally, works hard, shows lasting affection, and acts with judgment and integrity in his art.

III

Seeking a demonstration of widespread error in a particular book is not irrelevant to the promised definition of intrinsic romanticism. Just as in dealing with historic Romanticism it was important to show the difficulties that come from equating the upsurge against liberalism with Romanticism, so in dealing with intrinsic romanticism it is important to show the impossibility of matching up the term with the current commonplaces about irrationalism, sentimentality, and the like. I will go even further and say that none of the usual scholarly definitions, whether sympathetic or not, seems satisfactory. Romanticism is not a return to the Middle Ages, a love of the exotic, a revolt from Reason, an exaggeration of individualism, a liberation of the unconscious, a reaction against scientific method, a revival of pantheism, idealism and catholicism, a rejection of artistic conventions, a preference for emotion, a movement back to nature, or a glorification of force. Nor is it any of a dozen more generalities which have been advanced as affording the proper test. It is not any of these things for the simple reason that none of them can be found uniformly distributed among the great romanticists. Mention any such characteristic and a contrary-minded critic will name you a Romanticist who did not possess it; he may even produce one who clearly strove for the opposite. It is this truth that has led a number of critics to abandon the search—and to abuse romanticism all the more for not yielding up its secret on first inspection.

This is not to say that many of the tendencies enumerated in the textbooks were not present in the romantic age. They obviously were, and it is in romantic work that scholars have found them. But a collection of features defines nothing unless

it is common to nearly all the individuals examined. The error
has consisted in supposing that what unites an age are common
opinions and common traits. If this were true what would become of the war of opinions which characterizes every age?
If it were true, how could John Dewey and T. S. Eliot belong
to one and the same culture? If it were true, how could there
be any traditions handed down through time? There would
be, on the contrary, blocks of unanimous people holding the
stage for a century or so, followed by other solid blocks of an
opposite complexion.

In other words, what we want as a definition of intrinsic
romanticism is the thing that gave rise to—and that incidentally
explains—all the other attitudes I have enumerated. Why did
some romanticists attack Reason, why did some turn catholic,
why were some liberal, others reactionary? Why did some
praise the Middle Ages and others adore the Greeks? Clearly,
the one thing that unifies men in a given age is not their individual philosophies but the dominant problem that these philosophies are designed to solve. In the romantic period, as will
appear, this problem was to create a new world on the ruins
of the old. The French Revolution and Napoleon had made a
clean sweep. Even before the Revolution, which may be taken
as the outward sign of an inward decay, it was no longer possible to think, act, write, or paint as if the old forms still had
life. The critical philosophers of the eighteenth century had
destroyed their own dwelling place. The next generation must
build or perish. Whence we conclude that romanticism is first
of all constructive and creative; it is what may be called a
solving epoch, as against the *dis*solving eighteenth century.

Because the problem of reconstruction was visible to many
men does not mean that they all proposed the same solution, or
saw all its aspects in the same way. The divergences were
due to differences of temperament, geographical situation, and
special interest. A poet such as Wordsworth or Victor Hugo
saw the emptiness of eighteenth-century diction and the need
of creating a new vocabulary for poetry; a philosopher such
as Schopenhauer saw the illusoriness of eighteenth-century
hopes of progress and the need of recharting moral reality, with
suggestions for better enduring it; a political theorist like

Burke, who apprehended the wholesale destruction of the social order, had to propose an alternative means of change; a
thinker like Hegel, who was at once philosopher, political
theorist, and esthetician, saw creation as the result of conflict
in history and in the mind, and proposed nothing less than a
new logic to explain the nature of change. He then showed
how to use it for rebuilding on more lasting premises.

These men clearly cannot be made into a romantic *school*,
but they equally clearly partake of a romanticist *temper*.
More than that, they share certain broad predilections in
common, such as the admiration for energy, moral enthusiasm,
and original genius. It is because an era faces one dominant
problem in varying ways that certain human traits come to
be held in greater esteem than they were before. The task of
reconstruction manifestly does demand energy, morality, and
genius, so that the new passion for them was thus not a whimsical or useless trait in the romantics, but a necessity of their
position.

By the same logic, one is led to see that romanticism was
far from being an escape from reality on the part of feeble
spirits who could not stand it. The truth is that these spirits
wanted to change the portions of reality that they did not
like, and at least record their ideals when the particular piece
of reality would not yield—both these being indispensable
steps toward reconstruction. Our modern use of the term "escape" is unfortunately vitiated by smugness and double meanings, and one should refuse to argue its application with anyone
who will not first answer this question: "Suppose a primitive
man, caught in a rainstorm, who has for the first time the
idea of taking shelter in a cave: is he facing reality or escaping
it?" The whole history of civilization is wrapped up in this example, and a universal test for distinguishing creation from
escape can be deduced from it. The mere fact that a man is
seen making for a cave or heard declaring his intention to build
a hut is not enough; what is he going to do *then?* What is the
relation of that single act to his whole scheme of life? Applying
this test to romanticism, we shall see that on the whole it was
infinitely more constructive than escapist.

But, it may be said, other periods faced with the task of

creation have not produced cultures resembling romanticism. The very system which preceded romanticism and came to an end with the eighteenth century was created around 1650 and it took the form that we call classical. True enough; so to understand romanticism we must add to the fact of its creative mission the further fact that it conceived its mission in a certain way. It conceived it in the light of a great contradiction concerning man. I mean the contrast between man's greatness and man's wretchedness; man's power and man's misery.

It would be tedious to give citations from one romanticist after another in which this contrast is noted and commented on. But one cannot help being struck by the repetition of this independent "discovery" in the works of the romantic epoch. It obtrudes itself in many forms and contexts, whether or not one is seeking common elements in the many-sided activities of this generation of men. Moreover, there are other supporting facts outside the period that are worth remembering. Where do we find the most famous expression of this contrast in the nature of man? Surely in the *Thoughts* of Pascal, historically not a romantic, but a seventeenth-century author whose whole temper, social and religious, made him a dissenter in his own time. Whom does the classicist Voltaire most persistently attack in his own eighteenth century? It is Pascal. Voltaire wrote an *Anti-Pascal* and looked upon him as the most dangerous enemy of the Enlightenment. In much the same spirit Condorcet brought out an altered edition of the *Thoughts*. When does Pascal emerge in his full stature? and with his full meaning?—not until 1843, in the first half of the romantic nineteenth century.

The core of the conflict is Pascal's view of man's fate—the antithesis of greatness and misery—which leads him to an analysis of art and society as merely conventional and relative; justice on one side of a river, Pascal points out, becomes injustice on the other. In short, man is first of all a creature lost in the universe and he *makes* his shelter, physical, social, and intellectual. This was bound to be also the view of the later romanticists, who found themselves at odds with the remnants of the old regime, without protection from the universe, and forced to build a new order.

But in a thinking reed, as Pascal terms man, the contradictory state of having powers and of feeling one's weakness is not one to be dumbly endured. Some resolution must be found even while the protective social order is being built. Indeed, many men feel that the imperfect social order is inadequate to resolve the inner conflict. Hence the search for a philosophy, a religion, a faith, which will transcend and unify the felt disharmony. Pascal himself, as we know, found this faith in ascetic Christianity. The romanticists, a hundred and fifty years after Pascal, found it in many different objects of belief—pantheism, Catholicism, socialism, vitalism, art, science, the national state. To fill out the list would be to give a catalogue of the contributions of romanticism. What matters here is the interconnection of all these faiths through their roots in the double problem of making a new world and making it in the knowledge that man is both creative and limited, a doer and a sufferer, infinite in spirit and finite in action.

If we must now answer the question, Is romanticism dead or alive? we are able to put forth some tentative answers that may lead us in the sequel to a decided Yes or No. In the light of the distinctions here proposed, *intrinsic* romanticism, that of the particular individual, is just as alive today as it has ever been; it is bound to be, for it is a human constant. But if we are tempted to say that the present age is still, or again, romantic, we must make sure that our period is one of creation according to the view of man I have just described. If modernism is thought classical, we must show in what sense it is in reaction against its predecessor. And if the cultural present is of some third kind, its relation to the other two must be made clear. None of this can be done until we understand somewhat better the historic romanticism of a century and a half ago.

II

Rousseau and Modern Tyranny

I

Our current ideas, it is clear, fail to encompass the many diverse facts that we call Romanticism, and the search for a common denominator in some single product of the movement is futile. Hence the need to re-create the atmosphere of the situation in which the romantics found themselves—that of having to fashion a new set of institutions and conventions after the decay and destruction of the old—and also to recapture, if possible, their vision of man as simultaneously great and wretched.

To be sure, the shorthand expression "creating a new world" has an air of paradox and courts contradiction. I can imagine some disciple of the late Irving Babbitt receiving with a skeptical smile the notion that there is any connection between romanticism and the creation of a social order. "Rousseau," he would say, "Rousseau is the father of romanticism: no one disputes it. And Rousseau is also the father of anarchy, the destroyer of established social values, the scorner of civilization, the preacher of individualist license, the man who said 'Back to Nature' and who idolized the Noble Savage in hopes that we would once again take up savage ways. Moreover," the anti-Rousseauist would add, "Rousseau comes historically before the Revolution. He died eleven years before its outbreak and therefore can have felt none of the anxieties that assailed the men who came fifty years later, after the Napoleonic Wars. Except for his sentimental yearnings, Rousseau's work is wholly destructive."

These are indeed the commonplaces of Rousseau criticism and the only thing the matter with them is that apart from the dates involved they are contrary to fact. It may seem strange that after a century and a half of writing and arguing critical opinion about Rousseau should still be in the dark about what he meant. I incline to think that on the contrary it was to be expected: Rousseau and Romanticism have not yet become a part of the dead-and-buried past. They are still among our living concerns, as I have already suggested and as nearly all casual references to Rousseau's ideas will demonstrate.

The work of Rousseau has been so pervasive that everybody knows enough to cite and abuse him. He has affected in one way or another all those who have come after him, so that to speak of his influence without further word is not enough. We must know *what* influence: a would-be disciple may adopt the sentiments of one chapter or book; another, those of another; yet the parts may belong together and convey something different when so taken. With Rousseau and the romanticists, precisely because they are architects on the large scale, nothing less than the tendency of whole works or movements will supply correct conclusions.

But the uncertainty about Rousseau tells us something besides, which may be even more important. Because of his widespread influence, everybody thinks he knows what Rousseau said, without taking the pains to study him. He is hotly arraigned and seldom read. There are libraryfuls of books about him, but not a dozen, perhaps, represent his views accurately. In the beginning his enemies were blinded by prejudice, and he has not yet been abused intelligently. With the weight of routine, the first crude notions have superimposed themselves upon the author's text, so that when he says "white" everybody reads "black."

If we can forget catchwords for a moment, we may be able to recover the impression Rousseau made on his contemporaries and near successors in time. Let us begin by asking why we should be so angry—his critics always are—when speaking of him and his ideas. Surely, it is because he was glorified by Robespierre and the Revolution, because he was of the eighteenth century and yet not with it; lastly, and perhaps mainly, because he wrote his *Confessions*, which a political theorist should never do. The man himself, or what we think is the man, together with his immediate reputation, stands between us and his ideas; for although no one is bound to like Rousseau, it is hard to resist impatient disgust on finding a man who has not even the grace to make his crimes splendid, but relates contemptible faults such as we too, perhaps, have been guilty of. On top of this, Rousseau pretends that he is a good man—obviously a contradiction; in fact, *the* contradiction we noted before between man's consciousness and power of good and his frequent conviction of sin—a very Christian contradiction.

But having read *The Confessions*, what do we gather from them beyond this opinion of the author about his own character? The book holds an important and neglected clue, not only to Rousseau's work, but to the history of the old regime. We can see from *The Confessions* that Rousseau was the only man of genius who traversed eighteenth-century society from the bottom to the top. He was the only one who did not take root and stay fixed. In the course of his career, he was by turns a vagrant, a seminarian, a successful composer, a hack musician, an artisan, the secretary to an ambassador, a servant who waited on table, a distinguished guest in the houses of the great waited on by others, the protégé of the nobility, the husband of an ignorant working girl, the friend of Voltaire and the Encyclopedists, the enemy of their atheism and frivolity, the bête noire of the Jesuits, a Protestant, a Catholic, a persecuted Frenchman, and a patriotic citizen of Geneva. By the accident of fortune, Rousseau was forever being dislodged from the society that his mind examined and condemned. He was in effect outside it, because he had passed through so many of its artificial niches; he got an anthropologist's view of his culture, which is why, belonging to the eighteenth century and using eighteenth-century ways of arguing like any rationalist, he was bound to become the enemy of the *philosophes*, the prophet of revolution, and the prophet of a new world.

In short, Rousseau achieved by chance and genius that sense of primitive nakedness in the face of nature which Pascal had felt a hundred years before, and which the romanticist generation was to feel half a century later. With them all it was of course a primitivism born of ethical judgment. None of them physically stood on barren ground amid heaps of literal ruins. There was to all appearances a flourishing civilization about them. Hence Voltaire's anger at a man who seemed to be throwing overboard all the gains of civilized man—for what? For an ideal order only dimly perceived in the future. But history proved Rousseau right about what was alive and what was dead. That astute observer of modern society, Mr. Peter Drucker, though an anti-Rousseauist, judges the situation as I do when he says in *The Future of Industrial Man:* "They [the rationalists] tried to define man as within the laws of physics. But Rousseau saw man as a political being acting upon impulse and emotion. . . . No doubt he knew more about politics and society than all the Enlighteners taken together. His view of man in society was realistic. . . ."

If this is contrary to the usual view of Rousseau as a "visionary dreamer," so much the worse for the usual view. It was rather Voltaire, Helvetius, Condorcet, and the rest—whose work we may still admire for its courage and intelligence—who were spinning the agreeable dream of painless improvement. By 1762, the date of Rousseau's *Émile* and *Social Contract,* the rationalists were of the past, doomed with the society in which they held the position of critical and destructive profiteers.

II

Having seen Rousseau's unique position as a man whose youth belonged to the Enlightenment but whose maturity was of a later age, we can now return to the slogans associated with his ideas. The most famous is certainly "Back to Nature," a phrase he never used but which serves as a very condensed way of putting his objections to the artificialities of a superannuated regime. Rousseau never intended that we should return to living in caves and wearing skins. He clearly saw that this is neither possible nor desirable, but he also saw that the complication of life resulting from civilization disturbs or destroys in man something valuable; something that cannot be flouted with impunity. This he calls nature. He found, for example, that in his century children were dressed and reared as if they were miniature men; he found the mothers of the well-to-do classes sending their infants to baby farms, which resulted in neglect and high mortality; he found pregnant women lacing themselves in corsets. He saw a useless nobility and clergy given over to gambling, intrigue, and etiquette. He saw a widening gap between idle rich and toiling poor. Tragic or trivial, these were social symptoms as indicative of the precarious state of France as the complex inefficiencies of public finance or the 285 different codes of custom law which defined the rights and controlled the relations of men.

Now all this can be called artificiality and complexity without suggesting that its extreme opposite—the absence of all laws—is what Rousseau desires. But if he attacks existing conventions as artificial and yet declines to return to savagery, what does he propose; what is a natural society? The symbol of the tree, which Rousseau often uses, gives us a standard by which to apprehend what he means by nature. The tree is a natural product. It remains natural even if "artificially" watered, and tended, and protected by the hand of man. But if the hand of man begins to twist the growing plant into fanciful shapes for topiary ornament, the tree suffers from artifice. It will not do to argue that storms and north winds will twist trees in nature itself. We recognize these as freaks, and so does the tree, which no matter how acted on always seeks to grow straight upward. In other words, what Rousseau means by nature is the given norm that we can discover under any deformation, like the eighteenth-century gentleman's hair under his wig.

This discovery of the "nature" of anything is always tentative, never absolute; but the desire to discover it is a guide which old civilizations generally neglect. Layer upon layer of convention acts as a cushion which society is reluctant to give up. He who proposes to strip off the upholstery and see whether the framework is still solid earns the name of anarchist, for it is always easier to combat the idea of man's natural wants than to remake society and fulfill them. One of the anecdotes told of Voltaire expresses the contrasted viewpoints very neatly. A young man had written a bad book and was berated by the philosopher: "Why did you do it?" "A man has to live," said the young man. "I don't see the necessity," retorted the old rationalist. The rationalist is "rationally" right; there is no philosophical necessity at work to keep a young man from starving. But there is something in a young man—Rousseau would call it his nature—that prompts him to use every means not to starve, even the desperate means of writing a bad book.

Similarly with old-established societies that neglect the claims of whole classes of men to life, liberty, or the pursuit of happiness: Reason, custom, legality, are against any change. But something in mankind breaks through the crust. It is in pointing this out and in making plans for a new society that Rousseau is revolutionary, that he is an individualist and an apostle of freedom. He attacks legality in the name of human nature, just as men have always done when social conditions became absurd or unbearable or both.

But he is far from attacking laws as such. The first sentence of Rousseau's political treatise, the *Social Contract,* is often quoted in support of the view that he is an anarchist. That sentence runs: "Man is born free; and everywhere he is in chains." That is to say, we can suppose the newborn infant to have no notion whether he is a prince or a pauper, but he grows up into one or the other. But do not go on to infer that Rousseau wants to break all chains. It is sheer assumption to believe that that opening sentence is a call to revolt. Read what follows right after: "One man thinks himself the master of others, but he is an even greater slave than they." In other words, society binds all the freeborn in a network of duties and compulsions. "How did this change come about?" asks Rousseau. "I do not know." (Those who repeat that Rousseau believed in the historical existence of a social contract, please note.) "What can make it legitimate? That question I think I can answer."

Rousseau's *Social Contract* is thus an attempt to make clear under what conditions social chains are legitimate, to reconcile the rights of free individuals with the requirements of society. Men have a will to be free ("To renounce liberty is to renounce being a man," says Rousseau) but they are compelled by their nature to live together in society. So far from believing that society as such is bad, here is what Rousseau says about the passage from an imaginary pre-social condition to the civil state: It "produces a very remarkable change in man, by substituting justice for instinct in his conduct, and giving his actions the morality they had formerly lacked. Then only, when the voice of duty takes the place of physical impulses and the right of appetite, does man, who so far had considered only himself, find that he is forced to act on different principles, and to consult his reason before listening to his inclinations. Although in this state he deprives himself of some advantages which he got from nature, he gains in return others so great . . . that did not the abuses of this new condition often degrade him below that which he left, he would be bound to bless continually the happy moment which took him from it for ever, and, instead of a stupid and unimaginative animal, made him an intelligent being and a man."

Thus speaks the philosopher who is still universally believed to have glorified instinct and repudiated reason, to have scorned society and urged the free pursuit of physical impulse. This is also the man whose works are widely supposed to be one long rhapsody, addressed to the emotions and defying sober analysis. Such are the imaginings of ignorance. Anyone who has the time to read the 123 small pages of the *Social Contract* will soon convince himself of this truth. He will find a closely reasoned and concisely put statement of what can make social compulsion legitimate, that is to say a statement of what constitutes the good society.

But the bare words "social compulsion" and "legitimate chains" have frightened another group of critics—readers of Rousseau, but blind in one eye—who have decided that Rousseau's *Social Contract* is simply a charter of despotism. In our day it is these critics who find in the totalitarians the apt pupils of Rousseau. To clear up this second and opposite misrepresentation, one need not follow Rousseau's deductions about law and government. It is enough to say that he favored a mixed form which he called "elective aristocracy" and which corresponds to our modern representative systems. Pure democracy—the Swiss or the New England town meeting in which all citizens govern—he thought too pure for an imperfect world and unworkable on a large scale.

Underlying these opinions are the more important principles applicable, in Rousseau's view, to all governments. They are two in number—first that a true social order must "express the general will," and second, that each citizen being "a member of the sovereign," he obeys himself when he obeys the dictates of society. The abstract form of these propositions serves a double purpose. In an age of censorship and persecution like the eighteenth century, the generalizing tone permitted Rousseau to make a covert attack on an absolute monarchy composed not of citizens but of subjects. Again, the theoretical form was a way of providing for a variety of local situations. Rousseau was not dictating a form of government, but giving a statement of what an intellectually and morally respectable society must live up to. No one can appreciate the need for first principles better than ourselves, living as we do in a time of upheaval, of boasted new orders, and of promises of welfare dictated by a sense of men's natural wants.

But what does Rousseau mean by the term "General Will"? It is easy enough for us to understand how society exists to guarantee individual rights, and why the concrete form of these rights must differ with different times and places, but how can the individual who finds himself in a minority, for instance, be said to obey himself? It seems as if, on the contrary, his wishes are being violated and his rights trampled upon. This is the hard nut to crack in any theory of government. The wishes of the governed and the good of the state are so often two separate things. To meet the difficulty, Rousseau distinguishes between the General Will, which is equivalent to the good of the state, and the Will of All, which is the majority opinion at any given time. At that given time, nobody can know absolutely what the good of the state is, and majority opinion must prevail. This opinion can turn out right or wrong. The test of it is pragmatic, it appears in the sequel. As an illustration, take Lincoln's decision to make war on the seceding states. In Lincoln's view, this means of saving the Union expressed the General Will, and we are now in a position to see that Lincoln was right. But the many individual wills were far from unanimous. Against him were the secessionists and the anti-war group in the North. Lincoln had to levy war on the former and to use compulsion on the latter. He had, in Rousseau's words, "to force them to be free." It was equivalent to saying: "You will wish to have done this; therefore, as your elected representative, I am forcing you to do it while there is yet time."

This is the point where Rousseau's accusers charge him with propounding a tyrannical doctrine. The answer to the charge is that any doctrine can be put to bad uses. The parables of Christ became text and pretext for the Inquisition. In Rousseau, the whole bent of the argument shows that the outcome he desires is the utmost individual freedom; or, better put, the utmost degree of individual self-direction and self-control. As G. D. H. Cole has said: "He takes his stand on the nature of human freedom; on this he bases his whole system, making the will of the members the sole basis of every society." Will, here, is the opposite of force, which, as Rousseau takes pains to point out, creates no right.

But Rousseau is above all a concrete thinker who does not for a moment forget the existence in society of conflicting wills. He is not content, like the later Utilitarians, to offer as a guide an empty "greatest good of the greatest number," nor, like the Marxists, to assume that the interests of one class can automatically represent the interests of all. Consequently he suggests as a guide the notion of a General Will which ideally expresses the will of each individual in the society. In practice, the opinion that prevails is most often a compromise that satisfies no one fully, though it is more acceptable to each than any one of the particular wills: hence its name of *general* will.

The fact that such a will can only be roughly ascertained puts the political problem as it is and as it ever will be. There is no way of bridging this gap between theory and practice, but the recognition of its existence is the best way to reduce it to a minimum. Just as the imperfect efficiency of a steam engine does not invalidate the theory of mechanics, but, on the contrary, knowledge of theory improves the construction of steam engines, so does Rousseau's theory serve the ends of practical government.

What makes it hard to think of Rousseau as both reasonable and creative, revolutionary and practical, is that we approach him with a series of unhistorical images in our mind's eye. We think of him as "a romantic who loved country walks," and we jump to the conclusion that he could not see reality; we think of him as an old man with a persecution mania and this blinds us to the thousands of accurate observations that he made—not only in political science, but in education, philosophy, botany, and music. We are not prepared, in short, for a many-sided genius when we have been told to expect a vague rhetorician. Perhaps ignorance is a good preparation for only a very few pursuits. Many people seem to think, for example, that Rousseau invented the Social Contract theory and that it proves him a fool, when as a matter of fact it is as old as Aristotle, and Rousseau disposed of it once and for all. He used it because it was the mode of thought of political theorists in his day and for two hundred years before his time.

Other critics show by their remarks that they think John Locke, because he was an Englishman, and Montesquieu, because he was a lawyer, were more "hardheaded" than Rousseau. But Locke's timidity and inconsequence do not bear comparison with Rousseau's grasp of fact, any more than does the sentimental utopianism which Montesquieu displays whenever he leaves ancient times. Rousseau, to be sure, owes something to both Locke and Montesquieu, but he belongs to the tougher tradition of Hobbes and Machiavelli, whom he supplements and perfects by showing that they do not go far enough. They show the necessity of government at all costs; he shows the possibility of reconciling government with liberty—this is his distinctive contribution, and that is why no one who reads them and him, bearing in mind the historical conditions affecting their respective aims, can possibly deduce tyranny as the logical fulfillment of their devices.

I have been speaking of political theory. When, in order to take up the challenge of Rousseau's detractors, I refer to the doctrine of tyranny, I mean its political methods: force, arbitrariness, the war against individual expression about the Gen-

eral Will, and so on. Insofar as totalitarianism asserts the need
of satisfying neglected human wants, it is of course in the
tradition of Rousseau, and so are the western democracies
when they espouse the welfare state. The whole quarrel in
political science is about the way to reconcile the legitimate
demands of the individual and the legitimate requirements of
the group. And on this point we should observe that Rousseau,
like most of the Romanticists, is a proponent of balance—of
contradiction, if you will—rather than of unity achieved at the
expense of one or the other legitimate claim: proof enough
that the romantic style of doing things is precisely the opposite
of the totalitarian.

III

Rousseau is not, of course, the only political philosopher of
romanticism laboring under a cloud. Fichte and Hegel are
often made to share his guilt, and if nowadays we hear less
than we used to about Edmund Burke's "reactionary thought,"
it is because certain attempts to refurbish conservatism have
made the old song ridiculous even to self-repeating liberals.

This is not the place to give a full account of Burke's or
Fichte's or Hegel's ideas on government, nor are my remarks
those of a disciple. There is much to object to in their doctrines, but before criticizing any doctrine it must be seen in
historical perspective. What is that perspective? At first blush,
Burke and Rousseau are opposites. Burke attacks Rousseau by
name in the *Reflections on the French Revolution* as one of
those abstract politicians who think they can create governments on paper. Since Burke fought the French Revolution
and Rousseau has been accused of fomenting it, the two men
are deemed genuine antagonists. But they also have been
classed together as romanticists. Which of these two connections is the more fundamental?

There is no question that Rousseau is trying to build a new
society from the ground up; we have just seen in what sense
this is true. Burke, on the other hand, sees history as the only
maker and remaker of societies. For him the continuity of
tradition, the link between one generation and the next, are

such compelling forces that he must be a rash man who would cut them asunder and leave himself defenseless in the face of nature. To state this is to show the fundamental point on which Burke and Rousseau agree: their view of man is the same—a concrete creature existing in a particular environment, shaped by nature and by history, dependent for his very existence upon the existence of society, and yet having to change social forms as time and need require.

When the Revolution broke out, Burke watched its first steps with approval. He believed the French monarchy badly in need of reforms, but slow ones, a few at a time, and guided by experienced legislators. His approval turned to disgust and despair when he saw what he thought was reckless upheaval. Thirty years before, Rousseau had said: "How can a blind multitude, which often does not know what it wills, because it rarely knows what is good for it, carry out for itself so great and difficult an enterprise as a system of legislation? . . . This makes a legislator necessary." Both Burke and Rousseau grapple with the problem of making changes, but whereas Burke thought them feasible by an alteration in tradition, Rousseau, closer to the source of the evils, knew that the monarchies themselves were bringing about their own death. One must agree with him that revolutions are far more the work of those in power than of those who seek to gain it; and Burke's notions of what could have been done in France were in fact illusory.

But it is not difficult to see why the two men judged the case so differently. Burke was accustomed to the British method of appealing to the historic rights of Englishmen. He thought it dangerous to appeal to natural rights which everybody knew to be convenient fictions. What Burke forgot was that the appeal to historical rights is just as great a fiction. When Sir Edward Coke argued for Parliament against the King in 1634, he had to invent Magna Carta. I mean by this that he took one of a series of documents having little or no applicability to the case in hand and manufactured the relevance. "How much better," you may say, "than having a revolution." Yes, but six years after Coke, the English *had* their revolution, followed in due course by dictatorship and military rule under Cromwell. Moreover, Rousseau's horizon was a little wider than Sir Edward Coke's. Suppose a people has not even a Magna Carta to twist to new uses. What historical rights can it appeal to? Those of Englishmen? They have no validity outside England. No, if the world is some day to be free and reasonably well governed, as Rousseau hoped, the appeal for making it so can only be to natural, that is to say, universal rights.

While the divergent procedures that seem proper to Rousseau and Burke can be explained by their respective situations, their unanimity appears in their common assertion of the organic, as opposed to the mechanical, character of the state. Burke stresses the genetic aspect of continuity: the state lives in its subjects, who inherit it as well as continually re-create it. Rousseau stresses the function of the will of the citizens: they are responsible human beings in whom all sorts of conflicting impulses have to be harmonized, and the state is the greater harmony expressing the equally conflicting wills of its members. This goes counter to the rationalist hope of devising "a few simple laws" that every sensible man will respect. Against the notion of abstract Man, both Burke and Rousseau —and later de Maistre—maintain the reality of diverse men. Thinking as a lawgiver, that is, as a statesman, Rousseau blames Peter the Great for having tried to make Englishmen and Frenchmen of his subjects when he ought to have made Russians. And for the same reason Rousseau refused to propose a best form of government for all mankind; when he was consulted by Count Wielhorski on a proper constitution for Poland, or again, for Corsica, he gave in each case advice that Burke would have approved, that is to say, advice at once practical and principled and which took account of history.

Burke's position, then, does not contradict Rousseau's; it parallels and adds to it by supplying all the color of history and example which Rousseau's strictly theoretical design did not permit him to use. But this did not prevent Rousseau's influence from reaching men who were steeped in historical considerations, and indeed caught in historical catastrophes. I refer particularly to Fichte and Hegel, and more widely to the German School so frequently abused.

The principal charge against them is that they desired a

strong, unshakable state and preached the submission of the individual to it. They drew the idea of submission from Rousseau, we are told, and they drew the idea of the immortal state, greater than the individual, from Burke: romanticists all. Quite so. But one is entitled to ask what other theoretical choices men can make, given the facts. Does not the state survive the individual? And is it not a source of protection to those living and to be born? If so, is not submission to the state desirable, as well as essential to its continuance? These principles are not specifically Germanic or romantic, even though they were made vivid and explicit in romantic Germany. The error is to suppose that the principle of coercion necessarily means wicked, unjust, inhuman coercion. In democracy as we understand it, the compulsion of the laws, the right of eminent domain, the imposition of taxes and military service, sometimes even the enforcement of vaccination and other health measures, are so many applications of the principle that the state can, does, and must coerce the individual.

The difference between one state and another consists in the degree to which this coercion follows general rules, and further, in the degree to which the general rules are made by those to whom they apply. Without going into the details of political programs, it can be said that nowhere in Fichte or Hegel is there anything to indicate that they favored arbitrariness and despotism. On the contrary, the ideas they inherited from the Enlightenment, plus those that they acquired direct from Rousseau or from him through Kant, made them veritable pillars of liberty and moral righteousness. So true is this that for thirty years after his death, Hegel was considered throughout reactionary Europe as a dangerous liberal and an agent of revolution. If subsequently his insistence on a cohesive state was used by others to establish tyranny, the utmost guilt with which he can be charged is that of overemphasis.

But there is even a good reason why Hegel, Fichte, and their peers committed this error. They had before them the same menace of despotism that we fear again today. The menace was Napoleon, and Napoleon had to be dealt with. It was the need to defeat him that lent to their utterances that harsh militant tone. Napoleon was the tyrant, the aggressor, the man who tramped in and out of Germany at will, who ruled through puppets over enslaved provinces. To defeat him and drive him out was the first dictate of self-respect. Hence Fichte's *Addresses to the German Nation,* Stein's great internal reforms, and the resulting wars of Liberation waged from 1806 to 1813. The times called for unity, a strong state, the merging of individual interests into a common overriding purpose.

One must remember also that culturally, and not merely politically, Germany had suffered French overlordship for a century and a half. In these circumstances, freedom could only mean political and cultural nationalism. When Fichte said that there would never be a cultural Germany until there was a political Germany, he was speaking from experience and without aggressive purpose. But a territory cannot be freed from enemy occupation without aggression; so that practical necessity grafted aggression upon a move toward freedom. When we ask what Fichte's ultimate goal was, we find that he hoped the human race would some day unite itself into a single political body, in which the benefits of culture would be extended to all without distinction.

Again, when Hegel summarizes the course of history as a progress in three stages toward freedom—first the stage of the Oriental despot who alone is free; then that of the ancient city-state, where only the masters of slaves are free; finally the modern period when all men are free—there is no reason to suppose that he was insincere and secretly plotting the enslavement of his people and the world. On the contrary, in his *Philosophy of Right,* published in 1821, he demanded representative institutions for his country—a full generation before they were granted. In the year of his death, a favorable article of his on the then pending English Reform Bill was suppressed by the Prussian censorship. He cannot therefore have been what he has often passed for—a Prussian propagandist. His final view of the state was very explicit. Since the time of the Revolution, he believed, the peoples of Europe had become deaf to the voice of freedom and had swung from mob tyranny to princely despotism. A settled, conservative order was therefore the first requisite of freedom.

All this should be admitted for the sake of clarity, if not of justice, even by those who, like myself, are repelled by Hegel's philosophy as a whole. But there is more to say, for with a bland disregard of the facts, many western Europeans continue to believe that *all* German political theory is for the state and against the individual. This overlooks the tradition begun in the 1790s by Wilhelm von Humboldt's *Treatise on the Limits of State Action,* to which John Stuart Mill expressed indebtedness for his own *Essay on Liberty* half a century later. Immediately after Humboldt came Kant's outspoken and courageous tract on Religion, which contains the axiom that "men only become ripe for liberty when they are set free." Kant's next political work was his *Philosophy of Law,* dealing, among other things, with the individual's inalienable rights, of which the most important is that of being considered an end in himself and not a means to an end; and this was followed by the famous *Project for Perpetual Peace*—so famous that few people know how practical some of its provisions about diplomacy, armaments, finance, and foreign intervention really are.

From Kant, the true liberal tradition passed into the hands of the historian and politician Dahlmann, whose writings animated the generation that strove to win representative government and failed in the Assembly of 1848. It is from this failure that sprang the contrary movement toward the absolute state. Its first theoretical outline was given by Treitschke in 1860, and its definitely militaristic contents were not added by him until after Bismarck's successful war against Austria six years later. There are undoubtedly some points in common between the theories of Treitschke and his followers, on the one hand, and those of the generation of Kant, Fichte, and Hegel: they all write about the State, for one thing; but the emphasis, the final goal, and the means are nonetheless radically different in the two groups. Nowhere in the earlier men do you find individual freedom held negligible and aggrandizement and war regarded as goods in themselves. Which leaves as the single important idea held in common the so-called mystical view of the state—a view which liberals rarely share.

But what does it mean to accuse a man of being mystical about government? Searching as they did for a metaphysical absolute, we are told, the conservative romanticists found it embodied in the state. And they proceeded to worship that very earthly institution to the detriment of Habeas Corpus and the Bill of Rights. This is a true indictment of certain extremists, like Adam Müller, whose importance in his own day has been exaggerated. But let us for the sake of argument, admit the general charge as true and see what the alternatives are. I shall take up later the curious fact that the objectors to this particular absolute cherish one of their own which they would strictly enforce if they could. At this point I would only draw attention to the fact that it is not only Germans and romantics who have waxed mystical about human government. All ancient classical peoples made religion and the state one institution. Later it was Bossuet, a French Catholic Bishop in the classical seventeenth century, who gave the best account of the divine right of kings. In England, Hobbes, who was neither royalist nor Parliamentarian, called the state "a mortall god" and was in such awe of it that he forbade revolution. Burke's feeling was only a little more secular, yet he has never been accused of wanting to replace the Constitution by a tyranny.

Nor were these mere superstitious beliefs, for what the divine-right theory of kingship expresses is the double mystery of society's being and beginning. It is because no one can explain its beginning, and because this unknowable origin must nonetheless be discussed, that a "state of nature" and a "social contract" were invented, long before Rousseau. It is because the bare continuance of society is no less a mystery that its divine character has so often been proclaimed. Who but a god could ordain a condition of things in which a few rule the unruly many and use the strength of the many to accomplish this, the power deriving from a tacit faith which is stronger than any laws and yet which a moment's disorder may shatter beyond repair? No wonder that from the dawn of humanity, peoples have worshiped their kings and lawgivers, and that in more modern times secular thought has transferred the worship to the abstract marvel of the machine. To this day, and for the same reasons, the question whether any government can subsist without a common religion—by which I do not mean a common theology—remains an open one.

The romanticists had seen the breaking of nations and the tumbling down of kings and thrones. Historically they were quite exactly in the position of Hobbes. Some of them were tempted like him to sink their whole faith in the state, provided a strong and just one could be created. They knew how a society went to pieces and what had previously held it together, namely, the mystery of custom. They knew that force alone could hold nothing—witness Napoleon; but that heroism and leadership could transfigure a given nation—witness, again, Napoleon.

After Napoleon, kings had lost their prestige, and sovereignty had descended to the peoples of Europe. Who would lead them and according to what rules? The voice of the people was traditionally the voice of God, but now more than ever there was need for a protecting order—chartered, constitutional—which would resolve man's primitive distress: alone, he is wretched and weak; in society his individual powers are released and multiplied; he can be not only strong but happy. He can purge his selfishness through devotion to tasks that transcend his short life and temporary interests. The state, in brief, can become an object of reverence like any other, and as such can direct the energies of men. The use that is made of these energies, and not the fact of their having been directed, is the pragmatic test by which a nation can be judged. The error of linking Rousseau with modern tyranny, like the error of linking Romanticism with modern Germany, consists in neglecting this test, while recklessly filling the broad principles of philosophers with the particular contents of subsequent history.

III

The Classic Objection

I

Two conclusions have so far emerged from our concern with romanticism. One is that it is a complex movement, whose direct connection with any doctrine in our own day cannot be asserted offhand or lightheartedly. The other is that romanticism has to do with creating a new society different from its immediate forerunner. Since we ourselves are living in an epoch of travail, perhaps of creation, and since there is fear of what some are pleased to call a new romanticism, we must, before going further, attend to the pre- or anti-romantic outlook; the old order which romanticism left behind when it repudiated—as the phrase goes—classicism and rationalism.

Given the native absolutism of the human mind, we may take it for granted that every epoch looks for unity—unity within the human breast and unity in the institutions sheltering man. Now the straightest path to unity is to choose from all possible ways of living those that seem to the ruling powers most profitable, most sensible, most general; and to enforce these as a code for public and private behavior. The laws soon give rise to attitudes by which any man may shape his feelings, and this in turn brings about a ready understanding among men. For no matter how arbitrary, conventions are useful and can be relied upon in proportion as they are held inviolable.

Such a system produces stability in the state and with it all the attributes of the static: fixed grandeur, dignity, authority, and high polish; while in the individual it produces morality and peace by showing him that values are rooted in the universe, rather than dependent upon his fallible and changing judgment. This, I take it, is the view of life properly called "classical," irrespective of whether it is enforced upon Europe under Louis XIV, or advocated anywhere today by the proponents of a new or old order. It is an attractive view and it draws out the best in those who make themselves its masterbuilders. It calls for intelligence, discipline, unselfish renunciation of private desires, a sense of social solidarity, and punctilious behavior towards other members of one's own caste.

From these premises, it follows that everything the romanticist thinks and does is wrong: far from taking the short cut to unity and peace, he insists on the reality of double-mindedness and self-contradiction. He denies the beauty and fitness of the conventions that bind men together and prefers the loose human diversity. Sharply aware of his own desires, he argues that the social rule is oppressive and unjust, so that he becomes, potentially at least, an anarchist. Being an anarchist in an anarchical world, he places a high value on effort, strife, energy. He is therefore in the position of constantly bewailing a condition for which he is solely to blame: Having refused all help from social conventions, his art, philosophy, and religion are bound to remain diversified, many-shaped, chaotic —hence unsatisfying.

This, I believe, is a fair copy of the classic objection—classic because it has been so often uttered and because it has been uttered in the name of classicism. In common speech, certainly, the sentiments aroused by the word "classical" are those of repose and serenity, while the connotations of "romantic" suggest restlessness and disorder. It is perhaps inevitable that something of these associations should always cling to these two words; but it is desirable for the moment to make a conscious effort at forgetting them, in order to look upon both classicism and romanticism historically. Instead of two neatly paired abstractions, of two contrasted ideals falling into familiar formulas, consider classicism and romanticism as recurring facts. Let us try moreover to imagine some concrete case for every generality and to generalize from the examples we are about to take up.

For the contrast I began by describing is obviously and

falsely heightened. It takes the abstract perfection of classicism and matches it with the concrete imperfection of romanticism. If the comparison were historically fair, we should properly expect the men of a classical age to be as completely happy as it is possible for humans to be; and we should expect the men of a romantic age to kill themselves en masse, like lemmings. But this has not happened. The wails of the classical gentlemen about existence differ in tone, but not in subject matter, from those of the romanticists; and beneath the difference in tone we shall find certain facts which afford a better test of cultural meanings than the routine antitheses about *the* classicist and *the* romanticist.

To begin with, the opponents of romanticism are strong on generalities but rather weak on particular cases. This is indeed consistent with the other tastes that make them prefer classicism. It is because they are bewildered by romanticist concreteness and diversity that they seek refuge in the simplicity which classicism achieves by generalizing and abstracting. And here comes the pragmatic test: how far can abstracting and generalizing be carried as a device for organizing society? Clearly some unity of opinion, some common ground, is indispensable to every social order. Romanticism does not deny it, either in theory or in practice. The romanticists may have defied certain conventions, but they did not go about naked. They praised originality but they did not talk each in his own private language. Still, let us suppose for the sake of argument that on the basis of some degree of uniformity one desires to abstract and generalize, so as to build a stable classical order. One decrees that Man is a clothed creature, whose proper, because logical, language is French, and whose destiny is to live according to the Christian religion under an hereditary monarchy. How far can one go without meeting some actual instance that defies the universal rule? The world being what it is, not very far. There are then two courses to follow: one is to remove the exception by pretending that it does not count; the other is to remove it by enforcing conformity.

The reasoning here proposed is not so fantastic as it seems. It is neither a straw man nor an imaginary instance, but simply one feature of the historic ideal embodied in seventeenth-century French classicism. The absolutist temper of that century removed the "exception" of the unclothed man by calling him a savage "who does not count," while the unorthodox habit of speaking a foreign tongue was removed by declaring French the universal language and successfully imposing it on all Europe.

This suggests that if a just comparison is to be made with the historic romanticists, we must look not at a theoretical classicism found in books or fancied in ancient Greece, but at an actual classicism found at work in modern history. This is another way of saying that we must look behind the Versailles façade of the Age of Louis XIV, with its alliance between an absolute monarchy and an absolute church, and assess the work of the half-century 1661–1715, which established a new order and succeeded in enforcing it upon manners, behavior, language, art, and thought. This classical age followed appropriately upon a period of political disorders, national disunity, and dynastic troubles. Once established, it entered upon a career of territorial aggrandizement and it spread its culture by snobbery and force of arms to the rest of Europe. The pattern of conformity came to England with the restored Stuarts who had lived in exile at the French court; and everywhere in the following century it evolved into a cosmopolitan classicism, during which its ideals became less and less compelling or productive, until the ground was cleared for the romantic revival.

To sketch in this way the career of a modern classicism is to treat it as it were from outside. Within, the first important fact confronting us is that classicism must begin by making, by manufacturing, its unity. Then, when this artificial unity has been enforced long enough to have become habitual, classicism is sure that it has been found ready-made in nature. This explains why the classical period used the two words Reason and Nature interchangeably, and why the romanticists, in repudiating classical Reason, had to give Nature an entirely different meaning.

What lent support to the seventeenth-century view that reason and nature are one is that the classical scheme of society coincided with a great scientific epoch; an epoch, moreover, specializing upon the one branch of science most congenial to the classical temper. I mean mathematics. For mathematics also abstracts and generalizes and yields simplicity and certainty while appearing to find these ready-made in nature. Seeing the beautiful demonstrations of Descartes and Newton as they explained the heavens with their coordinates, the great classical minds sought to rival this perfection and simplicity on earth. Philosophers used the geometrical method to arrive at moral and religious truth; social scientists reduced government to mechanics; the tragic muse imitated the tight deductive gait of Euclid; and I am not merely playing upon words when I say that poetry itself adopted one common meter as if scientific accuracy depended upon it. In all the imponderables of life, conduct, and art, the test was no longer the flexible, "Is it good, true, or beautiful for such and such a purpose?" but "Is it correct?"

As the classicists are wont to boast, the tremendous pressure of all these restrictions and rigidities produced some magnificent expressions of human genius. Racine and Boileau, Dryden, Swift, and Pope, Lully, Rameau, and Handel, the English portraitists and the French landscape school, created an abundance of great works to which we return with ever-renewed pleasure and admiration.

Yet there is to this brilliant period a darker and a neglected side. It is surely no accident that Pascal's *Thoughts*, written at the height of classicism, but undermining it, should begin with a distinction between the geometrical mind and the intuitive. Pascal's actual phrase to express the latter is *esprit de finesse*, which means the ability to distinguish and deal with concrete things, with living beings, as against the geometrician's ability to manipulate abstractions and definitions of the nonexistent. The geometrician's universe is articulate, colorless, and clear-cut; the *esprit de finesse* on the contrary sees the color, continuity, and indefiniteness of things. The *esprit de finesse*, in short, is the instrument of romanticist perception, though romanticism does not necessarily begin and end in the realm of concrete detail.

The two types of mind contrasted by Pascal are alike capable of subtlety and greatness, but the geometrician works in a closed universe, limited by his own axioms and definitions; the romanticist works in an open universe, limited by concrete imperfections—imperfections which have not all been charted, which may change, and which need not be the same for all men. Classicism is geometrical in its assumption that human shortcomings must be disregarded in order to be corrected, correctness being stated in the form of an exact rule. Romanticism is *finesse* in the belief that exactitude is only a guide to thought, less important than fact, and never worthy of receiving human sacrifices. Classicism is therefore stability within known limits; romanticism is expansion within limits known and unknown.

An enforced choice at this point would, it is true, probably still incline us toward the classical as meeting more nearly the requirements of such a wayward creature as man. Since man wants certainty and stability, it seems better to have known limits and known ways of moving towards them. As a seventeenth-century English poet, Robert Herrick, phrased it under the title *Rules for Our Reach:*—

> *Men must have bounds how farre to walk; for we*
> *Are made farre worse by lawless liberty.*

But there is a great doubt concealed within the safer choice: does a geometrical order yield stability when imposed on life? The question can perhaps be answered by comparing this same seventeenth century with the agreeable fictions that are current about it. Modern critics who are avowed enemies of our century and the last, yearn for the classical order as having given to the best men full scope, high honors, and true peace. Under classical rules, they say, the artist is not a rebel at war with society and his public; he satisfies a settled taste and is a willing supporter of the established regime. Under classical morality, the good man is reasonably happy; he is not, as with us, driven by the chaos of manners and codes into morbid guilt and fanatical efforts at reform. Lastly, under classical religion, the human mind finds an unshakable embodiment of its own permanent values, making impossible that modern freakishness or irresponsibility of belief which turns every man into a puzzle or threat to every other man and robs the state of all cohesiveness. In a word, the classical order acts as an infallible balance wheel to steady the human emotions.

Yet on looking at the classical centuries in biographical detail, one is struck by the amount and kind of ill-repressed human feeling beneath the crust of serenity and politeness. The number of converts to the forbidden religion of tears, self-mortification, and enthusiasm which goes by the name of Pietism was considerable. They include Pascal, Racine, and Fénelon. The names of Mme. Guyon and of the convent of Port-Royal will suggest many more; and a famous chapter in Voltaire's *Age of Louis XIV* tells us in a satirical vein about the unhappy quarrels and tribulations of those the historian mocks as fools and bigots. Far from keeping a religious balance, Louis XIV and Mme. de Maintenon themselves ended their reign as extremists in superstition and devoutness, an excess which swung the early eighteenth century into libertinism and atheism.

As for the standard comparison between the classical geniuses, thoroughly in harmony with their age, and the romantic rebels divorced from their society, it is simply not true. To take France alone, the first case we meet is Corneille's compulsory retirement after his quarrel with the Academy. Some may feel that Corneille was a belated romanticist harking back to the Renaissance. We must then recall Racine's struggles with his critics and the cabals which cut off his career at thirty-eight. Another genius, La Fontaine, was forgiven his nonconformity only because he seemed a child, a "natural," who loved the woods, and would not be acclimated to the only classical life —city life. Molière himself, supposedly the great interpreter of classical moderation and social sense, harbored a dissenter within. It was the dissenter who created the Alceste of the *Misanthrope* in his own image, who maintained the tradition of popular speech against refined diction, and whose death robbed the world of a projected satire on the highest classical product, the courtier.

The poets were not alone in feeling out of joint with the times. What we find among the philosophers, from Descartes to Voltaire, is one long story of persecution and flight from authority, only a little less violent than the harrying out of the Huguenots after the Revocation of the Edict of Nantes.

Because of the force of authority in all departments of classic life, it has become a commonplace that the romantic cry for freedom reveals an egotist. We take it for granted that the classic ego is silent if not subdued. But this is mere forgetfulness on our part. Compare the prefaces of Boileau, a classicist, with those of Victor Hugo, a romanticist. Contrary to your expectations, you will find that whereas Hugo is chiefly concerned with the principles of the artistic battle he is waging, Boileau seems to be interested only in reporting the praise that has been lavished on him and in disputing the statements of fault-finding critics. Hugo is "objective," historical-minded, occasionally grandiloquent; Boileau is "subjective," autobiographical, downright pettish. Or again, turn to Racine's prefaces—there are usually two to each play, the first rather grumpy and quarrelsome about the play's reception, which was seldom satisfactory; the second more complacent, because, after all, Racine knows what he is worth.

I am not saying, of course, that Racine and Boileau were egomaniacs. I believe rather that the reason their egotism seems so personal and small is to be found in the very nature of the classical scheme of things. It is the worst of the classicist beliefs that all true judgments are absolute and universal. As the King rules, so is the law. By extension, what is decreed by that vague abstraction, polite society, must be correct; for standards are common and public and there is no such thing as individual taste. In reality the polite world is a single cabal or critic. Hence any attack on an artist is fraught for him with grave consequences. Unless repelled it may mean ostracism, because society pretends to be unanimous. In any case it means battle, which explains the fate of Corneille and Racine, and the narrow escapes of Molière and La Fontaine. Indeed, the story of Poussin's or Bernini's misadventures with officialdom, and the function of the Royal Academy under the dictatorship of the First Painter to the King, Charles Lebrun, form a tale of coercion, jealousy, subservience, and war against all but mediocre talents, such as must give pause to the most sanguine neo-classicists. Pascal himself was not secure in his private retreat from a classical church and state jealous of all individualism.

In other words, the classical hierarchy maintains an unruffled front behind which all the fighting passions of men go on just as usual. But these passions take an especially heavy toll because there is no legitimate shelter in some other group —a second, or third, or fourth party—based on diverse interests and tastes. For the artist, the classic society is like a disunited family that is compelled to live together in a single room. There is hatred but no fair field for it. At the same time the issues lack magnitude; they are personalities. To read the memoirs of Saint-Simon gives one a painful impression of frivolity, even of immaturity at the root of the system. His admirably drawn figures are like schoolboys, kicking and cuffing one another under the table while the royal master is not looking.

II

These conflicts of authority and individual wills are not peculiar to classicism; only their form, and the pretense that no conflict is there. All of which naturally brings up the classical antithesis between Reason and Emotion. With its bent towards social unanimity how does classicism cope with man's emotions? Classicism does not of course deny their existence. It merely says that for the sake of decency certain feelings only can be exhibited—pleasure, amusement, ridicule, surprise, a few others—and these in their mildest form. For the same reason, gestures, fervor, eccentricity, must be suppressed, so that the social stage—the salon or the court—shall be peopled by human beings whose contacts will resemble those of perfectly smooth and well-lubricated ball bearings. With this ideal, incidentally, go some admirable rules of conversation which it would be well for modern man to meditate. But the trouble with the social device of repression throughout is, again, that there is no outlet, no elsewhere, for the force generated by pressure to expend itself, either harmlessly or productively.

This force, it may be said, has no right to intrude itself on society's attention. It is for the individual to dispose of it, since it is, by definition, irrational. More than that, it is *the* Irrational. Granted. But it is precisely called the Irrational because it cannot be argued out of existence, "it" being the blind and resistless force that we call life. Abstract reason is here simply irrelevant. Rather we must look for the socially accepted channels that may help drain off these energies. Whether admitted or concealed, these channels exist.

What investment, so to speak, could the classic century make of its fund of unreasoning passion? Taking for granted the ancient tradition of love-making, we discover several other institutions for expressing emotion. One excellent object of enthusiasm was the person of the King. Whoever thinks the romanticists worshiped heroes foolishly had better see for himself how much time and effort went into deifying the *Roi Soleil*. Certainly there is no extravagance in the nineteenth century comparable to the folly uttered and acted out when Louis XIV crossed the Rhine in 1672. One would suppose he had actually fought a battle and built a bridge like Caesar. His virtue, his grandeur, his words, his appetite, his form—nothing seemed too slight to deserve exaggeration. Perhaps the nation was worshiping itself through the King: it was a time of aggressive imperialism; the fact remains that it was hero-worship, and concentrated upon a non-hero.

At all times, in spite of his title of Most Christian Majesty, the monarch was reverenced—and painted and sculptured—as a pagan emperor-god, and the state followed imperial precedent by exacting (or purchasing) from its most brilliant talents the most profuse expressions of praise. The King could see his figure reflected from every wall and outlined in every square. In an Academy presumably devoted to letters, it was customary rather than strange to hear a new appointee—often an ecclesiastic who had never published a line—signalize the cultural greatness of the regime by saying:—

What have I been doing thus far? Why have I spent so much time admiring in Antiquity examples of virtue which I deemed without equal? Our age has gathered them all up, greater and more pure, in the person of the monarch to whom Heaven has subjected us for our

greater happiness . . . [and to whom we owe] a great
state better organized in all its parts, order more solidly
established . . . our frontiers more gloriously extended,
our enemies more promptly conquered, our neighbors
put in greater fear or respect towards us, . . . everywhere a more perfect union between the Head and the
Members. . . .

All these great and wonderful qualities . . . united in
him whom we have the honor to obey . . . will hence-
forth furnish me with a nobler object for my admiration
and my studies, and a fitter subject for my praise than
any of those I have found in ancient history.

Though the pension system will account for much of this
adulation, we must remember that even without bribes flat-
tery is a binding medium between the layers of classical society. For in its effect upon the emotions the theory of rank
serves a double purpose. According to it, each man is absolutely better and nobler than the man below him, hence energy can go into emulation, *noblesse oblige*—and social climb-
ing. But at the same time, the single code common to all men
of honor restores a kind of equality and releases a certain
amount of passion, by giving egotism an outlet through the
point of honor.

King-worship, love-making, intrigue, etiquette, dueling, will
certainly take up a good deal of slack in the sphere of the
irrational, but there were still other socially approved channels for feeling in the seventeenth century. The playhouse—
not quite so orderly then as now—was one. Watching public
executions was another, a pastime which in eighteenth-century England degenerated into the worship of the highway-
man. The life of leisure and the constraints of politeness
encouraged pleasures that were violent and exhausting. Sport
embraced gaming, hunting, and the playing of murderous
practical jokes; not to mention lavish entertainment, which was
often so extravagant that the expense ruined the host if the
King did not rescue him in return. In all these it is not the
thing itself, but the lengths to which it is carried that is a significant comment on "reason."

Such were the energetic manifestations of feeling tolerated under classicism. There were also more passive ones. The literature of the seventeenth century, we must not forget, was not limited to the high tragedies and comedies that we still read. The age consumed a great quantity of long-winded romances about Grecian heroes, shepherds and shepherdesses, swooning lovers, and marvelous adventures. Books like *The Great Cyrus* and the *Astrea* were not read by the lower classes but by the aristocracy; they were not confined to France but were translated or imitated abroad. Parlor games grew out of such reading, and nature imitated art to the pitch that Molière records in *Les Précieuses Ridicules*.

Lastly, classicism had to recognize, though perhaps it did not relish, two flaws of temperament that we are likely to forget in speaking of classical balance. One was melancholy, a familiar yet half-hidden manifestation of the strength of the feelings. The other was vindictiveness. We should like to know more about the settled sadness of the moralist La Rochefoucauld, whose melancholy, as he tells us, came not only from his constitution, "but from elsewhere." We ought also to ponder the strange irresoluteness of Dryden's faith, the true source of Swift's "savage indignation," and the mental depression which the young Alexander Pope suffered during his four years at Binfield. Perhaps Pope recovered by main strength of Newtonian reason. Certain it is that in *The Dunciad* he discharged passion enough for a lifetime. Yet characteristically this passion was the undiluted one of hatred, turned upon men whose crime was either to have offended him or to have remained lowly and poor. Finally, in the supposed paragon of sound eighteenth-century common sense, Dr. Johnson, emotional troubles and the fear of death were so deeply implanted that a sympathetic critic can only describe him as "melancholy almost to madness, radically wretched, diseased, indolent," and unpredictable in his actions.

Historic classicism is therefore not the blessed epoch that some modern critics like to imagine. Without taking Pope or Racine or Dr. Johnson as typical—for they are the finest products of the age and its best recommendation—we can nevertheless infer something from so much covert rebellion, hate, and misery. The least we can infer is that classicism does not necessarily bring peace to the individual and stability to the state. Making "admirable rules" is one thing; enforcing them, another; and still another, having them enforced upon oneself by the eternal knaves and fools whom Racine suffered or Pope pickled in vinegar.

If it is objected that the facts I have presented are only the by-products of a fine distillation, I fully agree. No one should argue that classicist art, philosophy, or science are diminished by stating the conditions under which they were created. Nor is personal taste involved. I for one enthusiastically admire many of the seventeenth-century masters, and am not so foolish as to think less of Johnson as a critic because he showed psychiatric symptoms. The argument is not about the undisputable merits of classical genius; the argument is about the feelings and behavior of representative classicists, and the political, social, moral, and esthetic forms within which they worked. The point is quite simple: the usual comparison between classic and romantic depicts a wonderfully ordered greenhouse as the nursery of the former and a desperate battleground as the ungrateful soil of the latter. That comparison is false.

More than that, the catchword "tradition," which is monopolized by the proponents of classical order, helps to conceal the important fact that seventeenth-century classicism was nearly everywhere a break with European national traditions and a return to an imaginary Graeco-Roman past. It was just such another "break" as that of the Renaissance before, and Romanticism after. Classicism naturally borrowed from the Renaissance, but looked upon itself as civilized order replacing barbaric chaos. Quite specifically, the French classicists were asserting their independence from the Italians who had been their masters during the previous century and a half. But whether in politics or art, nothing could be further from the *ancient* classic spirit than the products of seventeenth- and eighteenth-century Europe.

To be sure, poets, painters, and academic critics ceaselessly invoked the ancients and pretended to follow them humbly, but the rules they tried to respect and enforce upon one an-

other were as arbitrary and as "original" as those of any "revolting" romantic. It is precisely because modern classicism
was an original creation, and not a copy, that it deserves to
be called great. It differed from romanticism in seeking greatness through the adoption of common forms which it tried to
make exclusive. In this sense it is "traditional" and resembles
other periods of thoroughgoing orthodoxy—incuding the earlier phases of ancient civilizations—where individualism in art,
action, or belief is sternly repressed.

Pro-classical critics are wont to say of some romanticist they
half admire, "If only he had had discipline!" It would be easy
to retort of a classicist, "If only he had been let alone by rule-
ridden mediocrities!" Both statements are anti-historical. The
choice does not exist, for artists find themselves inspired or
crushed by institutions which they are not alone in making.
That is why it is important to know what is achieved when
the general will produces a classical order, and at what cost.
To suppose that one can have classicism without authoritarianism is like supposing that one can have braking power
without friction. Conversely, romanticism is not simply love of
ease or impatient rebellion. It is a different way of fulfilling
human wants after the breakdown of an attempt at eternal
order.

III

The question of human wants brings us back from historic
to *intrinsic* classicism, for a second look at the classical meanings of Reason, Nature, and Feeling. The classic objection to
romantic psychology is that it accepts an inner dualism—the
"two souls in one breast" which publicists in wartime like to
think especially German, if only because it is exemplified in
Goethe's *Faust*. In romanticism, the two souls can be variously
interpreted. I have chosen as most basic man's double consciousness of power and weakness. Another expression of the
feeling is the Christian awareness of grace and sin. A third is
the conflict between man's sense of values and his knowledge
that nature is indifferent, this last being another form of
Pascal's loneliness in the eternal silent spaces.

The classicist view of man's mind also recognizes the split but makes it fall in a different place. Following one of Plato's myths, it sees the soul as a charioteer driving a team of wild horses. The charioteer is Reason, the wild horses are the emotions. Some emotions are good, some evil; the driver is of the same sort as the good. Classic man is a kind of Centaur—man above and horse beneath. Now, one of the features of classical Reason is that it can be put into words and become common property. Hence a society can be built which embodies Reason and helps each individual to drive his equipage on the straight road of duty and decency.

So natural is this psychological metaphor that we still speak of reason and emotion as opposites, we use the Head and the Heart as images of rival powers. Even when we repeat Pascal's phrase "The heart has its reasons which the reason does not know" we tend to mistake its meaning and to use it as an equivalent of: "It is sometimes good to do something which our judgment disapproves." We go so far in our slipshod use of words on this subject that we commonly characterize certain people as "emotional," as if they were cursed with pure emotion, or with more emotion than others. Freudian psychology is doing something to correct this error by pointing out how deceptive is the calm of so-called repressed personalities. The task is difficult because common speech imputes the wish to go berserk to anyone who challenges the classic figure of the charioteer.

Fortunately, in this same classical seventeenth century there lived a philosopher of blameless and even stoical life, who can act as a character witness for the anti-classical view of emotion. I refer to Spinoza, and to his demonstration that the only way the human mind can conquer an emotion is by attaching its thought to another and stronger emotion. According to Spinoza, Reason is not a charioteer; it does not play the role of a guardian angel pushing back the demons into the pit; reason is but a guide, always moved by some emotion and pointing to an object. By effort and training, ideas can be detached from one deep-lying motive and reattached to another. As William James showed, will power consists in the ability to sustain an idea against its competitors from within the stream of thought. It is imagination plus attention. Hence there is never an emotion without an idea, nor an idea without an emotion. In the so-called reasonable man there is an awareness of motives and consequences which gives the impression that reason is wholly aloof from passion; but this is an illusion —the illusion upon which classicism builds its society.

This corrected view of the human passions explains why it is not sufficient to know the good in order to achieve it. It explains why copybook maxims always seem empty words until "something hits us." If this is true, we should cease to qualify a man or a mob as "emotional" when what we mean is that the ideas of the one or the other are crude, oversimple, and destructive. If we ever come to feel this difference clearly enough to change our clichés, we shall know that it takes as much emotion to solve a differential equation as it does to write a sonnet, and we shall stop speaking of "cold reason" and its counterpart, the "hot fit of inspiration," as if the categories of the plumber would suit the psychologist.

Spinoza is a doubly telling witness, for it so happens that, like Pascal, he was neglected by his classical age and rediscovered by the romantics. On the point we have been discussing, they all saw alike, and what they saw was not a need to glorify emotion or to give up thinking; it was something much more subtle and important, namely, the need to find organic unity within the human animal—the mind harmoniously expressing the demands of the feelings. Pascal who said "The whole duty of man is to think well"; Spinoza who said that the freedom of man lay in concentrating his passions on a proper object; the romanticists who said that the highest development of the self was true morality—all agreed that the task was one of reconciling the two souls as a prelude to social harmony. Blake put it with his usual forthrightness when he denied "that energy, called evil, is alone from the body; and that reason, called good, is alone from the soul." Contrary to the charioteer theory, he asserted that "energy is the only life and is from the body; and reason is the bound or outward circumference of energy."

It is urged against this view of reason and emotion that it sets men no common goal, and that the romanticists in particular did not seem to agree on the good life. Shall a man be a saint or a civil engineer, a gentleman of leisure or a social reformer? The disagreement exists, but it may point to an eternal feature in the world of men—its pluralism. In any case, Romanticism declined to be deceived by the sleight-of-hand with which classicism pretends that the truth has been found and can be handed to each shareholder in its limited-liability company. Classicism forgets that its truth has not been found but made; that its social order does not represent concurring wills but is imposed by a caste; and that its boasted reason is mere maxims of prudence, useful in their place, but incapable of stilling forever the diverse claims that men do in fact make upon life, and make good. There is, in short, as much weakness in mankind as classicism sees and tries to conceal, but there is also much more power than it allows room for.

In calling classicist reason "maxims of prudence," I mean that they are negative commandments, whose application to life can only be mechanical, since they fail to recognize temperamental differences among individuals and the organic bond between feeling and thought. Too much ignored in the seventeenth century, this bond was rediscovered in the eighteenth. The men of the Enlightenment did not underrate the irrational, but they still dealt with it abstractly. Voltaire's *Candide* is a complete demonstration that the world is largely the product of impulse. But of what use is the maxim "Cultivate your garden" except to a wise old man like the author, who has indulged his passions for many a year before prescribing this capsule of wisdom? Surely it is rank unreason to expect of the young Candide, at the beginning of the book, that he should cultivate his garden instead of the lovely Cunégonde's acquaintance.

The difference, then, between classical man and romanticist on the point of irrationalism lies wholly in a difference of judgment and intellectual bias. It is not a factual difference. Nothing can be more false than to represent the rationalist as natively able to get on without trouble from his feelings, or even as wishing to forget them. Those who have tried to palm off this picture of a rationalist superman might be surprised if one asked, "Who was the first great French writer to say that the passions were all good?" They would certainly shout "Rousseau" with one voice, but the correct answer is Descartes, who concludes his *Treatise on the Passions* with that blanket approval. His rationalism lay in recommending a "simple method" for controlling these all-good energies. Hume, too, saw very clearly that "without passion, no idea has any force": and the psychologist Hartley was far from ignorant of the importance of the sexual passion in shaping human character. But they all believed in a simple common rule of reason, almost a recipe, for maintaining equilibrium and keeping not only the individual but society static.

When reason itself suggested that society might stand in need of improvement, what did classicism offer on the perplexing subject of social change? Nothing, unless we adapt the words that Pope applied to fashions:—

> Be not the first by whom the new are tried,
> Nor yet the last to lay the old aside.

In other words, let a romanticist begin. Let Columbus discover America: the classicist will come when de luxe passage has been provided. In truth, under classicism, innovation and discovery cannot be underwritten by society, because they are destructive, venturesome, uncertain; and because all the necessary forms and truths are known. Classicism assumes its own highest perfection and the individual who departs from it does so at his own risk. Rousseau is accordingly compelled to define genius as that which has the power to create from nothing, and to add that only fiery souls ever accomplish anything.

But why should there be creation and social change? Because although the great classical word is "restraint," classicism is impotent to restrain the forces that keep society alive. In the eighteenth century, the most perfect of neo-classical ages, the stirrings of unchanneled emotion were the most tangible force disrupting the old order. No sooner had "civilization" reached its high point, as all agreed, than restlessness set in and the South Sea islands began to seem a better world. Throughout Europe new interests developed—in popular ballads, in Gothic architecture, in natural scenery, in sentimental stories, in informal gardens, in tales of horror and mystery, in the Celtic and Germanic literatures as against the Graeco-Roman—all having the common feature of a pleasing *ir*regularity.

All these new tastes were at first affectations, for things which have been formerly neglected can only be taken up by a conscious steeling of the person against public censure. The innovator has to pretend that faddishness is a merit, and the new does not sit as lightly upon him as upon his successors. The modern connoisseur of cathedrals is a man like any other, but the first gentleman to like Gothic architecture made himself ridiculous by building false ruins.

The significant fact is that the new taste was for pleasing irregularity. Each innovation was just another fad, but all together amounted to a shift in outlook. The results were to mark an epoch not only in art and society, but in political forms and natural science. What happened in these four realms may be summed up in the words which apply particularly to science: it was a Biological Revolution. The term says plainly enough that the absolute reign of physics and mathematics was over, and with it the dominance of the Reason patterned upon these two sciences. By the end of the eighteenth century new branches of knowledge—the sciences of man—had come of age: anthropology, ethnology, and zoology were offering new facts, new analogies, new modes of thought. Cartesian and Newtonian mechanics were taken for granted; the new principle was vitalism and the new theory, evolution. The mechanical materialism which had threatened to overcome all rival philosophies was in full retreat.

The clearest manifestations of this unexpected reversal are to be found in the careers of three famous rationalists—David Hume in England; Diderot in France; Lessing in Germany. All three had won fame by battling for the Enlightenment, for Deism, for the classical view of art and life. But by dint of sticking to their method and leaving nothing untouched by it, they dethroned Reason herself—Reason, that is, with a capital *R*, the Reason of the eighteenth century. A curious parallel unites the last thoughts of these men—they are consigned in dialogues, all three posthumously published. Hume's *Dialogues concerning Natural Religion* undermined Deism, and did so by means of biological comparisons and suggestions, including the notion of the survival of the fittest. In France, Diderot adopted the evolutionism of Buffon and Bordeu and became a virtual pantheist. At the same time, in his extraordinary dialogue, *Rameau's Nephew*, he plumbed the irrational depths of a human specimen chosen as if on purpose to disprove that man is a machine and to forecast the dilemmas of the romanticists.

It was Goethe who first drew Diderot's masterpiece to the world's attention. Meantime, Lessing in Germany had been having conversations with a young publicist named Jacobi, of which the burden was Lessing's enthusiastic adherence to Spinoza's psychology and Spinoza's religion. When Jacobi published an account of these conversations it caused a scandal throughout Germany: the philosophy of the Enlightenment had been dealt a mortal blow.

Why should this be so? What does biology imply that mechanics does not? It implies that life is an element and not merely a combination of dead parts. It implies organic structure and organic function. It implies that the primary reality is the individual and not either the parts of which he is made or the artificial groupings which he may enter into. This is, in a word, individualism. Within the individual, the motive power is, as its name reveals, emotion. Consciousness and intelligence remain at the top of the hierarchy of values but they are not disembodied or centered upon themselves. They serve larger interests, which are those of life itself—the survival of the individual and of the species.

Survival in turn suggests that the first law of the universe is not thought but action. As Goethe has Faust say, "In the beginning was"—not the Word, or Thought, but "the Deed." Action means effort, energy, possibly strife and certainly risk. The world is a world of novelty, in which changing situations cannot always be met by rules previously learned, though imagination can foresee and forearm the creature, who thereby becomes also an agent of creation. But imagination and creation carry with them no guarantee of success. The sustaining principle in man and his new world is therefore not reason—which is merely the already acquired and codified experience—but faith, which is hope plus the power of hope to realize itself. Why this power should work as it does is a mystery. It is the mystery at the heart of nature, which reason can guess at but not pluck out. When successful, man's reason —man's sense of power—is justified, and equally justified when he fails is his sense of weakness: in denying neither he has become a romanticist.

As a romanticist, his task is to reconcile the contraries within him by finding some entity outside himself vast enough to hold all his facts. He has become once again a religious thinker. For religion is more than a description of the Unseen. It is a theory of energy—the energy that animates nature and that animates him. To the romanticist, religion is no longer a superstition or a bald statement that the universe must have a First Cause; religion is an intellectual and emotional necessity. As Pascal said, man must wager on the existence of God, "because he is embarked." In the romantic period, man wagered on the existence of the Catholic or Protestant God, on pantheism, on art, on science, on the national state, on the future of mankind: but in all the pattern is the same. The solutions differ in concrete particulars only because salvation is ultimately individual.

With these premises, classicism—at least in its old form—cannot subsist. It had built a shelter for man on too narrow an enclosure. It had supposed society to be static, emotions compressible, and novelty needless. It had selected what seemed to it best and truest and most eternal—monarchy, orthodoxy, courtly etiquette, mathematics, and rules of art and of morality so simple that their universality could be deemed self-evident. But what had it selected these elements from? Clearly from a previous romanticism, that of the sixteenth-century Renaissance, an age of exploration and creation.

That is why, when classicism had twinges, they were like pre-natal recollections of romanticism. When Corneille drew his heroes, they were medieval knights and religious martyrs in seventeenth-century dilemmas. When Molière drew Alceste, the prospect of retiring to the country did not frighten the so-called misanthrope, but only the coquette and the flatterers he left behind. When Racine was melancholy, he wrote a simple song in which he says he feels two souls within his breast, two men struggling with each other; and on hearing the song Louis XIV is reported to have leaned over to Mme. de Maintenon and said, "How well I know these two men!" In short, the protection and certainty that classicism gave were only temporary. It is no discredit to the genius or the strength of the classicists that it should have been so. It is merely a reflection on their self-knowledge, and a damaging flaw in the anti-romantics' classic objection, that they should mistake the man-made and temporary for what is given and permanent.

IV

Romantic Art

I

An historical review of the classical epoch nearest to us has enabled us to measure the distance between its ideal of peace and serenity and its actual tendencies toward repression and formalism. The psychological presuppositions of that age naturally threw light on the differences between rationalist and romanticist; differences which, speaking figuratively, correspond to the difference between physics and biology. This contrast faces, as it were, backwards from the nineteenth century to the eighteenth and seventeenth. A second usual contrast, that between romanticist and realist, presumably looks forward to a movement later than romanticism. Since these terms belong first of all to the realm of art, I want now to argue against this postponement of the realistic label and to suggest that, on the evidence just set forth, romanticism *is* realism.

If this is too great a shock to common usage let it be softened by a modification of the ideas behind each term. By the equation romanticism = realism I do not mean that there is no difference between romanticism and the artistic movement known after 1850 as Realism. I shall speak later and at some length of that important difference. What I am concerned with here is to show that what the romanticists of the period 1790 to 1850 sought and found was not a dream world into which to escape, but a real world in which to live. The exploration of reality was the fundamental intention of romantic art.

Before we come to particulars, the general setting may be

put in a few words: classicism perished from an excess of abstraction and generality. This was most visibly true in the several arts, and nothing shows more clearly the romanticists' realistic purpose than their refusal to go on imitating forms whose contents had evaporated. Seeing this refusal, we believe too readily in the miscalled "romantic revolt." We imagine a sudden and irresponsible rebellion of brash young men against the wisdom and experience of their elders. It was nothing of the kind. The breaking away was reluctant, painful, and deliberate. After much soul-searching and abortive efforts to continue in traditional ways, a whole generation of talents came to see that to write or paint in the manner of Pye, Gottsched, and Delille, of David and Reynolds, was no longer possible.

There was no choice but to begin afresh. The romanticist was in the position of a primitive with the seven arts to create out of nothing. At the same time, he labored under the handicap of having "inimitable" classical masterpieces held up to him to imitate, even though the substance of these great works had already been rendered threadbare by repetition and refinement. The romantic revolt consisted solely in refusing to do the undoable.

Having perforce given up conventional abstractions, clichés, poetic diction, and classical rules, what did the romanticists turn to? The answer can be generalized: for substance they turned to the world about and within them; they tried to meet the claims of every existing reality, both internal and external. For form, they relied on earlier romantic periods and on their own inventive genius.

The characteristics of romanticism which the textbooks list as if they were arbitrary choices by eccentric artists are merely the embodiment of what I have just said. As against poetic diction and "noble" words, the romanticists admitted all words; as against the exclusive use of a selected Graeco-Roman mythology, they took in the Celtic and Germanic; as against the uniform setting and tone of classical tragedy, they studied and reproduced the observable diversities known as "local color." As against the antique subjects and the set scale of pictorial merits prescribed by the Academy, they took in the whole world, seen and unseen, and the whole range of colors.

As against the academic rules prohibiting the use of certain chords, tonalities, and modulations, they sought to use and give shape to all manageable combinations of sound. As against the assumption that no civilization had existed since the fall of Rome, they rediscovered the Middle Ages and the sixteenth century and made history their dominant avocation. As against the provincial belief that Paris and London were the sole centers of human culture, they traveled to such remote places as America and the Near East and earned the name of "exotic" for their pains. As against the idea that the products of cosmopolitan sophistication afford the only subjects worth treating, they began to treasure folk literature and folk music and to draw the matter of their art from every class and condition of men. As against the materialistic view that only the tangible exists, they made room in their notion of reality for the world of dreams, the ineffable in man and nature, and the supernatural.

All this they did knowingly, deliberately, with the patience and tenacity of pioneers and explorers. Hence to the scoffer who would dismiss the "romantic revolt" one must reply as Liancourt did to Louis XVI: "Sire, it is a revolution." To assure oneself of the magnitude and seriousness of the upheaval, one need only do two things: read the considerable body of critical theory that the romantics left about their art; and examine the art itself, not piecemeal in anthologies, but in the bulk. Then, hark back to what Addison, quoted with approval by Hume, says on the range of classicist reality: " 'Fine writing,' according to Mr. Addison, 'consists of sentiments which are natural without being obvious.' . . . The pleasantries of a waterman, the observations of a peasant, the ribaldry of a porter or hackney coachman—all of these are natural and disagreeable."

They are disagreeable to the classicist not only in themselves, but because of their irregularity as compared with a standardized reality. Hume says again: "As the eye in surveying a Gothic building is distracted by the multiplicity of ornaments and loses the whole by its minute attention to the parts, so the mind . . . is disgusted and fatigued . . ." by a work lacking in simplicity and refinement. After this read Wordsworth on King's College Chapel and Victor Hugo's descriptions of Notre Dame.

But first, perhaps, read Wordsworth's preface to *Lyrical Ballads*, in which he states his intention to disregard the expectations of his readers and to treat a variety of subjects, including the emotions of common men. With Wordsworth's ballads one finds Coleridge's *Ancient Mariner*, which it is tempting to regard as an example of romantic unreality. It is rather an example of the romanticist interest in the supernatural and its use of the folk style. Being inclusively realistic, romanticism has no typical works, in the sense that to read one is to read them all. It has typical genres, just like classicism, but covering an immensely greater range.

Unfortunately, the very mass and variety of romantic interests have disturbed criticism into the hasty conclusion that the dominant note is some one or other of these interests. This is frequently done by taking, say, Scott as the symbol of the romanticist "return to the Middle Ages." Few people read Scott nowadays, so that a reference to *Ivanhoe* seems enough to settle the dispute. But Scott's novels are not all about knights and tournaments. His best work consists in close-grained studies of the Scotland that survived into his day, in scenes of humor or drama that have been fitly compared to Shakespeare's, and in historical intuitions which Professor Trevelyan, himself an historian, credits with having changed the mind of Europe and taught it history. As for the Black Knight and his kind, Scott was the first to point out their weakness and lack of interest for him. They were put in, like the attendants in classical tragedy, to help out the management of the main business. This does not mean that one is obliged to like Scott; nor that as a novelist he is better or worse than one or another of the classical writers. The point is that he was essentially a realist, who ought to be judged on what he wrote and not on what a generation that does not read him thinks he wrote.

The pattern of this rectification applies, *mutatis mutandis*, to all the great romanticists that we think we have outgrown. This is a generality without exception. But for the sake of re-enforcement it may be well to say a few words about Shelley. The Shelley of the textbooks is a disembodied spirit, living on air and fluting about Intellectual Beauty. The Shelley of history was a man with a precociously sharp eye for the political and industrial realities of his England, a poet with a "social consciousness" most fully developed, a psychologist and observer of considerable scope, and one who, incidentally, did not wait until the advent of Naturalism to use the word "garbage" in his poetry. To displace the image of Shelley the dealer in moonshine, it is of course necessary to read *The Mask of Anarchy*, the poems written in 1819 about English poverty and discontent, and the *Philosophical View of Reform*, particularly the second chapter, "On the Sentiment of the Necessity of Change."

This should be enough but there is more. Shelley's realism did not stop at the observation of social fact. Although his famous biographer, Dowden, found that Shelley was incapable of thought, we have come to see, through more careful scholarship, that he was a hard and able student of physical science, metaphysics, and psychology. Professor Grabo of Chicago calls him "a Newton among the poets," and Lionel Trilling, reviewing the latest *Life*, says: "Shelley is often spoken of as a man without tradition, but that is because his tradition is so wide that its limits cannot easily be seen. . . . Shelley, with most of the romantics, was passionately reverential of fact, though, like them, realistic enough to include under this head the mental fact as well as the physical. . . . A good case, for example, might be made for his having foreshadowed many of the essentials of Freud."

One need not know at first hand the total output of the romantic period in art to agree with this generalization. As a body, there has never been a group more persistently curious of fact than the romantic artists. The greater part of their poetry was the record of observation, whether of their own souls or of the world outside. The accuracy is sometimes painful and the detail excessive. But there have been few see-ers and reporters as minute and comprehensive as Wordsworth, Balzac, Hazlitt, Goethe, Victor Hugo, and Stendhal. One may not enjoy what they saw or approve what they said of it, but wherever one begins looking for the "authority" behind their reports one is likely to find some actual and factual experience.

What is true of the poets is, *a fortiori*, true of the painters. The romanticist revolution in painting was achieved by the simple means of stepping out of the studio and observing nature. From Constable rushing out of the room with a violin to show his skeptical friends that grass is really greener than old varnish, to Géricault, Bonington, Turner, and Delacroix filling notebooks with effects of color, motion, and shadow under every conceivable light, the school—if it must be called one—was a realistic school.

In music, once allowance is made for the difference in medium, the same thing holds true. I do not speak of the melodic inspiration that composers such as Beethoven, Weber, Mendelssohn, and Berlioz tell us they drew from nature, for that is a kind of mysterious transformation of mingled perceptions into sound which has nothing notational about it. I mean that the romantic musicians' concern with expressiveness in melody, harmony, and orchestral color implies a desire to mold musical form as closely as possible on psychological and dramatic truth. The contour of a Schubert or Schumann song is, in this sense, the fruit of observation, just like the shades of Chopin's harmony or the expressive choices in Berlioz's orchestration. These are not decorations laid on, but facets of a new conception, whose intent is correspondence with experienced reality rather than correspondence with established general forms. And the way to it was already being trod by Mozart and Haydn at the end of their careers.

Whatever one may think of the results achieved, it is a fact beyond dispute that the romantic artists worked like scientific researchers. Their notebooks, their critical writings, their letters and treatises on composition are there to testify that technique was to them as important as subject matter. Indeed they reasserted the old truth that the distinction between the two is one for the critic rather than the creator. The artist has said nothing until he has found the right form. Accordingly, form, or rather forms, preoccupied the romanticists to a degree we hardly recognize now that for a hundred years we have used their discoveries and inventions. We have come to think of them as ready-made for their makers as they have been for us. A volume on each of the arts and one on each of the European nations would not suffice to discuss the successful creation or adaptation of forms by the romantic artists. Let anyone conversant with poetry imagine English poetry without the forms bequeathed by Wordsworth; French poetry without Victor Hugo; German without Goethe. And in their obsession with variety, as close examination shows, the romantics acted not merely as innovators and revolutionists but as great restorers and wise conservatives.

II

The comparison of the romantics with scientific researchers may be objected to in some quarters, not so much because of the light it throws on romantic realism but because it contradicts the "well-known" opposition of the romanticists to science. It is so well known, apparently, that it is seldom documented. One is referred to Keats's toast confounding Newton and to a pair of lines in Wordsworth: "We murder to dissect," and "Peep and botanize upon his mother's grave." This hardly seems conclusive evidence, particularly Wordsworth's usually misread phrases, one of which states a biological fact (an organism does not survive its dissection into parts), and the other expresses a moral judgment on the fitness of a particular act. There is here no blanket condemnation of botany or any other science.

Nor is it recorded that when Wordsworth and Sir Humphry Davy climbed Helvellyn together, the poet tried to push the scientist down the abyss. One might rather imagine that it was this expedition which suggested to Wordsworth his later description of science as "a succedaneum and a prop To our infirmity." The passage where it occurs shows the precise esteem in which Wordsworth, like most poets, held science: it is a prop, but not "our glory and our absolute boast"; a reservation which did not keep the poet from paying Newton a tribute of a sublimity yet to be matched by a scientist speaking of poetry:—

I could behold
. . . Newton with his prism and silent face,
The marble index of a mind forever
Voyaging through strange seas of Thought, alone.

On the whole it is fair to say that the romantic artists were respectful admirers and sometimes active propagandists of science. I have mentioned Shelley's studies. Goethe's are justly famous, as are or ought to be those of Thomas Lovell Beddoes. Other writers, such as Victor Hugo, Vigny, Coleridge, Hazlitt, Novalis, Büchner, Berlioz, Schiller, Schopenhauer, Stendhal, and Balzac, come to mind as friends or students of science. Keats himself, according to a recent editor of his poems, has been misinterpreted as an enemy.

The truth is that at the beginning of the nineteenth century, specialization had not gone so far that a man could not combine an intelligent interest in science with every other liberal pursuit. This worked both ways, and many of the scientists of the period showed clear signs of being romanticists as well. Without going back to the scientific poems of Erasmus Darwin, one can list Sir Humphry Davy, Dalton, Oken, and Faraday as men of science who were not strangers to the poetical spirit of romanticism. Faraday, we are told by his biographer, responded to "sunsets and thunderstorms with a kind of ecstasy," which did not prevent him from being the founder of the science of electricity. As for the philosophers of the period, particularly the Germans, it was their faith in science that moved them to reconstruct metaphysics so that the warfare of science and religion might come to an end.

The attempt to reconcile experimental fact with spiritual truth may in fact be the reason why romanticism has been falsely interpreted as the enemy of science. Both the romantic philosopher and the romantic artist agree in thinking science valuable, but they clearly perceive that science can deal only with a restricted field of experience. Scientific method proceeds by exclusion and achieves wonderful results; art and philosophy are, on the contrary, inclusive disciplines—none more so than romantic philosophy and romantic art. This is the point of the romanticist attack, not on science, but on materialism: materialism narrows down the universe to a fraction of itself. The romanticists were realists precisely because they admitted the widest possible range of experience as real. They made mistakes as to particular facts, for they were fallible men, but they made no mistake as to the endless variety of things that are. Their critics cannot have it both ways: the romanticists' "thirst for experience," which is condemned as a dispersion of effort, is at least a proof that phenomena as such were to them of infinite concern.

One may then ask, "What about the unreal phenomena that so plentifully adorn romantic work: Coleridge's and De Quincey's opium dreams, Scott's and Goethe's demonology, Blake's and Hoffmann's visions, Shelley's and Hugo's revelations of the divine? Have we not here lost touch with reality—the reality which the Greeks and the classicists knew so well how to discern?"

Three elements are here being questioned: the psychological, the religious, and the supernatural. Consider first the supernatural, of the kind we find in *Faust*. Its reality is of course disputed by eighteenth-century reason as well as modern science. But surely it is vindicated by history. Not that I believe in witches, but that as an historian I cannot disbelieve in the force that witchcraft has exerted on history, New England history as well as European. What Goethe and Scott found in demonology was the popular expression of mysterious nature —the dark and seemingly evil forces at the core of living things. These poets adopted the folk imagery and turned superstition back into significance. In so doing, they were precursors of Freud. They were also fulfilling their role as challengers of convention. Coleridge, for example, was aware of the value of familiarity with the supernatural for inducing that "willing suspension of disbelief" which is as essential to scientific as to artistic work. Poetry has always had the duty of attacking crusted common sense, and it is on seeing the ghost that Hamlet tells Horatio there are more things in heaven and earth than we commonly suppose. Even if it is taken as a purely literary device, the supernatural belongs to the great ancient and medieval tradition, which classicism merely interrupted. This should be enough to legitimize such embodiments of the fantastic as Goethe's *Faust I* and *II*, Corot's painting of Macbeth and the Witches, and the last movement of Berlioz's "Fantastic Symphony."

It is incidentally curious that would-be classicists bred on Greek mythology should object in the romanticists to an element that figures so largely in the literature of the ancients. Are we not asked to believe in the Sphinx, the Minotaur, and the Eumenides? in the dooms and curses cast on Prometheus, Atreus, and Phaedra? This question raises another, the question whether all of ancient literature is indeed classicist—a subject outside our present limits. Yet it must be said in passing that students of antiquity find a period of romanticism in Greek letters, beginning—oddly enough—with the man upon whose work the seventeenth-century writers thought they were patterning their classic drama—Euripides. Even before him, in Homer, the unprejudiced critic finds elements that cannot be called classical or realistic in a literal sense: most of the *Odyssey*, and in the *Iliad* such conceptions as the making of Achilles' shield or his battle with the river Scamander.

So much for the fantastic. The second charge of unreality instances the romantic predilection for the world of dreams. This complaint answers itself. Dreams are facts, even daydreams. Hence the artistic use to which Hölderlin or Gérard de Nerval or Coleridge or De Quincey puts dream-stuff is legitimate and points to the real. The important thing is not that the Pleasure Dome of Kubla Khan would remain invisible to the traveler looking for it on Hampstead Heath, but that it could be seen by Coleridge in such a fashion as to impress us still 150 years after the vision. Pragmatically, what is true about the vision is what it does to us; its source is interesting but irrelevant. As for De Quincey and Nerval, their study of dreams seems to have proceeded from a desire to capture the most fleeting of human experiences and turn them to the uses of deeper understanding. I need only add that in the *Confessions of an English Opium-Eater*, always cited as typical romantic pipe-dream literature, one comes upon some extraordinary realistic passages—not only in the pragmatic sense just defined, but in the modern vulgar sense, as for example in the passages about poverty and prostitution in London in the first decade of the nineteenth century.

The third cause of critical confusion is the status of the subjective. The romantics are described as invariably or excessively "subjective," and it is often from this description that their lack of realism is inferred. Worse still, subjectivism is sometimes made to imply an "adoration of the ego" productive of irresponsibility in belief and technique. The question is partly one of fact, partly one of language. I shall speak of egotism and individuality in the next chapter, which deals with romantic life. Here I want to take up artistic subjectivism. It was the romanticists, by the way, who taught us the word through their discussions of Kantian philosophy. But we have distorted its meaning. Too many use "subjective" to mean false and "objective" to mean true. There is no warrant for this, except the probability that several people or "subjects" are less likely to be mistaken than one. But this is by no means a certainty: a good observer is worth ten mediocre ones, and good ones are rare. What is properly meant by subjective is the fact that any experience occurs as an event in the mind of some observer. Experiences that are shared should accordingly be called inter-subjective. What we usually think of when we use "objective" is simply those very common (subjective) experiences which in our culture have long been inter-subjective as well.

Now to return to the romanticists. They were forced, as we know, to take stock of the universe anew, like primitives, because the old forms, the old inter-subjective formulas, had failed them. There was consequently nothing for them to do but report individually on what they saw. They entertained the reasonable hope that individual reports on reality would lead to generalized and probable truths. This is the method of scientific induction. To the extent that we can say of a poem or picture, "Yes, I see and am moved by it," the subjective perception of the artist's ego is verified.

To be sure, human perception, as William James pointed out, is guided by interest: we see what we think will help, or interest, or edify us. And, as we saw, the romantics put their desire for facts before their interest in consistency. They chose to record the grotesque and the mystical side by side with the trivial and the sublime, which makes their revelation of the world through art a multiverse rather than a universe. It is this representation that we find hardest to accept. We try to reduce the many to one, both with respect to the cosmos and with respect to art: we want "romantic" to mean some one thing. So we find romantic art labeled "naturalism" by those who are thinking of Goethe, "idealism" by those who are thinking of Novalis or Carlyle, "mysticism" by those who are thinking of Blake, "conservatism" by those who are thinking of Burke, Scott, and de Maistre, "liberalism" by those who are thinking of Byron and Hazlitt. None of the labels has a chance of being true, for romanticism and its great men were diverse. Though it had a purpose and a direction, the movement was not "purely" some one thing: only to the purist are all things pure.

Having dropped the "nothing but" attitude we readily see that it was neither caprice nor egotism that made many a work of romantic art subjective; it was the conditions of the search and the modesty of the searcher. The romantic artist said in effect: "I have been there and this is what I have seen." Blake saw visions; if he were a pathological liar, we could dismiss him. But his work shows that he knew how to observe and express hitherto neglected aspects of reality: he was an artist in the specifically romantic sense of art. He saw the previously unseen or elusive and he caged it for our pleasure and instruction. It is a part of man's power that he can do this, although it remains his weakness that he can never eliminate error.

We are of course free to say that Blake's visions are error, just as we can dispute the statement that "life is real, life is earnest," but we cannot dispute the fact that some people see visions and others find life earnest. In this regard—which is important not only philosophically but also politically, for true democracy hangs upon it—the romanticists are more "objective" than their critics. Though it is but one ego, a mere subjective self, that does the recording, he is able to record the feelings and perceptions of others as well as his own. The single consciousness of the subject turns dramatist and uses the self as a sensitive plate to catch whatever molecular or spiritual motions the outer world may supply.

Doubtless not every romanticist answers this description at all times, but it is remarkable how many do, and how aptly this fact explains a number of otherwise puzzling appearances. In the Preface to an early work, Victor Hugo says that the romantic period is "dramatic and thereby eminently lyrical." This statement has generally been accounted a paradox; in the light of what I have just said it ceases to be one. The lyricist is not always speaking for himself. He captures and reproduces the diverse, the conflicting essences of other beings. Who but an artist could do it? The result is drama in the literal sense of conflict and in the figurative sense of contrast.

On the dramatic quality of romanticist art there is little disagreement. Whatever the medium, the romantic abounds in contrasts, oppositions, antitheses, strife, and color. It is no accident that it was the romantic generation that first found Shakespeare the supreme artist of modern times. This admiration, as well as the lag of theatrical habits, may account for the absence of any great romantic drama in the form of stage plays; just as the enthusiasm for the neglected Gothic may account for the absence of any great romantic architecture. In both these marked deficiencies, romanticism suffered from an excess of its own qualities. In the one, historical fidelity turned architects into simple restorers and archaeologists; in the other, critical insight turned playwrights into self-conscious imitators. The expectations of theater managers and their public reduced Hugo's plays to mere experiments in verse form, and indirectly stifled the two or three born dramatists of the period—Beddoes, Kleist, and Büchner. But the lyric forms were free and hospitable to dramatic contents.

It is this fusion of speech in the first person with the playwright's vision of diversity that sometimes makes the romantic artist seem inconsistent and enables the facile biographer to call him "a bundle of contradictions." Yet closer study will show that in spite of their dedication to diversity the romantics achieved a high degree of organization among elements that seem at first to jangle. In any single case incoherence will be found to come from fidelity to received impressions, that is, objectified fact is the cause of disorder in expression; so that even in his failures the romanticist—true to his awareness—is a realist.

III

If the anti-romantic whom I have imagined still protests, he is probably saying, "Granted: romanticism is an inclusive kind of realism, lyric in form and dramatic in content, but is there not over the whole a particular coloring which is properly called romantic because it distinguishes the works of this period? If so, that coloring is what we *mean* by romantic unreality, or, if you prefer, romantic idealization and sentimentality."

Only a review of the actual works can supply a conclusive answer, and I have in mind not three or four samples selected from memory, but a systematic survey of all the arts, including the dance, and of the several nations of Europe, including Italy, Spain, Poland, and Russia. For romantic art was an inter-European phenomenon, and not a series of successive importations from some single point of origin. To suppose that Mme. de Stael or Wackenroder or Macpherson or even Rousseau "started" the romantic movement, which was then copied by two generations of alleged "egotists," is at once to contradict oneself and cast doubt on one's ability to write cultural history. That there is in truth a "romantic coloring" argues, not a process of imitation, but a community of response to similar perceptions and similar technical problems. This type of similarity is a constant for all artistic periods. There is a family likeness among the works of the Italian Renaissance, among the Elizabethans, and among the Romanticists. But it is strictly a family likeness, which allows of wide divergences among individuals. The prose of Stendhal differs from that of Balzac, the verse of Byron from that of Shelley. To obtain an all-embracing view one must step back and lose sight of detail. This is not to deny the general coloring but to point out its coexistence with individual and cultural traits.

The works of the romanticists are difficult to classify for this reason as well as for the ones rehearsed earlier. Romantic art is, in Henry James's vocabulary, "thick." Many moods and tendencies are harmonized into one whole. That is why our recollection—of Scott, for instance—is so imperfect. We do not reproduce in ourselves the several kinds of substance that are there. We pass from confession to revery and philosophy, from autobiography, learning, and criticism to social and political animus. At its best, romantic art is perfect art, that is, complete in the manner of Homer, Dante, and Shakespeare, though it has not always the shape of that very different thing, a perfect work of art.

Where then does the atmosphere of idealization and sentimentality come in? It is obvious that some sort of idealization occurs in all art and thought since they cannot avoid selection and emphasis. But idealization can take various paths. In classicist doctrine, idealization consists in approximating a common norm. Here is what Delacroix says about his early academic training: "In order to draw the ideal Negro head, our teachers make him resemble as far as possible the profile of Antinoüs, and then say, 'We have done our best; if in spite of everything he is not beautiful, we must abstain altogether from drawing this freak of nature, this squat nose and thick lips, which are so unendurable to the eyes.'"

The romanticist idealizes, not in the direction of a common norm, but in the direction of complete expressiveness. This is the desire to make each object disclose itself as fully as possible under the most favorable conditions. Now just as classic idealization can be carried so far that it denies the difference between one cast of countenance and another, so romantic idealization can be carried to such excess that more is squeezed out of the particulars than they can possibly contain. This is true for example of some of Wordsworth's poems in which a dumb animal or a trivial incident is made into wisdom incarnate. But if it is foolish to deny classical power in painting because of the excessive idealization of David, so it is foolish to equate romanticism solely with the failure of its method.

Romantic error is no doubt still too near to us to acquire that quaintness which we enjoy in its classic counterparts. For example, the traditional costumes of Racine's Greek heroes and heroines are so comic as to escape criticism, and the same might be said of the narrow intensity of his *Andromaque,* in which the entrances and exits of the passionate lovers come dangerously close to suggesting a farce in a revolving door. There is a sense in which all art is absurd, and we are reminded of it by the excess—or near-excess—of the very method which insures triumph.

But we must take note of yet another form, another idealizing which is common to the arts, with no difference of principle discoverable between classicist and romanticist techniques. That is the method of combining several experiences into one representation or, what is often the same thing, doing what Racine did in *Andromaque,* namely, distorting for the sake of drama. The romanticists made frequent use of both these devices and have been somewhat roughly handled for it. Criticism has only slowly come to recognize, for instance, that Turner's painting of a particular spot is truer in virtue of his alteration of the separate details. Likewise, a scene such as Victor Hugo's bringing together of Danton, Robespierre, and Marat in *Ninety-Three* incurs the charge of false drama and idealization, until an historian like H. V. Temperley says of it: "No historian in such short compass gives us as good an idea of the gross manly breadth of Danton, of the feline caution of Robespierre, or of the insane suspicions of Marat. Victor Hugo was always the most learned of writers. . . ."

Idealization by deliberate distortion is nothing more than the old Aristotelian teaching that poetic truth is sometimes truer than history, a dogma which one is glad to have from the pen of an ancient Greek, for it would certainly have been put down as an untenable romantic paradox had it come from a writer of the last century.

The final problem on our hands is that of sentimentality, which in vulgar usage is often equivalent to romanticism. Here again we must distinguish. Some observers call sentimental whatever seems agreeable. If a young man likes an attractive young lady, he is said to be "sentimental about her" just as if her attractions were the figment of an ill-judging brain. This use of "sentimental" discloses a hidden assumption that everything being bad, any report of good must be a sign of blindness. In the criticism of romantic art, this error dots every other page. When, for example, the Russian novelist Gogol describes nature with enthusiasm and delight, he is dubbed sentimental and "romantic"; when he describes with equal power scenes of sordidness and bestiality, he is praised as a realist. Much the same treatment is meted out to Balzac, Scott, Hugo, Wordsworth, Byron, and the rest. It is apparently difficult for the modern critical mind to accept the ugly and the beautiful as sometimes coexisting and sometimes separate. Anyhow, they cannot both be true, hence the romantic artist who yields to pleasure or admiration lapses from realism. He is then said to "escape" into the beautiful, whether it be scenery, art, religion, or the love of woman.

Since for many persons this curious assumption is the whole content of the word "romantic," it seems a good moment to digress here and relate how the word came to be used at all, after which it will be easier to speak without confusion of sentimentality properly so-called. The word "romantic," I need hardly say, comes from romance. A romance is a type of story that derives its name from the romance languages in which it was originally written—that is, the vernacular tongues which grew up as the offspring of Latin in those countries that had been provinces of Rome. Since these stories were largely about love and adventure, the word "romantic" became associated with these two things. Moreover, since these stories were often laid in an attractive natural setting, the phrase "romantic spot" came in time to be used as the opposite of ugly and commonplace. The last ingredient of the romances of medieval and classicist times was the improbable, or fairy-tale element. This gives us five overtones for the *original* meaning of romantic. The word suggests love, adventure, scenic beauty, improbability, and make-believe. It needs but a glance to see that these meanings are not inescapably bound together: scenic beauty is not in itself improbable; adventure is not necessarily make-believe. From which it follows that we cannot tell by the mere use of "romantic" applied to a person whether he is a hero, a lover, a fairy prince, a liar, or a mountain climber.

Significantly enough, the adjective romantic occurs only once in the writings of Rousseau, where it describes the shores of a lake. Its use was revived in his period, however, to make

intelligible to the French, not Rousseau's works, but those of
Shakespeare, which Letourneur had for the first time translated. This enthusiast said in his preface that one must wander
through the countryside, see mountains and the ocean, and
come upon an airy landscape before one could sympathize
with Shakespeare's genius. Letourneur's intention was no
doubt to overcome the rationalist and city-bred prejudices
against Shakespeare which Voltaire had confirmed, and to
open the mind of the eighteenth century to an art which required faith in the existence of natural beauty, mystery, heroism, and adventure.

In short, whenever the word "romantic" is applied to art or
artists, the overtones of falsity and improbability remain to be
proved in each particular case. It follows that to call the works
of Scott or Byron or Landor romantic does not convict them
of untruthfulness, or even of error; the probability of a tale is
not enhanced by the mere fact that it is set in a slum. An age
which welcomes surrealism ought to sympathize with this
view, and perhaps amend its use of "romantic" in the deroga-
tory sense.

The contrast of Voltaire and Shakespeare brings us back to
the question of sentimentality as such. The term is perhaps
as loosely applied as any that deals with the moods of man,
but if it is to mean something in criticism, its scope must be
better defined. I submit that sentimentality is not the mere
display of feeling, nor the possession of excessive feeling—who
shall say what amount is right?—but the cultivation of the feelings without ensuing action. Habitually to enjoy feelings without acting upon them is to be a sentimentalist. If this is so,
it would appear that sentimentality belongs to the late classicist period, the eighteenth century, rather than later, when the
French Revolution had translated feelings into deeds. The
presence of sentimentality among the romanticists is consequently a regrettable hangover from the past or an isolated
individual trait.

No blame need attach to eighteenth-century sentimentality,
nor need we be surprised that reason should have reveled in
it. It is logical that a period which repressed feeling should
come to lead a double life. To say: Don't be an enthusiast,

don't be a poet, don't fall in love, don't take a risk, *nil admirari*, is an infallible way to make sentimentalists. At any rate sentimentality flourished in such representative eighteenth-century figures as Richardson, Fielding, Gibbon, Horace Walpole, Sterne, Young, Mackenzie, the Abbé Prévost, Marivaux, Diderot, Voltaire, Marmontel, and Greuze. It was the classical Voltaire who said the best works of art were those that made one weep the most, and it was the romanticist Chateaubriand who disputed the criterion.

This does not mean that Chateaubriand had no sentimentality in him, nor that Voltaire had only sentimentality. But the eighteenth century was certainly the age of effusiveness about arrivals and departures, dead donkeys, long-lost brothers, old soldiers, and dairymaids. It was the age of the domestic play and the tearful comedy, of easy moralizing and good intentions. Where Rousseau is sentimental he is as bad as the rest, but his sentiments are not always sentimental. It is important to distinguish feeling hung upon some conventional peg for the sake of obtaining easy credit for good nature, and feelings expressed about some new or old object of human concern, where feeling can discharge itself in action—by changing the world or the self.

The stock illustration in these matters is Goethe's *Sorrows of Young Werther*. It will not do to forget that this was an eighteenth-century book, published by a young man of twenty-five in 1774. We know that its influence lasted into the nineteenth century and that many young men of the later age felt a kinship with the unhappy lover who committed suicide. But to say only this overlooks the important fact that the novel is not a eulogy of its hero but a case study. Human beings, particularly young men, feel like Werther, yet the young author's self-analysis in the book is on the whole unsympathetic. Goethe understands Werther's feeling for Charlotte, for her children, for Klopstock, the thunderstorm, and the slices of bread and butter; but another and a stronger emotion is at work displacing the weaker. The one that prevails is the desire for psychological understanding which is to lead to self-mastery. That the effort succeeded is shown by the fact that Goethe lived to the age of eighty-three, having presumably shot his hero so that he himself could get on with his other work.

In the imitations or echoes of *Werther* the same devotion to psychological truth can be found, sometimes reaching the point of cruelty. It exists in Constant's *Adolphe,* in Leopardi's *Dialogues,* in Byron's *Harold,* in Musset's *Child of the Century,* in Vigny's poems and tales, and in Schopenhauer's stoical essays. Whatever these works may say of their authors' first hopes, none preaches a turning away from the facts that destroy hope. They are warnings, not models. In actual life, only one of these men—Musset—came to a bad end, though after producing much good work; Chateaubriand purged his sentimentality and emerged as the terse and lucid writer of the *Memoirs from Beyond;* Constant had a political career; Byron —a good-tempered, sensible man, as a critic and politician said of his letters—ended as a capable leader in the Greek revolt. None of them "escaped," each acted out his feelings. Indeed, most of them—Byron and Rousseau among the first—proclaimed that the goal of life is not happiness (in the sense of enjoyment) but activity. Unlike the sentimentalist who has a compartmented existence, the romantic realist does not blink his weakness, but exerts his power.

Romantic Life

I

Romantic art, then, is not "romantic" in the vulgar sense, but "realistic" in the sense of concrete, full of particulars, and thus congenial to the inquiring spirit of history and science. Romanticism is not simply a synonym for subjectivism, over-expressiveness, or sentimentality, though when strictly understood these terms suggest respectively the philosophy, the technique, and the inherited accident of romantic esthetics. Can it be that "romantic" meaning "wild and foolish" applies exclusively to a way of life? What was said about sentimentality should help settle that question, for it showed that the test of feeling is action, and action is also the touchstone for life as the romanticists conceived and tried to live it.

The most casual reader will have noticed that whenever a romantic artist is talked or written about today, the facts of his life seem to outnumber and overwhelm the facts relative to his work. Rarely does one find any discussion of Byron or Berlioz, for example, which does not very quickly lose itself in biographical detail. The obvious comment to make is that it is their own fault for telling us about their lives, and for being such good writers that we continue to read their memoirs and letters. Two centuries earlier, Hobbes and Boileau carefully recorded and doctored their biographical legend, but no one bothers to look it up. Once more it seems to be Rousseau who successfully showed the way with his *Confessions*. In him and his fellow romanticists, it is clear that life is of considerable importance in the shaping and testing of thought.

Hence as critics we must think biographically, that is, historically. But have we developed a technique for assessing the relation of life to art? I doubt it. From comments on romanticism we gather only that romantic life is part and parcel of romantic art, and that the romantic career is more disorganized than that of other men. Can this be the sole contribution of so many printed pages? Again, it is charitable to doubt it.

At the outset the historian must acknowledge that what we know about the career of art we have learned from the romanticists. They considered art an important profession both socially and philosophically. Accordingly, they analyzed its difficulties and disadvantages with their usual minuteness. We are thus in a poor position to judge whether previous epochs aroused more or less daily disturbance in the breasts of its poets, painters, and musicians. Yet all that we have on this point seems to suggest a fairly uniform experience. Shakespeare's sonnets, Dante's poems, Cellini's memoirs, Poussin's letters, even the *Epistles* of Horace and the dialogues of Plato, indicate that artistic work has requirements which do not jibe with those of a world organized exclusively for business and domestic life. So on principle we should be suspicious of any statement that the romanticists showed more oddities and led more distracted lives than their predecessors.

Besides, any comparison is imperfect which does not take into account unequal lapses of time. For example, we know that Socrates was ugly and unbusinesslike and had a shrewish wife and homosexual companions. But it was all so long ago that the vividness has gone out of these facts, leaving us a clear view of the wise man. Had he lived but a hundred years ago, every Socratic thought would be partly obscured by the figures of Xantippe and Alcibiades. His enemy Protagoras would have a party of defenders and so would the judges who passed the sentence of death. It is by virtue of the gradual clearing away of neighboring detail that works of the human spirit acquire that dignity and grandeur which, confusingly enough, we also call by the name of classic. In one sense, then, the romanticists have not yet had time to become classic.

But what is a romantic life? An answer lurks in the influence of Napoleon's example upon the men of the romanticist gen-

eration. Though there are notable exceptions, it is astonishing
how many diverse minds of the first rank were caught in the
Napoleonic spell. Beethoven, Goethe, Byron, Scott, Hazlitt,
Stendhal, Victor Hugo, Chateaubriand, Vigny, Manzoni,
Mickiewicz, Foscolo, Balzac, are a few whose opinions on the
subject are copious enough to show us the depth and discrimi-
nation of their regard. Napoleon was tyrant, conqueror, and
faithless usurper—this the romanticists knew and said with absolute frankness. They condemned his destruction of liberty,
his mania for war, and his open contempt for morality, but
they found him nevertheless an indispensable symbol. He objectified one of their sensations: they used him as a shorthand
sign of what they meant by genius and energy.

For he was the living and historical embodiment of his own
phrase: "Careers open to talent." One ought even to say "careers open to genius" since he was no common performer in
anything he undertook. He was *extra*-ordinary, and as the
dominant figure of his half century he centered upon himself
the gaze of all those who were pondering the nature of man's
fate. As Joubert said in Bonaparte's early days, "Without him,
one could not have felt enthusiasm for any living thing or
power. Thanks to him, admiration has come back to rejoice
the saddened earth." Napoleon was power, and fittingly—as
Byron notes in *Childe Harold*—he proved to be also weakness.

Out of admiration for him grew the wider attitude that has
been called the "cult of energy." In its worst aspects it could
of course become mere waste motion or violence. It could be
destructive of the individual, as in the career of Julien Sorel
in Stendhal's *The Red and the Black;* or demoralizing, as in
Balzac's insatiable heroes; no doubt the age devoured its men.
But we must not forget that when we speak of the romantic
life we mean a model held up primarily to men with the requisite balance of gifts for art or public life. If we apply the test
of fruits to both these groups during the romantic period, we
find that "romantic energy" is no vain phrase. Energy was not
merely a cult but a fact. Whatever we may think of its products, the products are there in abundance. The labors of Scott
are legendary but true, so are those of Balzac. The historical,
editorial, and political work of Guizot, of Gentz, of Macaulay;

the threefold career of Goethe; the nine hundred canvasses of Delacroix—not counting his murals; the patience of Blake, the incredible output of Turner; the herculean activity of a Weber, Berlioz, Paganini, or Liszt in creating a new musical world— all this means work if it means nothing else.

And to each man's share must be added his particular studies, avocations, and political acts. I spoke before of the romanticists' concern with history: in France it was a committee of literary men who unearthed, edited, and published within half a dozen years sixty-five volumes of historical documents for the then newly founded Société d'Histoire de France —an enterprise carried on as a side line to the production of plays, novels, books of verse, editions of older poets, political speeches, and a staggering mass of critical journalism.

This summary is not meant to overvalue the artistic merit of mere bulk, but to connect it on the one hand with the cult of energy, and on the other with a disputed quality of romantic life—robustness. On one occasion, Goethe is reported to have said that classicism was health and romanticism disease; and this has been repeated as a final judgment. But Goethe later modified the dictum and pointed precisely to the fertility of the Romantic impulse. It would be interesting to go into what Goethe and Schiller meant by their own "classicism," but it is enough to say that Goethe was content to call his second *Faust* "Classic-romantic," and to eulogize in it the spirit of modern poetry under the shape of Byron. Moreover if we apply Goethe's own excellent test—the test of seeing whether a man's outlook paralyzes his will to create—we find a full refutation of the disease theory in the mere mass of romantic work. Chateaubriand's declaration: "I was overwhelmed with a superabundance of life," characterizes the group as a whole and explains its labors.

An equal measure, though of a different form of strength, is the situation in which Hazlitt found himself when courting a very ordinary coquette. Driven to despair by her contradictory antics, the essayist felt he had to relieve his anxieties by writing down the facts and observations which compose that remarkable document, the *Liber Amoris*. Here we think we catch sight of romantic life in its most typical aspect—the aspect of unhappy love, made worse by confession, that is, by self-pity and egocentric display. The truth is that this so-called *Book of Love* is a remarkable document of dispassionate introspection—a piece of analysis so far from futile brooding that its author was at the same time producing also the critical essays which form the second volume of his *Table Talk,* work of a quality as high as any he ever did.

This instance could be duplicated many times over from the biographies of the romanticists. It may be De Quincey at grips with opium and poverty, Balzac with his creditors, Byron and Shelley with their families and friends, Victor Hugo or Mazzini with the police—production goes on as if the issue of a war depended upon it.

Some critics who have perceived this priority given to work over concerns that would cripple most men have argued that the work must be "insincere" or "empty" or "a refuge." Such judgments would have to be tested one by one in their particular applications, a task beyond the scope of this book. But we note in passing that they contradict that other critical gravamen, of a romantic disease ending in artistic paralysis.

The chief cause of confusion in dealing with romantic careers is, as I have said, the lack of ethical principles for assessing lives and works. We forget, often willfully, that a biography or autobiography records only a few moments of a man's life, his spectacular encounters with mankind or the universe. Going from peak to peak, it does not explore the valleys where the quiet work is done, even on a day of storm and stress. We, and not the romantics, do the exaggerating. We take the entirely true statement that on a given occasion the artist was overwhelmed by a piece of news and remained distraught for six hours, and fail to compute that that leaves him eighteen in which to be himself again. We imagine, we like to imagine, we prefer to imagine, the romantic artist flying headlong from one crisis to another and doing his work in fits of absence of mind. We construct a storybook romanticism out of incomplete observations and then attack this fiction as if its faults belonged to the reality it conceals.

We should remember that in any biography the ratio between years and pages is always misleading, and in both directions: too much and too little. When one considers that many of the best-known romantics died before the age of forty, that most of them met with every kind of rebuff, and that even the temperamentally indolent or the physically disabled have left enviable memorials of their talents, one is forced to admit that these men, who are dubbed idlers, wastrels, and lovelorn egotists, had a remarkable knack for getting things done.

Even with the unfortunate German school of Novalis, Kleist, Tieck, and Wackenroder, the facts and the appearances are much the same. A writer of the last generation, Ricarda Huch, thought she was being both just and sympathetic when she defined "the romantic type" as "one who is lazy and proud of his laziness"; but a less excited scholar put the matter more truly. Says Professor Silz: "Her chapter entitled 'The Character of the Romanticist' should be entitled 'The Character of Ludwig Tieck.'" In other words, as too often happens, a single example, or one imperfectly analyzed, is palmed off as the whole of the evidence.

In saying that energy is the distinguishing mark of romantic life, I am not implying that a previous or a later age did not also have its herculean workers. Voltaire and Diderot were certainly giants of activity, but I believe that apart from single instances that may occur in any time, energy as expressed in output bears some relation to the cultural lie of the land. I do not think it is altogether because Mr. T. S. Eliot and Mr. Paul Valéry are superhumanly fastidious that their poems are so few.

Meantime we need not be surprised that the romantic life was robust and productive, because, as we know, the romanticists were stimulated, pressed onward, justified by extraordinary events. The French Revolution and Napoleon had, in Stendhal's phrase, made a clean slate. But this stimulation was purely spiritual. No one was waiting with open arms to receive their gifts. One has but to read the lifelong complaints of Goethe—a relatively fortunate man as well as a stoical mind—to see that the energetic life had to be lived in a dampening milieu. For the habits of individual men change at unequal rates, and when it seemed to the young Goethe or Schiller "impossible" to go on turning out literature in the manner of their predecessors, it seemed to the good burghers not only possible but desirable that this should be done.

This state of affairs explains why we associate the struggle of the artist against his environment with the romantic period. Excepting Scott and the historians, there was hardly one to whom fame may be said to have come without a long struggle. The artists were often, but not always, the aggressors, because they felt it their mission to say truly what they saw. Nor were the times out of joint merely because the artist felt private wrongs; he had also formulated standards by which to judge the world and its institutions. Whether it was liberty or monarchy or economic reform, or religion that the romanticist advocated, he was confident that society could change; the revolutionary era had proved change possible. Under the old regime, if a Mozart rebelled against the intolerable servitude of a patron's household, all he could do was run away. In the nineteenth century, the artist starved just as much as in the eighteenth, but at least he made his grievance known, he analyzed the general conditions that made it representative, and he fought society's instinctive attempts to muzzle him. It is this rhythm of repulse and counterattack which lends to the lives of so many romanticists that defiant and assertive character which in looking back we mistake for egotism or misanthropic sulks.

But as we have just seen, the issues the romanticists fought for were larger than their personal selves. They were political, social, and esthetic issues. It is in the classicist epoch, under authority, that artistic hostility is as individual as the rivalry of courtiers: Dryden attacks Shadwell, Racine is egged on to compete with Corneille, and Pradon set up to undo Racine. The public character of romantic art—as against the coterie aspect of classicist art—helps to explain the deplorable confusion between the artist's work and his life. Already in the seventeenth century Pascal had expressed a preference for finding a man rather than an author between the covers of a book. The romantic period fulfilled his wish. But this continuity of art with life affected the artist's reputation. To the artist, life and work are distinct; he knows the relative importance of a temporary lack of funds and a completed symphony. But in the hands of a careless or ill-intentioned critic, the trivialities of existence can be intermingled with the finished work in such a way as to create an impression of misdirected energy, of powers out of control or successful only by accident. Finding the trivialities picturesque, we assign the same value to the anecdotal and the critical, and we end by projecting a kind of precipitate of all the anecdotes upon all the artists of the era.

What we call a "romantic life" in the vulgar sense is all too often a reflection of the mental confusion fostered by bad biography, just as our wish for peace is the cause of the serenity we find in the men of the classical period. What confirms me in this belief is the frequency with which the biographer who has studied a particular romanticist discovers a character differing from what he expected. The critic thereupon asks us to modify the meaning of romantic in that one instance while he continues to use it vulgarly in other contexts. Mr. Abercrombie does this for Wordsworth, Mr. Sackville-West for De Quincey, Mr. T. S. Wotton for Berlioz, Mr. and Mrs. Stebbins for Weber (as we saw earlier), Mr. Edmund Blunden for Leigh Hunt, Messrs. Grabo and White for Shelley, Mr. Stringfellow Barr for Mazzini.

This hardly exhausts the list, but let us listen to a few of the critics' cautioning words. Lionel Trilling says: "It is Shelley's life, more than anything else, that has hindered the understanding of his work, [so that] a biography like Professor White's is necessary not only for historical but for critical completeness." T. S. Wotton writes: "Berlioz's music may be now better known; still to many, the man is better known than the musician, and many of those who know something of the music have not yet disentangled their picture of the man from their appreciation of his art." Edmund Blunden: "Mistaken or malevolent notions concerning Leigh Hunt die hard in England. . . . We may therefore be the more particular in the correction of this ungenerous ignorance." Walter Silz: "A mere perusal of the fragments of Friedrich Schlegel and Novalis should suffice to disprove the myth of the vague, emotional, unreasoning Romanticist . . . they were men of intellect, of supreme intelligence and extraordinary analytical power, masters of incisive criticism and trenchant polemic. . . ." C. D. Thorpe:

"Any valid final estimate of Keats must take into account his quite complex nature. It is clear he cannot be lightly disposed of as a mere dreaming poet interested only in sensuous beauty. . . . No one who has read Keats's remarkable correspondence and has then turned to an earnest consideration of his poetry can fail to see that he was a man of thought and intellect."

The common element in these remarks is the insistence of the writer on the discrepancy between the factual evidence and the usual opinion. Unable to reconcile these two as regards the particular romantic case, and wishing to correct public ignorance, the critical biographer simply whittles away the name "romantic" by an ever-increasing series of exceptions.

This means either that we have no biographical standard of maturity or that we do not apply it justly. If we kept in mind the disordered lives of classical specimens such as Cardinal de Retz, Richard Savage, John Wilkes, or Voltaire; if we lingered over the love affairs of Racine, and cared as much about Descartes' mistress and illegitimate daughter as we do about Wordsworth's; if we had more vividly before us the falsifications of Pope; if we recalled Johnson's rowdiness or his bursts of weeping at the reading of his own poetry, we should perhaps form a more balanced conception of what human beings are like under comparable circumstances, and we should cease to find mad or monstrous the lives that the romantic artists led.

We could make these necessary inferences and correct our own "romantic" folly, if we could bear in mind that in all cases, classical as well as romantic, it is only on account of extraordinary achievements that the details of the life have been preserved. And by studying the art independently we could discover its solidity, order, reasonableness, and so work back to the character of its maker. Mr. Julian Green is a modern who can do this. He notes in his diary: "I read once more, with the utmost delight, Rousseau's *Confessions*. That admirable style can express anything it wishes by the use of the most ordinary words. . . . I know of no other example of an elegance of style that is so free from artificiality and pose; but what efforts that simplicity must have involved!"

Whatever the period or subject, we should learn to mistrust that lay figure of biography we keep hidden in our mind's closet, possibly an image of ourselves—the man who has never been crossed in love, never angry, nor poor, nor dejected, nor ridiculous, nor passionate, the man who is pure wax throughout and beside whom any living creature is bound to seem a crude specimen. In the absence of critical ethics, the least we can do is what the American historian Dunning recommended when General McClellan's reputation suffered a blow from the publication of his love letters to his bride: wait until the appearance of other generals' love letters. In other words, judge generals as military men, and romantics as artists, *first*.

II

So much for the most salient feature of romantic *practical* life—its energy and the harnessing of its energy to the production of large-scale works. A second meaning of "romantic life" is more abstract. It suggests a *theory* of life, born of a spiritual insight rather than of productive strength, though also full of consequences in action.

If I should allude to a masterpiece of modern times which described how a man came to doubt all the truths he had learned in the schools and grew disgusted with the professional arts; how he decided to leave his study and wander through the world, seeking experience and learning from the book of life; and how, at last, he came to devote himself to working on his own plan for his fellow men—if I gave such a description, almost everyone would assume that I was outlining the theme of Goethe's *Faust*. This would not be wrong, but it so happens that the same words would apply equally well to the autobiographical part of Descartes' *Discourse on Method*.

There is nothing strange in the similarity, for the situation in both these life stories is common enough. But *Faust* is rightly supposed to be the gospel of the romantic life. How then does it differ from Descartes' confession?—In this, chiefly, that Faust's life is the life of every man. In the romantic view, the lesson of Faust has to be relearned individually through experience. The lesson of Descartes can presumably be learned from reading the remainder of the *Discourse on Method*. Des-

cartes has alone done the perilous work; he has taken the risks
and wrested the true answers from his experiences. The lesson
that Faust learns can only be found in the undergoing of experience itself.

This agrees with what we should expect from the abstract
and authoritative character of classicism as contrasted with
the concrete and individualist character of romanticism. But
so much has been written about the romantic search for experience, and in praise or dispraise of the striving which goes
with the search, that we must look farther into their meaning.
First consider Descartes' or Faust's disgust with academic
learning. "Grey is all theory," says Goethe, and "green only
Life's golden tree." Is this a callow throwing over of tradition
by some impetuous and self-conceited youth? No. Descartes
—whom I may use interchangeably with Goethe up to their
point of divergence—is careful to point out that he is learned
in the knowledge his teachers gave him and even fit to be himself a teacher. Faust is also a learned man, a doctor in every
possible sense. Why then break the continuity of culture? This
is like asking, Why need there have been a romantic movement? Or if we want to particularize, Why did so many romanticists go through crises of rejection early in their lives?
John Stuart Mill's is the most famous, though not the first. Before him, Wordsworth had had such a crisis, Fichte and Carlyle
also; Vigny and Shelley likewise. The German romantics who
came immediately after Kant, Goethe, and Schiller had possibly the worst time of it. These violent "conversions" had certain points in common. In them all, we find studious youths
crippled by a vast emptiness of spirit. The crisis consists in
rejecting, with full risks, the inherited modes of experience and
taking up activity as the path to new ones. Carlyle's once well-
known words apply here: "The Everlasting No had said: 'Behold, thou art fatherless, outcast, and the Universe is mine';
to which my whole Me now made answer: 'I am not thine,
but Free, and forever hate thee. . . .' From that hour I began to be a man." This is, by and large, the way in which
Wordsworth, Coleridge, Shelley, and Mill put aside the eighteenth century and set about creating the nineteenth.

Obviously the "freedom to experience" in this sense is a

loaded phrase. These young men had been experiencing, in the ordinary sense, from the cradle. But nothing is a stronger proof of the fact that experience is made by choice, as well as given by nature, than the courageous *volte-face* these young men made when they became conscious spirits. The step was not taken altogether without help. I am thinking of the influence of Berkeley upon Shelley and Coleridge; of Spinoza upon Herder, Schleiermacher, and Goethe; of Marmontel and Wordsworth upon Mill; of the German philosophers upon Carlyle. These influences being nothing more nor less than tradition, or rather traditions, in the plural, it is a stupid literalism that supposes the romantic life to begin by cutting off its own roots. Rather, romanticism began by tapping deeper layers for its spiritual nourishment, having found the topsoil barren from overuse.

Through crisis but with a guide, then, the life of experience begins. What are its contents? A usual answer is that it is self-indulgence—in love, in drugs, in melancholy and pleasing thoughts of death—a fullness of impulse without self-control. The neo-classicist Paul Elmer More vivified this belief by suggesting that the definition of the romantic was a man with a bottle in front of him and who could not stop drinking. For a scholar and a Platonist, who should have been familiar with both *Faust* and Plato's *Drinking Bout,* the imputation was at once a blunder and a libel. The mere physical output of the romantic energies precludes the possibility that romantic Experience meant self-indulgence. We know that Faust is soon disgusted in Auerbach's wine cellar, but possibly one meaning of romantic experience is that it is not vicarious or abstract: having been in a wine cellar and learned disgust at first hand, Goethe could not, any more than Milton, praise a cloistered virtue.

Among the actual romantics there were indeed opium-eaters and melancholy poets. Of the former, the principal are Coleridge and De Quincey, neither of whom, as everyone should know, took up the drug for pleasure or "experience." In their day laudanum was regularly prescribed for stomach ulcers and other painful complaints, and what is remarkable is not that these two succumbed to the habit, but that they both exerted enough will power to overcome it—Coleridge twice and De Quincey four times. The fact that the evil itself yielded experience is incidental; what is not incidental, but an effect of will and genius combined, is that that same experience was transmuted into *Kubla Khan* and the dream fugues.

As for the drug called love, the historian has a right to be somewhat impatient with the common idea that it was invented by the romanticists. Classical society makes of love a much more exclusive object of interest, both in life and in art, than does romantic society with its wide and diverse interests. It is in any case impossible to exclude love from any conception of human experience. The only question worth considering is how that particular kind of experience shall be treated, individually, socially, and artistically. In the popular phrase, romantic love idealizes its object, that is, the romantic loves an illusion: an error that can always happen. Yet in the romantic period one is struck by certain recurrences which I shall simply enumerate. First, the idealization of the loved one by the artist is not incompatible with a sense of reality. Faust tells us that Gretchen is a pure soul—and she is. But he also knows—and tells us—that she is an ignorant girl, with red hands roughened by housework.

Other poets may put more or less emphasis on the imperfections of their beloved, or they may be interested in other things. Rousseau, for example, irritating as he is in the love passages of his "New Héloïse," is obviously trying to introduce more openness and simplicity in the relations of the sexes, and he knows that in describing what is new he strays from the possible. Again, what we call idealizing in romantic love is often the recognition that a woman is a person worth respecting, as well as an object of desire—it is a germ of feminism. At the same time, the romantics' demand for the fulfillment of desire is a complementary recognition of the fact that to love a dream picture, to pine away in silence like Marivaux's eighteenth-century heroes, is pure sentimentality.

If, however, repeated disappointments or lack of fixity in love is our test, the romantics seem to show about the same degree of perfection as any other group of men. Their relatively large output of love poetry need not be ascribed to flightiness but rather to the fact that they were poets and also young. Many died before middle age, like the soldiers of the Revolution. Those who lived to ripe years turned quite normally to subjects thought fitter for the meditations of the elderly.

But youth is also the time of melancholy and the first realization of death, so we should not wonder that Shelley, Keats, Poe, Beddoes, and Büchner, return to this theme. Yet even in their song it is possible to discern more notes than we generally hear. Poe is not always macabre. He is a great critic and writer of "scientific" stories; Keats's letters are not indited to "easeful death," they are boisterous and gay; Büchner is a revolutionist and a satirist; Beddoes a critic and a creator of grotesques, as well as a politician and medical man. The pace and variety of romantic life may be too fast for us, or we may be overimpressed by what is striking; but the truth remains that the romantic artist has often modulated to a new and different experience while we are still complaining of his "constant" addiction to a previous one.

The seeker after experience loves variety because the world is various, because life is made up of contrasts, because opposites help destroy the temptations of provincialism. Hence the romanticist travels. Foreign lands and customs and literatures truly exist, and not only one's own. Nothing, therefore, could be more inappropriate than the term "exotic" applied to romantic tastes, for exoticism implies the classic belief that one is at the center of the universe and that everything else is *ex*-otic to it.

This cultural relativism does not contradict the general report that the romanticists were also nationalists. But the label "nationalist" has considerably changed its meaning since the romantic period. The men of that time seldom, if ever, used the word to describe themselves, and if we must use it about them, it must be with the modifier *cultural* in front of it. The romantics' nationalism is cultural nationalism. They spoke less of nations than of "peoples," whom they considered the creators and repositories of distinct cultures. The romantics could hardly have overlooked popular cultures and remained good historians, or even good critics. But they went further and maintained that each human group, being a unique product of history, was worth preserving in its integrity. They compared Europe to a bouquet, each flower growing in its appointed soil, a simile which only slowly degenerated into the racial absolutism of blood and fatherland.

The romantics indeed repudiated the classical effort to impose a common speech and art on all of Europe. Whether we turn to Herder's *Thoughts on History*, where he rejects "those ignoble words, 'the races of men,'" whether we read Wordsworth's full exposition of romantic nationalism in his pamphlet on the *Convention of Cintra*, or whether we follow Victor Hugo's wanderings in *The Rhine*, we find this same nonaggressive cultural nationalism, which cherishes diverse folkways for what they are.

Modern critics of romanticism are prone to assert that out of this doctrine grew present-day mysticisms about nation and *Volk*. This outcome, they add, was all the more natural because the romantics preached the struggle for life—an idea, they go on, which is not only included in the Faustian myth but is a part of the biological view of man which twice in our century German imperialism has exploited.

This implication of descent is plausible but not true. By hurrying over the points of contact between one idea and the next it shows as inevitable and universal what was in fact only local and possible. We saw earlier how the peculiar condition of Germany under the Napoleonic tyranny put a premium upon aggressive energy. This energy developed around the idea of the state and was re-enforced by that of a nation united through its common culture. At this stage it was indeed cultural nationalism militant—but militant in defense. Even so, it was not a unanimous feeling. Many felt as Goethe did in looking back upon this period: "How could I take up arms without hatred? And how could I hate without youth? I have never shammed. I have never given utterance to what I have not experienced. I have only composed love-songs when I have loved. How could I write hate-songs without hatred? And between ourselves, I did not hate the French, though I thanked God when we were free of them. How could I, to whom culture and barbarism are alone of importance, hate a nation which is among the most cultivated on earth, and to which I owe so great a part of my acquirements?"

Out of his younger fellow poets' hatred grew, without question, the mood of 1870 and 1940. It was a progressive shift from defense to offense, about which I shall have more to say in the next chapter. But its setting and purpose have nothing specifically romantic. As for the idea of struggle, Goethe's oft-quoted text says *streben*, that is to say "strive," a word which can be filled with any contents, and which it is sheer demagogy to interpret as necessarily meaning human fighting.

Striving, to be sure, implies resistance, opposition, and ultimate victory or defeat. But these are metaphors that apply to exploring the Antarctic or building a tunnel as well as to winning battles. The romantic view of life did rejoice in risk, adventure, and heroism. It said that these things *were* life, and it still remains to be proved that life can be maintained individually or collectively without them. When the Western world as a whole adopts the creed of passivity, rewards those who decline adventure, and cherishes the lotus-eater above the doer, it will be time to scorn the romantic apostles of Faustian striving.

I said earlier that classicism provided a fixed greatness: the king was great whether he did anything or not. Romanticism could only admire an active greatness; it even admired failure if greatness had been shown, because it knew that it is by a succession of failures that man can overcome both himself and the indifferent universe. The goal and the reward were, as in Wordsworth, "Resolution and Independence"; and romanticism knew that these were not given, but won by striving.

The farther aim was salvation, the search for the infinite reality that corresponds to man's infinite longing. In this search romanticism reached out for many fulfillments. I need only list the pantheistic union with nature felt by Goethe, Schelling, and Berlioz; the Protestant revival led in Germany by Schleiermacher, Hegel, and Jacobi; the Catholic revival begun in England by John Henry Newman and the Tractarians and in France by Chateaubriand and Lamennais; the liberal or radical agitation of Byron, Hazlitt, Hugo, Mazzini, and others; the cult of science preached by Vigny, Goethe, and John Stuart

Mill; the socialist programs of Fourier, Saint-Simon, and Robert Owen; finally, the systems of philosophy, of history, and of art still subject to debate.

Among these, three may be called other than humane or humanitarian in purpose—the economic system of Adam Müller, the anarchical egotism of Max Stirner, and the Young Germany movement with its poets, *Burschenschaften*, and Wartburg Festivals. For excellent reasons—which are no excuse—these were solely German manifestations, though of a spirit which their authors might well say they learned from Napoleon and his French armies. If this is true, we should then have to discuss the self-perpetuating effects of wars of aggression, from Caesar to Hitler, and not the contents of philosophies elaborated for the most part by peaceable poets and speculative intellects.

Romantic striving may therefore be summed up as the effort to create order out of experience individually acquired. It is a striving because human experience does not automatically dictate its own forms or point out its own values. That the task of man is to discover these for himself is shown by his possession of energies and desires.

Accordingly, romantic life led in two directions—union with God, conceived either traditionally or pantheistically or metaphysically; and work for mankind, conceived in the form of either social improvement, or the creation of art, or the application of science. Faust dies, we must remember, upon perceiving that his happiness lies in the hope of helping men by the building of a great dike. His last words are an affirmation of things ampler and better than are remembered by those who use "Faustian" to mean egotistical and destructive:—

> *Yes! to this thought I hold with firm persistence;*
> *The last result of wisdom stamps it true:*
> *He only earns his freedom and existence,*
> *Who daily conquers them anew.*
> *Thus here, by dangers girt, shall glide away*
> *Of childhood, manhood, age, the vigorous day:*
> *And such a throng I fain would see,—*
> *Stand on free soil among a people free!*

Then dared I hail the Moment fleeing:
"Ah, still delay—thou art so fair!"
The traces cannot, of mine earthly being,
In aeons perish—they are there!—
In proud forefeeling of such lofty bliss,
I now enjoy the highest Moment—this!

The judgment of Mme. de Staël, aided by Schlegel's, that the
romantic view of life is basically Christian seems fully justified,
for it combines the infinite worth of the individual soul in its
power and weakness, the search for union with the infinite,
and the gospel of work for one's fellow man.

VI

The Four Phases of Romanticism

I

The two preceding chapters have concerned themselves with essences—those of romantic art and romantic life, insofar as they can be generalized about by disregarding differences of time, place, and temperament. From the conclusions arrived at, we gathered that the common meaning of romantic has to be radically modified if it is to accord with the facts, and that its usual sense is quite irrelevant to the purposes of cultural history. Leaving essences we now turn to the course of events and answer the query, "After romanticism, what?"

Any simplification of history such as is implied by a phrase like "the four phases of romanticism" is open to objections arising not only from local diversities, but also from differences of opinion as to when a given phase begins or ends. To illustrate this difficulty and set the stage for the "four phases" suggested here, I shall first briefly sketch the development of romanticism in its national and chronological aspects. Throughout the *eighteenth* century, all over Europe, signs appeared of new interests and new feelings about neglected elements in life and art. This is sometimes called eighteenth-century romanticism or pre-romanticism. It covers the period from Dyer and Thomson to Cowper, from Klopstock and Wieland to late Lessing and early Goethe, from Marivaux to Marmontel and Chénier—a fairly spontaneous rise of novelty everywhere, in spite of crosscurrents of influence. But this movement is not as yet romanticism. There is in it too great an intermingling of the old with the new, and the all-important new forms, which are the mark of decisive cultural change, are still lacking.

Departure in form appears at widely spaced intervals in the several countries of Europe, and first in Germany—partly because her eighteenth-century literature was largely of French importation, partly because her rich tradition of German folklore was never stamped out by a centralized absolutism. Under Lessing's vigorous and brilliant attacks, second-hand and second-rate classicism fell away and the new forms appeared as early as the 1770s with Bürger's *Lenore*, Goethe's *Götz von Berlichingen*, and Schiller's *Robbers*.

In England, the shock that broke the dominant tradition seems to have been the French Revolution. We can date romanticism from Burns and Blake. Then Scott and Wordsworth sharpen the break in the decade 1789 to 1799, all four deeply moved by the meaning of the events across the Channel. But understandably enough, those same events in France itself had the effect of delaying the outburst of new ideas. Dictatorship, at first revolutionary, then Napoleonic, stifled expression and directed energies to political ends. The most gifted French poet alive in 1789, Chénier, went to the guillotine in 1794. Three years later, the young Viscount René de Chateaubriand was in exile in England, where he published his *Essay on Revolutions*, a mixture of rationalism and the historical spirit, of Rousseau and traditional monarchism. It was not until 1800 that he returned to his native land and saw his fame assured with the *Genius of Christianity*, in which, as someone has said, Pascal triumphs and becomes a poet.

But there were further delays. The Napoleonic censorship suppressed original thought, and the encouragement that Mme. de Stael meant to give to the new ideas by her book on Germany was cut off by the police in 1810. It was not in fact until ten years later that the young genius of Lamartine made itself heard. Between 1820 and 1830, then, is the incubating time of French romanticism, which burst forth in full-blown vigor towards the end of the decade with Hugo's Preface to *Cromwell*, Stendhal's *Racine et Shakespeare*, Delacroix's *Death of Sardanapalus*, and Berlioz's *Fantastic Symphony*.

In Spain, Italy, Poland, and Russia, the establishment of

romanticism paralleled in time its coming of age in France. Italy—or rather Milan—was perhaps in advance of Paris, and Spain and Russia a trifle lagging, unless we except the ripe genius of Goya, which reached its high point during the Spanish war of liberation from Napoleon. Everywhere, the new developments were the outcome of deeply rooted national traditions, combined with a common recovery from the eighteenth-century blight on poetry. Russia and Poland offer particularly good examples, their romantic revivals being in fact their first great and original literary epoch since the Renaissance. It is now called, as a result, the "classic period" of their literary history. With Pushkin, Gogol, and Lermontov in Russia, Mickiewicz, Slowacki, and Krasinski in Poland, these two countries not only made lasting contributions to European literature, but explored and gave form to their own past and present, their own reality and ideals, with a fullness and power that nothing in their previous pseudo-classical and pseudo-French tradition could have led one to expect. Here as elsewhere, the quick reception of influences, as shown in, say, Pushkin's Byronism, is a sign, not of imitation but of pre-established sympathy between minds independently tending towards the same goals.

Romanticism as a European phenomenon, then, comes of age between 1780 and 1830, and remains undisputed master of the field until about 1850. This period constitutes what I find it convenient to regard as the first phase. By the latter date, 1850, some of the greatest names in romanticism belong to the dead: Burke, Burns, Byron, Shelley, Blake, Keats, Scott, Wordsworth, Coleridge, Hazlitt, Lamb, Pushkin, Lermontov, Espronceda, Goya, Büchner, Beddoes, Chateaubriand; Leopardi, Beethoven, Chopin, Mendelssohn, Schubert, Schumann, Bellini; Bonington, Géricault, Balzac, Stendhal, Gérard de Nerval, Goethe, Schiller, Hegel, Schelling, Schleiermacher, Hoffmann, Kleist, Hölderlin, Novalis, Wackenroder, and the brothers Schlegel.

This list reveals that in seventy years, two semi-generations —an older and a younger group—have made their contribution and left the stage; yet in the short working time of twenty to twenty-five years allotted to each group, all the forms, ideas, perceptions, tendencies, genres, and critical principles have been put forward which the rest of the nineteenth century is to make use of in its further development. What I am suggesting is that the first phase of romanticism is one of extraordinary, unremitting, "unspecialized" production in all fields. The next three phases, which we are about to examine, are efforts at specialization, selection, refinement, and intensification. Romanticism sounds all the themes of the century in its first movement. The next three movements develop one theme each. These next three movements are: Realism, Symbolism —which may also be called Impressionism—and Naturalism. The divisions in time are roughly: 1850 to 1885 for Realism, and 1875 to 1905 for the other two movements.

Each of these takes the form of a strong reaction against its predecessor, with the exception of Naturalism, which reacts against its own contemporary, Symbolism. This strong reaction is accompanied, of course, by theories which tell us that the preceding movement has failed, but which generally point at the same time to some part of that movement as containing the germs of a solution to the new problems of the particular art. Thus, for instance, the realistic Russian novelists admire and vindicate parts of Gogol, but separate them from what they are pleased to call his romanticism, as if the artist had not been himself in both aspects of his genius.

In the nature of things, the movements that follow the "failure of romanticism" are, like any specialization, easier to grasp and define. They are more consistent and concentrated; they have more the air of a school about them. But when closely examined they show such clear marks of stemming from the main trunk that no doubt can arise about the thesis here presented: romanticism does not die out in 1850 but branches out under different names like a delta.

This has sometimes been remarked, but usually in piecemeal fashion. The relation of the Pre-Raphaelites to Blake, and of the Impressionists to Turner and Delacroix, is perhaps the most visible, and hence the most often noted, but it is not necessarily the closest. In some cases, as with Zola and Flaubert, the debt to Hugo and Balzac has been admitted by the artists themselves. This is also true of the debt owed by the

Russian Five to Glinka, Weber, and Berlioz. That owed by
Debussy and the whole French school to Berlioz has also been
demonstrated. Often, where the kinship between a romantic
and a post-romantic may seem tenuous, the appearance can
generally be accounted for by a quantitative difference: there
is much more Impressionism in an Impressionist than in Delacroix, because Impressionism is all there is in an Impressionist.
What is plain in the later man is but one aspect of the work
of the earlier.

I need not add that opinions are free to vary as to which
of any two phases is preferable—the first, encyclopedic, or one
of the later, selective. With this question of taste we are not
concerned. Modern feeling, for understandable reasons, works
against a just appreciation of romanticist performance. Even
so, to choose among artists otherwise than in the light of one's
own enjoyable perceptions is foolishness, and to want styles
immutable is but to quarrel with history: there is neither the
need nor the possibility of a new full-scale renaissance or romanticism every twenty years, and after an epoch of revolutionary triumphs, artists can only refine.

If there were any doubt about this, the doubt would be
removed by the tendency, noticeable in many romanticists,
to end their career with a conscious effort at refinement and
simplification. Tieck and Pushkin, Berlioz and Goethe, are
good examples, for whom there is no need to invoke the misleading cliché of "reformed romantic" as if there were something of the repentant criminal in a change of manner. It is
very likely that if a certain type of artist lived for two hundred
years while his contemporaries lasted the usual span, he would
follow without constraint or imitation the curve of their successive changes of style. This is not artistic determinism. It
suggests not a cause but a condition of art, namely that its
problems and techniques follow an inner logic, at the same
time as they respond to that outside pressure of the times
which the greatest artists have seldom wished to resist.

II

With these generalities in mind, we are in a position to do

for Realism what I have tried to do for Romanticism: to see as far as possible through the eyes of its representative figures. Since Realism began with the assumption that romanticism had failed, what is meant by this failure? Obviously romanticism had failed to please the younger generation. But had it failed absolutely? It seems a paradox to speak of failure and yet go back to haggle over works and men as critics and artists have been doing for a century. If the first phase of romanticism ended in bankruptcy, why the waste of time over the wreckage? Undoubtedly what is meant is failures, in the plural.

For unquestionably romanticism failed at many things. It failed to establish a universal order, permanent peace, and a common language of art and philosophy. As E. M. Forster has said, history is a series of messes. From these, temporary and local achievements stand out like isolated peaks. This is in fact what romanticism asserts about the world, and the paradox would be to have its clearest perception belied by its own results. In classicism, the peak is the establishment of fixed order for a small class by the exclusion of real but disturbing facts. In romanticism the peaks are individual achievements, serviceable to others not by enforced imitation but by free choice. Consequently romanticism is rich in successes, and proportionately rich in failures. Who tries for much stands to gain or lose much. No concealment in mediocrity is possible, even if desire for concealment were present.

As heralds of defeat one thinks first of those disheartened German romantics who turned joylessly to Catholicism, neo-medievalism, and political nationalism, because a more inclusive and more perfect order did not win the support of their fellow nationals. Next, one looks at the so-called Victorian Compromise, which followed the Reform Bill of 1832 and the rise of industrialism. There one sees political order achieved by a class who voluntarily accepted the strictest code of morality as a substitute for force and a guarantee against revolution. That purpose was fulfilled by subtracting from the romanticist program a certain freedom of individual behavior and certain expressions of the feelings. At this cost intellectual freedom alone was saved out of the larger romanticist scheme.

On the Continent, where between 1830 and 1848 a similar

attempt was made by a part of the bourgeoisie, one thinks of the series of uprisings and revolutions which precluded compromise while seeking a short cut to the good life, that is to say, the concrete goods romanticism had desired: individual liberty within the social organism; the satisfaction of man's needs under the spur of imagination; and the pursuit of the intellectual, national, and religious life without superstition or intolerance. By 1850 all these legitimate aims were disappointed, whether they had been expressed as liberalism, as cultural nationalism, or as Utopian socialism.

The rebound from this disappointment was Realism. The very word wants to convey that what romanticism desired was not possible and that the romanticists' methods would not work. Realism is the fox in the fable who said the grapes were sour. This likeness does not prejudge the case against Realism, though to this day no one can affirm that the romantic aims are not achievable by the romantic means. Realism, meanwhile, was sure that they were not, and hence turned to two familiar devices—force and materialism. It developed *Realpolitik*, which means the abandonment of principle—on principle—and the adoption of cynicism in its place. The signs and successes of this new method were seen in the unification of Italy under Cavour, that of Germany under Bismarck, and the emergence of the second French Empire under Napoleon III.

In thought, materialism played the same role that force played in politics. In the highly symptomatic work of Karl Marx, the two are united. Force replaces either the concerted good will of the earlier socialists or the individualist-mutualist schemes of a Fourier or Proudhon. In German philosophy, the materialistic school flourished in the fifties with Moleschott, Ludwig Büchner—the brother of the dead romantic poet—and Feuerbach, whose writings influenced another symptomatic character of the period—Richard Wagner.

Behind all these manifestations of force and matter was the august authority of physical science, particularly chemistry and the new physics, which had just established the theories of the conservation of matter and the mechanical equivalent of heat. Here, too, unification was going on, and a new world system was being built which seemed a bridge reaching back to Newton over the dead body of romantic, vitalist biology. For this was also the time when the work of Spencer and Darwin once again delivered biology over to materialism. So ripe was the occasion that within five years after the appearance of the *Origin of Species,* the belief began to spread that science was synonymous with *Darwinismus.* The return to eighteenth-century mechanism was complete, and it looked as if romanticism had never been, except for the fact that Realism discovered and gave fame to a neglected romantic philosopher—not a materialist, but a stoic who had proclaimed the inescapable badness of things—Arthur Schopenhauer.

What had in fact occurred? A *reduction* of romantic perceptions and methods to a single term: Realism meant force *without* principle, matter *without* mind, mechanism *without* life. And what was the motive of this simplification? The quicker or surer achievement of some of the romantic aims: nationhood, social order, intellectual unity, the improvement of the human lot. Marx's socialism proceeds from all the motives of his so-called Utopian predecessors, but scorns morality and persuasion while presenting itself to the public as science. Finally, what method served this realistic reduction? It was the method of appeal to a common denominator. Liberals, conservatives, and radicals were united by their common desire for tangible, territorial nationhood; scientific hypotheses were tested by their suitability to mechanical representation or analogy—it was the heyday of the luminiferous ether; while force, which is by its nature the great leveler, was applied as the universal solvent of social contradictions and complexities.

This notion of a common denominator ruthlessly adhered to is of course essential to science, though it may make a difference to science itself which denominator is chosen. But Realism had as yet no inkling of this. It equated science with the common denominator of matter, which is why the postromantic period seems in all ways so scientific. It felt it had at last reached solid ground, not only in the study of nature but in that of history, philology, law, economics, and anthropology. It prided itself on correcting the errors and "extravagances" of the romanticists—though as one candid scholar pointed out, if the romanticists had not been, there would have been nothing to correct.

This pattern appears with identical effect in the domain of art. The Realist schools that sprang up in the fifties and sixties were inspired by the desire to correct and amend romanticism. Here again, what were the characteristic romantic failures? Some have already been mentioned—overexpressiveness; unsuccessful attempts at new forms; an exuberance of animal spirits, translated, as in Elizabethan England, into an exuberance of language; a too zestful appetite for dramatic contrast, intensity, and distortion. To these may be added a certain roughness and carelessness of treatment, side by side with the most finished and minute detail—Gothic or Shakespearean characteristics, which are frequent in the works of men conscious of their strength and indifferent to proving it.

Repelled and irritated by all this, the realists applied as their new criterion of the "really real" the denominator of common experience. Flaubert supplies the classic example of Realism so defined and made into a method. *Madame Bovary* is the bible of Realism as *Faust* is the bible of romanticism. We have often enough been told how hard Flaubert worked and we know from successive drafts of his novel what he was working toward. He strove for truth through the exclusion of subjective detail, by which—if the reader will recall our earlier definition—I do not mean fanciful detail, but simply individual and possibly uncommon perception. In the various stages of a description of rain falling on Rouen and the surrounding hills, for example, Flaubert flattens out every image, removes every salient word, docks every "original" idea, until what is left is what anybody might have said about the scene—though nobody, of course, but Flaubert could have said it. Scene and prose are objectified by being made completely intersubjective.

Now a noteworthy fact about the master of Realism is that he began as a romanticist. He himself recorded the transformation. "How did you spend your youth?" he inquires of a friend in 1858. "Mine was very beautiful *inwardly*. I had enthusiasms which I now seek for in vain; friends, alas, who are dead or changed. A great confidence in myself, splendid leaps of the soul, something impetuous in my whole personality. I dreamed of love, glory, beauty. My heart was as wide as the world, and I breathed all the winds of heaven. And then gradually, I have grown callous, tarnished. I accuse nobody but myself. I gave myself over to absurd emotional gymnastics. I took pleasure in fighting my senses and torturing my heart. I repelled the human intoxications which were offered me. Furious with myself, I uprooted the man in me with both hands, two hands full of pride and strength. I wished to make of that tree with verdant foliage a bare column in order to place on its summit, as on an altar, I know not what divine flame. . . . That is why I find myself at thirty-six so empty and at times so weary. Is not this story of mine a little like your own?"

The secret of Realism lies in this change, in these "emotional gymnastics." It was not only Flaubert's story but that of all his self-aware contemporaries who at the sight of the material conditions of their time determined to replace the "tree with verdant foliage" by a bare column. Flaubert, as we shall see, underwent another spiritual change and ended as a symbolist, but his importance for us here is that he first crucified romanticism in himself, knowing that had he not done so, his romanticism would have been secondhand, anachronistic, inadequate; just as it was in Emma Bovary, who, as we all know, read Scott in her adolescence and dramatized herself as a heroine throughout life. When Flaubert reached the point of saying, "*I* am Emma Bovary," the Realistic *coup d'état* had become history.

Because Flaubert had to blind himself to the realism in Scott and to pick and choose among the elements of Balzac does not mean that he was ungrateful or unjust as a critic. It means only that specialization had set in. A different order of genius was being used upon selected materials. "Flaubert," as John Peale Bishop aptly said, "already represents a deterioration of the romantic will in which both Stendhal and Byron, with the prodigious example of Napoleon before them, could not but believe."

For fifty years or more after Flaubert, the novel was to be the plausible and minute recital of commonplace events. More than that, because the setting and routine of life were being made increasingly drab by industry, the contents of the novel became more and more dreary and dull, until that moment in George Gissing's *New Grub Street* when the wretched Biffen loses the manuscript of the most realistic of all novels—so like life that its dullness will make it impossible to read.

That the great realistic novels of the mid-century are anything but dull hardly disproves the validity of Realism as a method. For though by it the real is defined as the commonplace and tends towards the sordid, it yet covers and cultivates so wide a field that to see it systematically exploited is in itself a pleasure. The romanticists—Scott, Balzac, Hugo, Stendhal, George Sand, Gogol—had shown in famous chapters what could be done with the commonplace and even the sordid. And the new, total Realism did not always achieve the naked form that Flaubert sought for. In Dickens, in Thackeray, in George Eliot, and even in Trollope—partly because they were born during the heyday of romanticism, and partly because of the Victorian moral tone—realism often appears side by side with an agreeable make-believe which I have termed secondhand romanticism. I mean such things as the story of Amelia and Dobbin in *Vanity Fair* or the change of plot forced on Dickens in *Our Mutual Friend.*

The result of this compromise between the real and what was thought more agreeable was unfortunate. For it reopened the door to sentimentality, of which the romanticists, as we know, had barely purged themselves in mid-career. The same condition that had created sentimentality in the eighteenth century—the split between reason and feeling—reproduced it after 1850. It accounts for the worst in the great Victorians up to Swinburne and Meredith. I mean not only the two distinct layers of substance in the English novel, but the corresponding attempt in a poet such as Tennyson to reconcile his solid ideas with a penchant for storybook conceptions; or in Browning to combine "tough" colloquial speech with secondhand adventure drawn from Renaissance history.

Worst of all, this same split is reproduced in Matthew Arnold, one aspect of whose influence canonized this effeminacy. Although Arnold's poetry usually succeeds in crystallizing deeply felt moods, it is deplorable that he should have been

the one to filter the romantic poets' output through his sentimental critical taste. It is to him that we owe our incomplete
view of Byron and of Wordsworth; it was he who, by coining
the phrase, helped create the legend of Shelley as an "ineffectual angel beating his luminous wings in vain"; it was he who
objected that Burns dwelt on the unlovely aspects of Scottish
life; it was he who by his methods for testing poetry narrowed
its scope to grandeur and nobility, thus masking the realism
of the romantics and disqualifying Dryden, Pope, and Swift
as poets; finally it was he who exhumed from their quiet rest-
ing places the least sturdy representatives of the earlier generation—Sénancour, Joubert, M. and E. de Guérin—and thereby
encouraged men to associate the romantic temper with droop-
ing self-pity.

On the face of it, Realism was most congenial to the literary
arts. To it the novel owed its supremacy, and in the theatre
Realism enthroned the well-made play, which was staged with
all the "accuracy" that nineteenth-century research and mechanical contrivance could desire. Through this visual art Realism also affected both music and painting. For in the mid-
century the dominant musical form was that in which material
realism has importance—the opera. Its masters were Meyerbeer and Verdi, both trading on the achievements of romanticist music and romanticist playwriting. I have shown at length
elsewhere how this tradition culminated in the *Gesamtkunst-
werk* of Wagner, which may be called pan-realistic through
its appeal to eye and ear by means of a junction of all the arts.

In painting, the school of Courbet, refining on the principles
of Delacroix, Corot, and the open-air school, followed the pre-
cepts of Realism by its choice of subjects from daily life and
by its treatment of them in as undramatic a manner as possible. Courbet paints animals, cliffs, men breaking stones by a
roadside, a picnic, a village funeral, himself arriving from a
walking trip and greeted by his host—the moment is seized on
as by a camera, for purposes of record. With the exception of
the large manifesto painting, "The Naked Truth," there is, as
in Flaubert, a conscious refusal to suggest atmosphere, individuality, or point of view.

This has been alleged as a reason why Courbet and the

realists generally were not successful as portrait painters. That may be stretching the influence of doctrine too far. But the part it still plays in vulgar criticism is well illustrated by the comments that a visitor to the National Gallery in Washington could read, some years ago, on the wall next to the two portraits of Alfred Bruyas by Courbet and Delacroix respectively. Bruyas was a southern French businessman interested in the arts, and he was painted by both artists in the same year, 1853. According to the notice Delacroix, being a romanticist, made Bruyas look "unhealthy and Hamlet-like," whereas the realist Courbet "has stressed the directness and acumen of the wealthy patron of Montpellier; the figure has greater weight and healthy energy." This faithfully reflects the attitude that the Realist would like the observer to share: business acumen is more *real* in a patron than thoughts about art, and bodily weight than expression of countenance. Matter dominates Mind.

III

It was Delacroix, nevertheless, and not Courbet, who was destined to lead the art of painting to its later development in Impressionism. But for chronological clearness, we must first cross the Channel and say a word about a school of painters and poets who, while Realism dominated France and caught their interest for its technique, were moving on to new things. I mean the Pre-Raphaelites, and particularly the Rossetti family, who initiate the third phase of romanticism by their conscious primitivism and new use of symbols.

The link between the style of Coleridge's *Christabel* or that of Keats's *Eve of St. Agnes* and the poems of the Rossetti circle is sufficiently apparent; a second influence was the rediscovery of Blake by this very group; a third was the inspiration of Delacroix, faint but real: "Delacroix specially," wrote Ford Madox Brown in his diary, "[Rossetti] now thinks the greatest painter of modern times." A fourth and final influence was the precept and encouragement of Ruskin, who as Turner's champion was prepared for both Impressionism and Symbolism, and in fact became the patron and preserver of the Pre-Raphaelite movement. Not all in the original Brotherhood turned into genuine Symbolists. Millais and Holman Hunt reverted to a modified Realism; but others who had had contacts with the group, notably Swinburne and Meredith, were in their own work to make a sharp break with Realism as we have defined it.

It remains to explain what symbolism means, since it is clear that all art whatever uses symbols. The specialization that deserves the new name consists either in new combinations of symbols—be they words or shapes—or in the unexpected transfer of a symbol from its usual meaning and context to a new one. The "scarlet cry" is the familiar poetic example, one of many in romantic verse. Blake's poems are almost wholly made up of such transferred and reshuffled verbal symbols, his difficult Prophetic Books, like their illustrations, being nothing but a systematic use of the device. We readily see its usefulness for reacting against Realism. By limiting itself to words and images that are universally current, Realism rapidly wears out its symbols. It keeps the context eternally the same, for fear of falling into an individual variation of the true. Artists tired of realism have no choice but to revivify symbols by putting them to unaccustomed uses in unaccustomed places.

Or rather, artists have a choice between this attempt to refresh the conventions and a return to an older set. And to put this alternative in its proper relation to all the post-romantic efforts, I must here digress. The marginal doctrine I have in mind is nineteenth-century neo-classicism. Being a purely individual, though recurrent tendency, it has no distinct place in the chronology. But some of the men who followed a neo-classic course are important enough to mention briefly. Puvis de Chavannes, who decorated the walls of the Boston Public Library and many public buildings in France, fairly represents the quality of the neo-classical mood. Its keynote is calm, austerity, determined anti-Realism as well as anti-romanticism.

It is in fact anti-present-day-ism. Though it takes the arts seriously, it regards them as the decoration rather than the expression of life; hence, like its parent classicism, it believes in rules independent of time and space. Thus did the poet Leconte de Lisle polish many beautiful verses about subjects antique and oriental; and thus in the second half of their careers did Brahms and César Franck seek to restore purity and "form" to music. They generally meant by this aloofness or piety combined with academicism. Matthew Arnold himself was tempted by an imaginary Greek ideal and produced the tragedy of *Merope* under its inspiration; but it was a vision that had obviously paled since the day when Sophocles saw life steadily and whole.

None of these five fully succeeded in welding their derivative subject matter to their would-be classical form. Theirs was a reaction against Realism which may be truly called reactionary, and it is this which lends a characteristic flavor to their work. What could be more refreshing than to see the contemplative Grecians who in Puvis's work represent chemistry and physics, industry and trade; or to think that in the middle of the toilsome nineteenth century he should paint "The Fisherman's Family" as a collection of pink and placid athletes, grouped about a smack that has never been to sea? Clearly, these are the fishermen of a golden age when the day's catch jumps ashore into the net. Neo-classicism is a sometimes moving expression of that distant hope, but in the century of romanticism the gap was still too great. Classicism had as yet no social role to play.

Having made this brief circuit, we can return to the third genuine and powerful phase of romanticism: symbolism. With the Pre-Raphaelites, as we saw, it took the guise of the "new simplicity" in order to work at the revivification of pictorial and poetic symbols. What we now call "arty" is the exaggeration of these tendencies, which Gilbert and Sullivan satirized in *Patience*, this play, incidentally being directed not at Oscar Wilde, as is usually said, but at the Pre-Raphaelites who were Wilde's forerunners. For symbolism did not stop with the relatively mild "strangeness" of Rossetti and his friends, still under the realistic afterglow. Symbolism developed in the direction of increasing subjectivism in word, image, and sound, and finally presented such a united front against the older Realists as to deserve the name of neo-romanticism.

Flaubert shows the gradualness of the transition very clearly. *Madame Bovary* is Realism: *Salammbô* is realism laid in a foreign setting, with the result that the commonplace for Carthage is nevertheless strange and wonderful for Europeans. This historical novel is, as it were, a way of playing truant from the Realist school without incurring the charge of romanticism. For the next step, Flaubert pulls out his old manuscript on the *Temptation of St. Anthony* and, by pruning it, shapes a work without plot, without visible bearing upon common life, occasionally without literal intelligibility, a veritable symbolist "prose poem." In it, as already in *Salammbô*, we find a sensuous pleasure in words, a sought-after musicality, which are contrary to Realistic tenets. In *St. Anthony*, there is added a multiple allegory that relates the work to symbolism. In a parallel manner, Wagner, the great idol of the Symbolist poets, straddles both movements. He appealed to the Symbolists by virtue of the allegorical, legendary, and atmospheric elements of his operas, while he taught them and their elders the meaning of the music "realistically" through its close association with concrete objects.

The musical impressionists, who came later and of whom Debussy is the best-rounded example, made the break with Realism complete. They not only chose their texts from the Symbolist poets themselves, beginning with Rossetti, but they were symbolists (or impressionists) in their disregard of the rhetoric of melody and chord, which they broke up and rejoined in new contexts. Here as elsewhere, the sign of the passage from realism to symbolism is the deliberate abandonment of established syntax.

The poetical creed of a Verlaine, the obscurities of a Rimbaud, the involution of images in Mallarmé, the impalpable atmosphere of Whistler's nocturnes, are but the working out of the premise that Realism is a very narrow and short-lived convention, which fails to give permanent unity to experience. Symbolism attempts the reunion of the two halves of experience—the inner or subjective part with the outer and communicable part—as against the divorce, productive of sentimentality and materialism, which Realism dictates. As we shall see later, and as indeed we all know from reading Proust, Joyce, and Gertrude Stein, the work of remaking language for the sake of a new synthetic experience is by no means over.

A comparable course of action explains the development of the school of painting known as Impressionism. By refining more and more on the perceptions of the human eye, by making use of the scientific truth that white light is made up of colors, and that complementary colors heighten each other's intensity when set close together, the Impressionists followed a worthy "realistic" bent which soon landed them clean outside the photographic reality. The effects achieved by their divided palette and the pointillism that gives such a wonderful brightness and shimmer to their canvases were so exactly studied and managed that the original beholders thought the painters were mad or making fun of the public. The retort was that realism was itself an arbitrary selection from among visible objects, and that the impressionist goal was to convey a new truth by means of a new set of symbols—dots and dashes of bright paint. Outline may have disappeared in the process, just as fixed views of natural objects had proved illusory under changing lights, "but"—prophesied the Impressionists— "you will soon see Nature as we do"; an outcome which Oscar Wilde was to erect into the principle that Nature imitates art.

Looking back on these three groups—the commonplace realists, the faithful impressionists, and the evocative symbolists—we are permitted to draw an important conclusion about the evolution of style. Strictly speaking, every school of art pretends to capture reality and every successful school does it. The classicist dwells on the reality of the abstract and the general; the romanticist on the concrete particular, both mental and physical; the Realist with a capital R, on the commonplace and physical; the Impressionist, on the individual impression of the physical; the Symbolist on the need to extend the range of his impressions and to make them vivid once more by defying realism and convention. Each doctrine takes in more or less; each doctrine at the beginning of its trial has validity; each doctrine, when repetition and imitation have set in, disintegrates from lack of meaning and conviction—and falls a prey to its successor.

This leaves us with one more wave of the romanticist impulse to discuss, namely, Naturalism. It is the fourth phase, but not in order of time, since its manifestations coincided with those of Symbolism and Impressionism. There occurred a split, in other words, in the generation that protested against dogmatic Realism. One group—generally the poets—preferred to exploit the subjective domain of idea, dream, word-music, and legend. These are the symbolist poets from Rossetti down to Rimbaud, Mallarmé, and Maeterlinck. The other group, chiefly novelists, were unwilling to forget the collective reality of late nineteenth-century Europe—its cities, factories and slums, its wars, social problems, and scientific beliefs. In this group Zola, the Goncourt brothers, Strindberg, Dostoevski, Huysmans, Sudermann, and Verhaeren belong. Some men, finally, divided their allegiance—the Goncourts, to begin with, who are the true precursors of modernism in taste as in style; and such men as Ibsen, Verlaine, Hauptmann, William Morris, John Davidson, and George Moore. I do not pretend to give a survey of the period or even to fit these names with finality, but to suggest tendencies.

In music, naturalism was made a conscious program by some members of the French school, principally Alfred Bruneau, and interpretation has extended the meaning of the word to apply to such composers as Moussorgsky, Chabrier, Charpentier, and most of all to Richard Strauss. In painting it may not be too farfetched to class Cézanne and the Post-Impressionists with the naturalists, as men who said in effect, "Objects exist—and not merely light—but Realism is too narrow. We shall restore the solidity of objects, but we shall paint either the commonplace or the uncommon, as we please; and in a manner suited to our temperaments, whatever the photograph-minded public may think." The Post-Impressionists also brought to light the genius of the romanticist Daumier, whom his contemporaries—excepting Balzac and Delacroix—had dismissed as a mere political cartoonist.

An interesting difference between the literary naturalists and the post-impressionists is that whereas the latter took their stand squarely on the artistic requirements of the situation in painting, the former pretended to treat of life according to scientific methods. At least the French naturalists, led by Zola, believed for a time in the possibility of making their novels "experimental researches" into the nature of reality. The de-

vice of accumulating genuine case histories from the news-
papers—a practice which Dickens and Charles Reade had already followed; the "working up" and insertion of technical
dissertations into the body of the novel—which Balzac and
George Eliot were wont to do; and more importantly, the selection of subjects that involved the study of social plague spots
—these things constituted the naturalistic stock-in-trade. The
contradiction between the claim to scientific dispassionateness
and the reforming zeal is only on the surface. Zola would have
answered that his work was *applied* science. But in applying
it, it was evident that the individual was re-entering the scene
he had left under Realist theory, and Zola ultimately admitted
that naturalism was a corner of life seen through a temperament.

When this admission was made, the outlook of science itself had begun to change. The hypothesis of materialism was
undergoing a thorough riddling at the hands of critics such as
William James, Nietzsche, Samuel Butler, Bergson. These men
did not attack science or its method, but only its temporary
ally, mechanistic materialism. It was becoming ever clearer
that science did not copy reality in full but selected from it
and created symbols—verbal or mathematical—to fit the relevant facts. The language of science was as arbitrary and man-
made as that of art: It was both Symbolist and Naturalistic.

The result of casting loose from narrow Realism was a kind
of scientific neo-romanticism: in biology and evolutionary theory, the work of De Vries and Bateson was creating a non-
mechanical science of genetics. In psychology, James and
Freud were displacing Spencer and overturning mid-century
dogmas. In morals and art criticism, Nietzsche had revised all
the "Realistic" values and discredited the authority of Darwin,
Marx, and Wagner. In physics, Max Planck and Einstein had
revised Newtonianism and raised more questions than Newton
or the nineteenth century could answer. For by this time we
have reached the twentieth, the first world war is on the verge
of breaking out, and the cultural work of western man is about
to suffer another of its periodic eclipses.

VII

The Modern Ego

I

Despite inner conflicts the three main schools that followed romanticism were intensive developments of themes enunciated during the first half of the century by the romantics proper. The frequent condemnation of the nineteenth century as one whole shows the compelling unity of the four phases, a unity which can legitimately be broken down for many purposes, but not for the purpose of singling out romanticism as a lapse of the European intelligence. Such a lapse could with better reason be found in the four years of the first world war, which did not merely waste the supply of mind and its energies, but broke in mid-career the fresh cultural impulse of the century.

If we take up the thread of history again after 1918, we find ourselves in a cultural milieu we cannot disown or separate from the present. The modern period in its contemporary sense is the quarter century since the Armistice.[1] Chaotic in appearance, our epoch has the same community of features which distinguishes every epoch, and which it is now our task to examine.

But I must make plain at the outset that in this and a part of the next chapter, I shall shift my point of view while also

---

[1] Written for the readers of 1943. By now, 1960, "Modernism" is just beginning to acquire the tone of the past. The name itself grows empty for us, though it is full of recognized and cherishable associations. For further comments on the current scene, see Chapter ix. (J. B.)

limiting my scope. Instead of trying to give a rapid but comprehensive notion of Modernism, I shall deal only with what seems to me its intellectual vices, its perverse critical deficiencies. I have set down elsewhere a defense of the modern period, particularly of its strong and healthy roots in the decade preceding the world war, and I am not now recanting the opinions I there expressed. The reasons for putting on blinders here are several: Modernism is vast and our space is short; I can moreover count on the reader's firsthand acquaintance with modern works and modern ideas and dispense with a descriptive appraisal. And most important, I want to show with what self-serving notions and attitudes the present day judges romanticism. In restricting myself to our ego, instead of encompassing our mind, I furnish an example of the very method that many moderns use in judging the romantic century.

I shall not consciously go as far as some of its detractors, but I shall generalize about modern traits that I recognize are incidental and temporary. Every age has its mannerisms and we too are marked by the indispensable quantum of illusion, the willingness to compromise where our interests are at stake, the vanity and bombast, provincialism and pride, which have long since been imputable to mankind. In short, we are alive and we show a partiality to ourselves which, were it applied to a past epoch, would seem like the absence of critical intelligence. This may for convenience be called ego, and I follow Pascal again in assuming that the ego is always hateful.

Though I admit all this and my purpose too, it may still appear that I am unduly lenient to the nineteenth century and unduly harsh to my own. I can only repeat that to be harsh is no part of my intent. A judgment is not necessarily a condemnation; and a judgment has to be both comparative and consistent with stated principles. The principles have been stated, the comparison drawn between a classic period and a romantic, and I now attempt a sketch of the sequel. Far from condemning it, I think the present period so much less fortunate than the early nineteenth century that it needs all our sympathy. It goes without saying that if cultural comparisons are to be fair, men and ages must be judged relatively, that is, achievements measured against opportunities. For how much men achieve is not wholly in their power, but our opinion of others' success *is* in our power or ought to be. With which Herodotean Oath of good faith, I turn to the "contemporary chaos."

The first striking trait of the modern ego is self-consciousness. I say self-consciousness rather than self-awareness, because I believe that in spite of much heart-searching, the modern ego is more concerned with the way it appears in others' eyes than with learning fully about itself and admitting its troubles fearlessly. The romantics were introspective, too, but they did not fear ridicule as we do, which is why we accuse them of indecently exposing their innermost souls. They were often wrong about the value of what they had to say, but they were unafraid of being wrong, of being themselves, and of being duped. The modern ego is desperately afraid of all three. It suffers from what the French call *mauvaise honte*. Let me cite as a hint of this the dedication of Ezra Pound's poems *Personae:* "This book is for Mary Moore of Trenton, if she wants it." This is the modern tone, it is the stance of awkward shuffling.

This trivial instance is a symptom of an organic ill, which is: the systematic distrust of one's perceptions and desires. Here are from the same book of Pound's the concluding lines of "Epilogue":—

> *Our emotion remains*
> *Your emotions?*
> *Are those of a maître-de-café.*

The assumption here is that something has been concluded about the worth of emotion, and also that the emotions of a *maître-de-café* are generically lower, coarser than even the worthless ones of the person addressed. The modern ego begins its career with self-contempt, and it expresses scorn by a violent, and indeed hostile, obtruding of the ordinary. We are far from Wordsworth's common emotions of common men; we repudiate these without quite knowing what ours should be. T. S. Eliot made the same observation more abstractly when he noted that the result of modern culture has been to obscure "what we really are and feel, what we really want, what really excites our interest."

One might reply that in order to have one's interest excited, one must first put aside mistrust and be willing to take a risk, be willing to be excited, instead of waiting to be galvanized convincingly. But most of the important work of Ezra Pound, Cocteau, Eliot, Apollinaire, and other representative moderns is a reiteration that things are not what they seem. This may be always worth saying because reality must always be re-discovered, but the modern ego is so perpetually hurt by this need that it hides its wounds under an affectation of toughness and expresses its uneasiness by bravado. In this ubiquitous, almost automatic response to life it betrays one quality which will not keep: youth. Open E. E. Cummings's *Is 5* and you hear the defiant note at once; it is not very imaginative: "My only interest in making money, would be to make it. Fortunately, however, I should prefer to make almost anything else, including locomotives and roses. . . . Whereas non-makers must content themslves with the merely undeniable fact that 2 times 2 is four, he [the poet] rejoices in a purely irresistible truth to be found, in abbreviated costume, upon the title page of the present volume."

Surely, this attack on the battered corpse of commercialism is ineffectual, this self-assurance is false. T. S. Eliot's early work shows the same kind of collegiate invention, side by side with lines of great power. I quote from the poem "Gerontion," which is precisely intended to show the rottenness and false-ness of our post-war civilization by dramatizing its cosmopoli-tan and acquisitive character:—

              . . . by Mr. Silvero
With caressing hands, at Limoges
Who walked all night in the next room;
By Hakagawa, bowing among the Titians;
By Madame de Tornquist, in the dark room
Shifting the candles; Fräulein von Külp
Who turned in the hall, one hand on the door. Vacant shuttles
Weave the wind. I have no ghosts,
An old man in a draughty house
Under a windy knob.

I have so far taken illustrations from our poets' early work, written soon after the war. This is simply to begin at the beginning. Besides, that decade is a decisive part of our history. And, for comparison, the ages of the writers correspond with those of Byron and Shelley and Pushkin. If most young poets are egotists we can juxtapose the two sets and gauge what has happened to the youthful ego in the intervening century. It has become thin, strained, weakly arrogant. It is the paralyzing egotism which Goethe feared for the younger men about him. The ego is indeed a constant threat, and in the 1920s there were excellent reasons for the disgust and paralysis of the finer self. The war just ended had been anything but heroic or meaningful to the young artists who suddenly found that they were called upon to speak. No wonder they could hardly find words for anything but a secret indignation transmuted into outward defiance. The continual check and its emotional causes have been ably rendered in a passage about a fictional poet:

". . . he tried the line over, hoping it might be poetry, but . . . found it on examination to be full of the very quality he spent his life in denouncing. Every word was wrong; every word was romantic and banal and . . . had probably been used by the so-called poets of the nineteenth century. Those impossible Romantics! He tried again: ochreous residue, heart's dregs. That was sufficiently unlike Tennyson, but it wouldn't do; 'dregs' was trite, and 'heart' was one of the bad old words, and anyhow the whole thing came perilously near being a statement. 'Excrement' would be better than 'dregs,' for neither Keats nor Shelley would ever have said 'excrement.' But why write about autumn at all? 'Autumn'— another prohibited word. It only shows how frightfully second-rate I am, concluded Brian. He was self-contemptuous and enjoyed self-contempt. He took a sadistic pleasure in analyzing his moods and disposing of his pretensions."

We now see that the objects of their indignation and defiance quickly became fixed points for their later course. So much so that its artistic expression may be given a name from

T. S. Eliot's work and called "the principle of Sweeney and the Nightingales," that is, the principle of dropping out the bottom from under any mood by the sudden juxtaposition of another. If we start with the disgusting Sweeney, we end with the nightingales singing near a convent; if we start with anything resembling beauty, we are catapulted into the mire. This is an old satirical device; it helps make Byron's *Don Juan* the masterpiece it is. But what becomes of its force if the sudden descent is required, expected, automatic? The will of the poet turns into the egotism of the prankster and the power of his art singularly diminishes. We are prepared for the doctrine of André Breton, the legislator of the Surrealist school: "To compare two objects as remote in character as possible, or by any other method to put them together in a striking fashion, remains the highest task to which poetry can aspire."

The various applications of this dogma have been defended as the rediscovery of a principle forgotten since the seventeenth century, that opposites coexist. In a very lively dialogue in defense of modern poetry, Ruth Bailey says that the seventeenth-century poets could be and do many things at once in their verse, and that after two hundred years modern poetry has relearned the technique of wit which a multiple awareness requires. But she rather damages her case for the need to go back so far by quoting Coleridge on the "necessary balance and reconciliation of discordant qualities."

She says moreover that the modern poet can "feel a thought." But this used to be one of the objections to romanticism, whose intellect was supposed to be impaired by the mixture. And of course it mixed other things productive of wit, as one can see not only in *Don Juan* but *Faust,* and also in Novalis, Heine, Blake, and much of Victor Hugo. If it is the ability to stand above oneself and the universe and look quizzically at the scene that is required, one need only turn to the German school which gave "romantic irony" its name. If, as Miss Bailey correctly says, modernism wants to offset sentiment with satire, seriousness with mockery, admiration with disgust, enthusiasm with reason, she will find in the romanticists the contrasts, the mingling of styles, the love of the grotesque, the ugly, and the trivial in conjunction with the beautiful and the rare, by the use of which they destroyed classical uniformity. Even the purposely prosaic squibs embedded in lyricism, such as T. S. Eliot's on the *Boston Evening Transcript*, find their parallel in Schiller and Goethe's epigrams against their contemporaries.

There is thus no need to invoke the seventeenth century, unless it be to accredit modern techniques as still another form of specialization based on romanticist models. This would be instructive about the modern ego, telling us of an insecurity that nothing allays, for in romanticism proper the possibility of a mood sustaining itself without jar was held to be real.

What modern man questions is whether this possibility has ceased to exist. If it has, then the ending of *every* lyric in sneers, the petering out of *every* tune in percussion and dissonance, and the decoration of *all* physical beauty with maggots is justified by the twentieth-century world of experience. But it is also possible that the incessant application of the formula is symptomatic only of the state of the will behind the ego, the condition of those who, in Eliot's words

. . . are terrified and cannot surrender. . . .

To trace the consequences would take us on a longer circuit than is here appropriate. It is enough for our understanding of modern self-consciousness that the damaged will accounts for the peculiar and obligatory sense of humor of our time, the defensive laugh coupled with every action, to forestall derision by someone else or one's later self. And from diseased will again comes the despair which represents acts of cruelty as funny.

Nor are these familiar occurrences part of a postwar mood which has passed. The crippled state persists and has nothing to do with individual circumstance. It is cultural and its effect on art is therefore fundamental, as Constant Lambert brilliantly showed: "It was the most natural thing in the world for Liszt to take his young countesses on Lake Como and read them Tasso and Victor Hugo. If anyone still thinks this spirit exists, let him visualize himself taking his young woman on the Serpentine and reading her T. S. Eliot. I don't want him to dismiss the argument as facetious or trivial, I just want him to spend a minute or two visualizing the scene. The various inhibitions, social and personal, which would prevent this scene taking place, or being in any way moving did it improbably take place, exactly explain why the modern composer cannot hope to write a movement like the Gretchen section in the *Faust* symphony."

I hinted earlier that perhaps it was not solely a more exacting taste that kept the output of our great modern poets so small. It is in part, of course, the paralyzing thought that everything has been done. It is also the conviction which Valéry and the Existentialists proclaim, that non-being is superior to being. It is, lastly, the recoil from risk, not out of cowardice but out of self-knowledge.

In a man of the older generation such as Stravinsky this inner check hides behind a variety of poses. The dominant one is perfectionism, which has been carried so far in the public mind that reputations can be made by maintaining an inverse ratio between time and output. An artist who publishes one work and says he has burnt a trunkful is acclaimed as a master. The implication is that in the periods of great production, everything is jerry-built or patchwork, whereas the slim column of the modern perfectionist will outlast the ages. It certainly concentrates the critical attention and earns the price of a planned scarcity. Another pose is that of the scholar who restores tradition. This is done by composing pastiches, not for amusement or virtuosity's sake, but as the next step on the main line. Whatever can be shown to be precisely "in the spirit of" some classical classic is authenticated. Still another affectation is to defy criticism in a manner that would have made the aged Goethe or Victor Hugo—Olympians both—blush and stammer. Here is what Mr. Stravinsky invites us to feel about the works of his third period: "There is nothing to discuss nor to criticize; one does not criticize anybody or anything that is functioning. A nose is not manufactured, a nose just *is*. Thus, too, my art."

Yet the modern ego is not without its characteristic mode of criticism, which has been given the name of debunking. This activity was first displayed in biography by Lytton Strachey, who discourses on method in the Preface to *Eminent Victori-*

ans. We discover there how, with perfect detachment, the historian's eye watches for the telltale sign that will reduce the stature of the great. The recurrent phrase throughout Mr. Strachey's works is "a bundle of contradictions." Newman can be hard-hearted and yet play the violin with tears streaming down his face. What a contradiction is man! The modern ego is apparently reassured by finding the fissure in the rock. The inference is that the weakness we feel is not ours alone.

The spectacle would be touching, were not debunking used to destroy admiration. No doubt, to admire what is false may corrupt judgment, but to admire nothing at all, for fear of being duped, is a progressive disease of the spirit. As G. M. Young pointed out: "Mr. Strachey has much to answer for. The skill with which he composes Variations on a Standard Biography cannot be communicated. . . . But when once he had written in fancy script on the back gate of Rugby 'Teacher Arnold's legs are too short,' it required no great originality in Mr. Kingsmill to chalk up underneath 'And M. Arnold's got a girl in Switzerland.'"

It would of course be exaggeration to say that the modern ego admires no previous artists, but it is certainly reluctant to admire the great of recent centuries. Its preference goes to the lesser or the distant figures. For example, the artists Stravinsky chooses from the nineteenth century are Bellini, Gounod, Bizet, Delibes, and the earlier Verdi. Sauguet, a modern, is to be respected because he is in the true line of Gounod. Beethoven also is great, but only because having been denied the gift of melody, his efforts to get on without it were remarkable.

Ought one, on this evidence, to infer that the modern ego, like water, seeks its own level? Perhaps not on this evidence alone. But the renewed study of minor poets, the onslaught on what bulks large—"the heaven-storming side of Beethoven"— the ostentatious preference for chamber music, in short, the preciosity coupled with the belief that subtlety is enough argues the wish to avoid overwhelming comparisons.

What seems conclusive is the modern ego's tenderness for the late nineteenth-century French poets. Whereas the contemporary critic scorns the romanticists as morbid, maladjusted, idle, and morally weak, he finds inspiriting and lovable the lives of Verlaine, Baudelaire, Rimbaud, Ducasse, and so on down to Proust and Joyce. Their diseases, aberrations, and antisocial traits, their turpitudes, shootings, and love affairs, claim his most generous attention. In France particularly, where anti-romanticism defines the true artist, the billing and cooing with the shade of Rimbaud reached such a pitch that in reviewing a book on the subject Denis Saurat began by saying: "There are some very good things about this book: one is, the authors do not believe that Rimbaud was a saint."

Let this point not be misunderstood: I have no objection to the minutest and most loving studies being made of the French Symbolists. But if the question of an artist's disease or distress is thought relevant to his merit, then the standard must be uniformly applied. If we are drawn to the Symbolists by their physical and moral mishaps, then we must not sneer at Chopin's tuberculosis or make a crime of Musset's drunkenness.

II

The modern predilection for the French Symbolists has other connotations. Men look back to an artist or a period because these seem earlier cases, already somewhat clarified by time, of present predicaments. It is noteworthy that the clichés of anti-romanticism can be found ready-made in the French *avant-garde* literature of the eighties and nineties. Obviously the bond between our mood and theirs is the artist's feeling of isolation from society, his difficulties in getting produced, and his rooted belief that the future is not brighter but darker than before.

Here one hesitates to judge. Comparisons of results achieved are difficult; comparisons of possibilities as they appear to men of talent and genius are beyond assessment. But the material conditions in which new art is born should not on that account be misconceived. The last hundred and fifty years have, on the whole, been kinder to artists than any previous culture. Certainly in the romantic period difficulties were as great as now. Where then were the museums of modern art, the foundation patronage, the universities eager to be baffled, and the predisposition of the public to think itself wrong and the artist right? Because it was the beginning of a cultural span, however, discouragement and despair were more readily taken in stride as part of the battle of ideas, which was in turn an aspect of politics.

This was particularly true in France, which lessens our surprise when we find modernism dependent on the French tradition for anti-romantic arguments as well as for technical models. To be sure, one should not underestimate the influence of the metaphysical poets on the moderns, but my point still stands, for, like Symbolism, that seventeenth-century school was a refinement and pruning down of the previous Elizabethan romanticism, and also a retort to the realism of its last playwrights.

In any case, the principal influence—by which I mean instinctive choice—is that exerted by the French poets upon Eliot by way of Ezra Pound. This soon became a direct connection between our poets and Rimbaud, Laforgue, and Mallarmé. No true poet, of course, is reducible to the sum of the influences playing upon him, but it would be interesting to take up the question of, say, wordplay in the symbolist school and trace its ramifications through the moderns, from Yeats and Amy Lowell and Joyce and Gertrude Stein down to the most unaware of journalists and advertising-copy writers.

Symbolism is, in truth, still our artistic creed, even under the forms of Dadaism and Surrealism. We have refined on a refinement. The elaborate joke, combined with the careful workmanship and wistful philosophy, is no invention of Cocteau or Dali; it had its models in Erik Satie and Aubrey Beardsley. Our angry playwrights and sermonizers unknowingly repeat Jarry and Ducasse. The bitterness of Debussy is already to the last detail the bitterness of the modern ego, and Kafka already peeps out of the pages of Villiers de l'Isle Adam.

In manners, of course, a great change has taken place between 1890 and now. Bohemianism has been submerged.[2] Constant Lambert was right to speak of "social and personal inhibitions." There is no valid attempt, as in the nineties, to make a caste or an institution of the artist. In daily life, the modern ego has reverted to the standards of Realism—the con-

2 Written before the emergence of the beat generation. (J.B.)

ventions. Within these self-imposed limits the artist and his readers commune by means of a fictional world of incredible toughness and sentimentality. The novels of Hemingway and Malraux draw cruel blood so that yours may run cold; the authors' calculated horrors are built up as a defensive reserve against the casual horrors which the modern world may at any moment produce. Writers and painters and playwrights prepare us for what they think we will not yet believe.

Still, when all the bottling up and fizzling out of feeling has been done, every epoch has to make some real disposal of its greater or lesser stock of native emotion and we accordingly find representative men throwing themselves into communism, into the Spanish War against Fascism, into a new scientific materialism, or (like Aldous Huxley) into successive cult-like beliefs. From the sidelines, too, admiration is expressed for D. H. Lawrence's repudiation of the whole "playing safe" philosophy, with its pedantry and preciosity. But respect is paid to Lawrence subject to the qualification that he is a "romantic" and probably a fascist, too.

One cannot mention Lawrence without also mentioning the modern topic which posterity will surely consider the sign of our broken life. I refer to sex. The very word is a volume of cultural history. For sex is not the despised romantic love, it is something scientific, realistic, and "very important." So important that we have coined a special phrase "sex life" to make clear the division we make between an individual ego and this part of his experience. I have even seen a reference—it was, I am sorry to say, in a work on English usage—to a book being "sex-filled." Can we imagine ourselves ever saying that a man's "food life" is deplorable, or that Dickens's novels are "food-filled"? Eating is still an integral part of life; loving has been detached and made into sex. It was this unorganic division that Lawrence sought to end by his passionate crusade.

How was it ever made necessary? The modern feeling about love owes a good deal to Havelock Ellis's useful volumes on the *Psychology of Sex,* to the encroaching idea of a "science of man," and to the unremitting onslaught that George Bernard Shaw made in the nineties upon the notion of romantic love. We sympathize with Shaw when we see what he wanted to get rid of—the coloring of every book, every social relation, with the pieties of literary amorousness. It was a misfortune that the name "romantic" was used to describe the sickly product. For it was Shaw himself who gave perhaps the best short definition of what the romantic felt about physical love—"a celestial flood of emotion and exaltation of existence" which prefigures what might some day accompany the experience of thought. Like Byron, Shaw refused to believe that love was man's whole existence, and like Carlyle, he told the tenth-rate littérateurs of love to stop their maunderings and get to work. This is what we should expect of a man whose gods were Shelley, Blake, and Turner, and who had the good taste to fall in love with William Morris's daughter. But the ambiguous word "romantic" implicated these men and the art of their time in a quarrel of limited import and which was further confused by Shaw's saying that sexual attraction was impersonal. What he meant was that it can spring up regardless of other qualities than immediate and visible ones. By these means, literary and scientific, love was conscientiously depersonalized and made into sex.

On top of this crusade, echoed naturally by Shaw's popularizers and then turned against him as a proof of his want of feeling, came the publications of Freud. The misunderstanding became complete. Freud happened to be encumbered with a materialistic notion of science, which gave added color to the crude supposition that at the root of man's being is sex; that all the supposed glamour and significance of love are "romantic," that is to say, spurious; and yet that a man's artistic creations, political opinions, and individual tastes are the direct, fated outcome of his sexual temperament. There followed the pseudo-psychoanalysis of everyone whose name could be read in the small print of a biographical dictionary. The vague public conclusion was that the romantic writers, from Rousseau to Oscar Wilde, were contemptible lunatics whose ideas had no applicability to life—much less to our life. It was not that the modern generation had wholly ceased loving in the romantic way of Hector and Andromache, nor given up reading the great love stories of the nineteenth century, but that the new interpretation of passion, which was a clear misinterpretation of Freud, served as a cover for the self-consciousness, the lack of spirit, and the dark fears which I have called the modern ego.

III

Another way of summarizing these lacks would be to say that the modern ego has lost its faith, and with it the willingness to take risks. It looks for certainties, guarantees of permanence and safety without, often, believing that they exist. Some, indeed, turned to Marxian communism not only because the hope it held out of remolding society was noble and generous, but because with it went a system, a set of sacred writings, and an authority enforcing orthodox readings. It was pathetic to see belated imitators of symbolism dropping their reveries and discovering, a hundred and fifty years after Shelley, that there was poverty in England. They found, besides, that to be a social-minded poet or scientist one had to give up obscurities and write like any journalist. The comedy and the pathos turned to tragedy upon seeing the converts grapple, long after Byron, with the politics of a party or the intrigues of a war for liberation.

It is nevertheless hard to resist the thought that so much naïveté and ignorance had in it a part of willfulness. One glance at the nineteenth century had apparently sufficed to estrange these otherwise thoughtful observers but not to warn them. The past century was stupid, gross, stuffy, and self-centered, albeit humanitarian, idealistic, intellectual, and revolutionary. Its abundance of ideas and programs repelled rather than spurred to study. It was as if the moderns had hoped to get their inheritance clear of the tax of organization —an estate already settled. They wanted a single system which should solve the pressing problems of the hour. For those not attracted by Communism there was Anglo-Catholicism; still others withdrew into Saint Thomas and the Roman Church; artists sought for classical models--Mozart, Ingres, or Aristotle-in-Dante. T. S. Eliot gave it as a prerequisite to poetic functioning that the writer command a ready-made body of truths; he must be freed from the need of devising his own philosophy. To make sure that no one should be misled by romantic errors, Eliot himself undertook the high critical task of assessing the literary tradition by means of classicism, royalism, and Anglo-Catholicism. He performed the delicate work of Murder in the Sacred Wood in the interest of peace, with pontifical dignity, much as Mr. Stravinsky now invites his hearers to consider his art "objectively—dogmatically . . . under the austere sign of discipline and order."

Order is the password, and since as yet no one has sufficient troops behind him to enforce it, recruiting is the first step. The choice is Aristotelian (Catholic) medievalism or Anglo-Catholic (Platonic) neo-classicism. I omit the Fascist and Communist options as belonging to our political discussion in the next chapter.

The laudable aim of both neo-Thomism and neo-classicism is to bring men to intellectual agreement. Both imply that the basis of agreement has been found; the only difficulty is to accept it. The authoritative source is Tradition, and the proof of its merit is the glory of the Middle Ages and the serenity of the seventeenth century. Tradition being all-important, the argument requires that the intervening time be considered a deviation, a long heresy, which advantageously explains our social and political troubles: we suffer because we have sinned.

The critics of the present naturally differ as to the beginning of the heretical deviation from Truth. Catholics naturally put it at the Reformation, but they except classical France from their strictures. Others exclude the eighteenth century as tainted with romanticism; some absolve it as more classic than the seventeenth. All concur, however, in damning romanticism as the fountainhead of our intolerable diversity of doctrines, all of them false.

By contrast, it is contended, the Middle Ages afforded an "orderly progression from truth to truth," the Church maintained a European community of language, learning, and belief, and until the undisciplined Renaissance broke loose, there was hope for a world order based on reason—as expounded in the *Summa* of Aquinas. The neo-classical argument varies from this chiefly in stressing the secular aids to order—a king, a state-supported church, and an aristocracy of intelligence. Long before the social malaise thus interpreted had become a commonplace, Irving Babbitt had written: "Men can really come together only in humble obeisance to something set above their ordinary selves." The so-called New Humanism, which survives as an atmosphere, if not as a movement, starts from this premise, a fine poet such as Allen Tate going so far as to say that when a social and political orthodoxy is lacking, the needful thing is military force. He asserts that for all its cruelty the fascist attitude toward the control of truth is simple and open compared to the chaotic struggle within the bourgeois democracies. His book on the politics of culture is aggressively entitled: *Reason in Madness.*

The state of mind which sees madness all about us and reason at the vanishing point is an extreme instance of the longing for the Golden Age. It is also the extreme of illusion—classical, this time, not romantic—for no student of history can point to an age that offered men the peace and certainty the modern ego is clamoring for. It is madness in reason to think that the scheme written down in Aquinas was ever reality. Why write it down if even a near approach to "order" had been achieved? The vindictive fury of Dante is there to remind us, in case we have forgotten, that the Middle Age was a time of chaos, social, political, and moral.

The belief, moreover, that the Church then afforded intellectual unity is belied by the quarrels of Franciscans and Dominicans, mystics and rationalists, Thomists and Occamites. Abélard was hounded for Sabellianism and his books were burnt; Aristotle was prohibited at Paris in 1209 and readmitted, on probation, in 1231; Thomas narrowly escaped being a heretic. He was found orthodox at last, for good reasons no doubt, but by means such as are used today in the comparable struggle among doctrines—argument, influence, and compromise. There is nothing surprising in this except to those who sentimentalize order.

What is true of the imaginary medieval serenity holds good for the classical epoch. We took note of its cultural stresses and strains, all the more galling for being concealed. In politics, classicism was the absolute monarchy, with its intrigues, religious persecutions, and dynastic wars—order at the expense of the loser. Modern champions of classicism sometimes think they strengthen their case by admitting the imperfection of Western neo-classicism and pointing to the perfection of the original classicism in Greece or the Roman Empire. But "this is a more exquisite song than the other," as Shakespeare's Cassio says. It takes only a copy of Thucydides and a little sense of history to recognize that the Greeks led the most chaotic, passionate, and disorderly life conceivable. They preached and praised serenity, no doubt, but calm composure and the austere sign of discipline were with them as they are with us, individual achievements. The unity of Greece was wrecked, not made, by whatever may be called "the Greek way of life." It was only after "the failure of nerve" which Gilbert Murray has studied that we find stoical calm, again in individuals. A society may now and again make these individual triumphs easier or more numerous, but the secret of their success will not be found in imitation two thousand years out of date, nor in the pretense of being the sole heirs of the lost tradition.

To conclude, what is alarming about the modern ego is not that it wants to create order or adopt a discipline or accept talented rulers, but that it is walking forward with its head turned back in fear and longing. This, and not its errors and affectations, is the signal of distress. It stamps it not only as an artificial survival of the last phase of romanticism—a kind of Mr. de Valdemar saved from putrefaction by hypnosis—but it also defines the revolutionary character of our era.

VIII

The Three Revolutions

I

If after listening to the complaints of the modern ego—complaints both in the sense of ailments and in the sense of protests—we pass from the symptoms of distress to the trouble itself, we find the disease due to the workings of a deep cultural change. Whether the name "revolution" is applied to it is a matter of taste: the important thing is that it matches in magnitude the transformation of a hundred and fifty years ago which has been the object of this study.

The reader will remember that like other students of the earlier period, I mentioned the French Revolution of 1789 as a major condition of the cultural revolution of romanticism. This suggests that by going back to look at the relation between culture and politics in that era, we may make a better guess at the meaning of our own revolution.

The first question is whether the French Revolution and the Napoleonic regime were themselves expressions of romanticism. This is not an idle question, and it brings us two cases for testing the relation of politics to culture. Yet it involves what seems at first sight a contradiction. It is commonly said of modern France that she, at any rate, is not a romantic nation like Germany. She had her "romantic fling" with Napoleon and was cured by it. Here, obviously, Napoleon stands for romanticism. At the same time, most textbooks represent Napoleon as a "true son of the Enlightenment" who brought France back to "her classic tradition" after the deviation of the revolutionary wars. From which it would appear that the revolution was romantic but Napoleon was not. Nor should we forget that the classical Louis XIV also "flung" France at Europe's head. What then has romanticism to do with revolution, with empire, and with war? The confusion grows worse if we reflect that conquest is but the political expression of the national spirit. The cultural expression is something else, however related to the first.

I shall return to culture in a moment. The political puzzle is solved by applying the definition of romanticism offered in these pages: man's sense of his energy and of his weakness. In this definition, no single goal is specified for the energy, even though the weakness may be thought of as common to all men. This means that any manifestation of human energy inevitably reminds us of romanticism. But romanticism, as I have said perhaps too often, implies not only risk, effort, energy; it implies also creation, diversity, and individual genius. This is why America is the land of romanticism par excellence and why her greatest philosopher, William James, asserted the doctrine in its fullness against all absolute, classical limits. In their heroism and energy, then, the French Revolution and the Napoleonic regime *resembled* romantic undertakings. This is consistent with what was said earlier of Napoleon's influence on the romantic poets, and it is also consistent with what was said of Louis XIV as a figurehead upon which the whole nation could project its spirit of enterprise.

Once again we see why it is so plausible nowadays to call totalitarian imperialisms romantic. Their energy and desire to create are akin to romanticism, but they express themselves—as did Napoleon and Louis XIV—through a unitary leadership based on oppression. A program of mass achievement through coercion is not a new romanticism, for its premises, methods, and goal are precisely the opposite. Two diametrically opposed schemes can be carried out with a like enthusiasm. This being so, we need a pragmatic test for judging the use to which human energies are put. The French Revolution, then, was an explosion which leveled the old regime and opened careers to talent. In meeting the coalition of foreign powers seeking to maintain the status quo, the Revolution stimulated heroism and afforded chances of greatness. Looked at from without, its activity was romantic. Its style and thought, however, remained thoroughly classical. Not only were its doctrines derived from the *philosophes*, but its imagination was cast chiefly in the molds of classical antiquity and abstract reason. It argued political issues with the aid of precedents found in Plutarch and in one of its phases it established the worship of reason. For their own national past, the French of that time had little use. Ancient charters were burned and a scheme was set afoot to destroy those "monuments of barbarism and superstition," the Gothic cathedrals.

In another, even deeper way, the French Revolution remained classical. Political necessity required absolute unity through dictatorship, and orthodoxy suited the revolutionary Committee of Public Safety as well as it had suited Louis XIV. That essential part of romanticism, the worth of the individual and of his testimony, could not be tolerated; nor yet that part which was seeking to recapture the spirit of early Christianity and led to a revival of religion. It was rightly held to be counter-revolutionary. Literature and the arts were muzzled. The struggle for power within, and the war for liberation and conquest without, were the only two goals which absorbed men's energies. There was no room for weakness any more than for diversity. Perhaps the single great figure of the period with a full romanticist consciousness was Danton. His policy was peace, and from the weariness of baffled versatility he let himself be guillotined. Because he was such a man, the romanticist poet Büchner chose him forty years later as the hero of his masterpiece, *Danton's Death*.

At the coming of Napoleon, the situation had hardly changed. The need for compulsion remained, and the new dictatorship still meant war. The Empire style mixed the neoclassic with the newly discovered Egyptian; energy and heroism continued to thrive. The single directing will hoped to re-create the splendors of Versailles and professed to want Corneille as a Minister of State, while sentimental Ossianism embellished the brutality and materialism of the conqueror. Only in the Catholic revival, encouraged for political reasons, was there any sign of a new direction, one upon which the centralized state did not proceed very far, as we saw in the condemnation of Mme. de Stael's writings on Germany. Classically enough, the minister of police pointed out to her that France had no need to seek artistic inspiration outside the frontier. Yet at the same time Napoleon was blaming his Minister of the Interior for the absence of a flourishing literature in the Empire. A clairvoyant might have replied that a young officer in the commissariat, later Stendhal, was too busy crossing the frozen rivers of Russia to be doing anything else.

It might be thought that with the return of the Bourbons after the fall of Napoleon, the old shackles would be reapplied. But the restoration of the absolute monarchy was a fiction. The King came back with a Charter, knowing that he must rule a people weary of constraints, of eighteenth-century reason, and of twenty-five years of unremitting physical energy. In these circumstances, and with the encouragement of German, English, and Italian examples, the romantic movement in France was born at last. Knowing at first hand what force and energy meant, it was not sentimental or confused about the meaning of these terms. It preached energy but it rejected the aim which twenty-five years of warfare had proved fruitless. In place of the one goal of unity for national self-assertion, it preferred diversity, freedom, and the arts of peace.

II

To this interpretation of Revolutionary and Napoleonic culture, which I mean to use as a touchstone for the present, one must add what has emerged from this study about historic romanticism. Alternately dominant and submerged, romanticism seems to be a permanent trait of Western man. It expresses and exalts his energetic, creative, expansive tendencies by recognizing that although he is but a feeble creature lost in the universe he has unpredictable powers that develop under stress of desire and risk.

In the course of history and of the individual career, Reason and Will keep pace with each other, now one leading by urging a want, now the other by stretching the use of a means; both together building up what in our sanguine moments we call civilization. In moments of dejection, we feel and see that

by the tests of both reason and desire civilization falls short
of its aim, and we are forcibly reminded of the romantic truth
that in his greatness itself man is weak.

It may be regretted that there is no "tradition of reason"
reaching from Plato down to us for the espousal of all good
men. But if there were, we should still be faced with the task
of sorting out its opposite strands; we could not avoid asking,
"Which Plato—the Plato of the authoritarian, puritanical *Republic*, or of the 'romantic' *Laws?*"

Often cited with Plato as supporting classic Reason against
romantic Will are the teachings of Jesus; though just as often
Jesus is classed as romantic, and Christian is opposed to Pagan.
These labels only serve to obscure the important, and to many
the disagreeable, fact that in its insistence upon faith the Christian tradition is sounder than the rationalist. Christianity sees
that mankind follows its conflicting purposes and beliefs exactly as it follows its religious leaders or its mathematical
axioms: *desiderio*, from desire, with no whisperings or guarantees from reason. Reason devises tests and records experience.
When conclusive, the results become mankind's "reason" in a
new sense—that of an accepted truth or article of faith. But
there is nothing final and compelling about these results. As
Shaw long ago pointed out: "The reasonable man adapts himself to the world: the unreasonable one persists in trying to
adapt the world to himself. Therefore all progress depends on
the unreasonable man."

The substance of reason, in short, is changeable. But its
great historic changes should not be thought the result of sul-
len pride or avoidable error. They answer needs which recur
rhythmically throughout the course of Western history. Periods of absorption alternate with periods of elimination; after
diversity, simplification. Though both tendencies are at times
present together, one dominates. Man explores and is romantic;
man wants repose and becomes classical.

Accordingly, the particular relation of nineteenth-century romanticism to twentieth-century anti-romanticism corresponds to a deeper need than that of the children to disown
their fathers. Could we but understand as well as feel it, we
would rid ourselves of a burden and recover our intellectual

honesty, for we cannot attack the nineteenth century as the breaker of tradition when we know that before it, in the ninth, twelfth, and fourteenth centuries, previous epochs of expansion and exploration followed upon attempts at fixed systems. What is more, we dare not any longer suppose that we are dabbling in the history of old mistakes; we must recognize that we are dealing with the cultural cloth out of which our present and future is to be cut.

Let me, for convenience rather than emphasis, recapitulate what I believe to be tenable and instructive about the great movement just coming to an end. The romantic era in Europe produced two generations of men who attempted, between 1780 and 1850, a feat of cultural renovation. The classical order, dying of overabstraction and false generality, had been devoured by its own children, the Enlightened philosophers. Political revolution and Napoleonic dictatorship buried the past and leveled the ground. The romanticists had the task of reconstruction. The vast horizons opened up by war and social upheaval gave romanticism its scope: it was inclusive, impatient of barriers, eager for diversity. It treasured fact and respected the individual as a source of fact. Accordingly, its political philosophy was an attempt to reconcile personal freedom with the inescapable need of collective action. Rousseau, Burke, Kant, Hegel, agreeing on the nature of the problem, differed only in lesser particulars. They were not anarchists or imperialists, but theorists of equilibrium in motion.

Alive to diversity, romanticism bound up patriotism with the life of peoples and gave form to a cultural nationalism compatible with international amity. Observant and imaginative, it rediscovered history and gave an impulse to the arts which has not yet died out. True to its inclusive purpose, romantic art was simultaneously idealistic, realistic, and symbolic; impressionist, expressionist, and surrealist. It produced forms and amassed contents only now nearing exhaustion, after furnishing the models for the movements which we enumerate through the past century as Realism, Symbolism, Impressionism, Naturalism, and Post-Impressionism.

The men who carried out this cultural revolution were both fortunate and ill-fated. Coming first after the deluge, they had the luck of position. They could and did infinitely more than it was given to their successors to do. Yet being men, not demigods, they often groaned and sometimes broke under the burden of their responsibility. Astounding in their energy, production, inventiveness, and moral fervor, they also found within themselves traits that led them to proclaim man both strong and weak. Their melancholy sense of failure and love of death; their recourse to opiates and stimulants; the retreat of some of their number to traditional havens, alike prove that their lot was tragic. The best of them are in fact like heroes of tragedy in that they simultaneously fail and triumph, irritate and impress us. They are out of scale with the common crowd and we can neither take them to our bosoms nor let them alone.

Though we cannot forget them, their lives were more arduous and more subtly organized than we remember. The striking generalities of the textbook writer about romantic careers are falser than most critical commonplaces, because the roles filled by the romantics are open only once in every century or two, and there clings something of the incredible to such human destinies. Moreover, in virtue of its very largeness and variety, romanticism is bound to seem vulnerable and loose. Whereas, to topple a classic orthodoxy, people must risk their lives to undermine it in secret, a romanticist position is breached at once by anyone who wants to tidy up the world by enforcing a few simple rules. Whereas the classical temper can be individually indulged within the romantic order, the contrary is impossible. But men's unstillable fear of diversity and impatience with failure are ever at work, and to them romanticism sooner or later succumbs. The age of Realism begins, and seeks to base a new convention on materialism. This is what happened in Europe around 1850. But its limitations soon generated a counter-reaction, a neo-romanticism, appearing as Symbolism, Naturalism, and Impressionism.

After so full a century, our own period obviously had little left to express and much to do. Nonetheless, from 1905 to 1914 signs of a new cultural start, the true work of impulse and reason, were everywhere visible. It was an era of socialism, internationalism, and buoyant futurism, following closely on the *fin de siècle* mood of decadence and despair. In many senses the pre-war decade created genuine novelty and laid down new techniques in art, science, and thought. But "practical" politics lagged behind, as usual, waiting for an unmistakable disaster. The first world war came and scotched the life of mind while failing to establish international order or even to restore the old balance of nations.

There followed twenty years of disillusionment, self-distrust, and futile promises of new realisms. In all that time, the main intellectual occupation has been either to complain or to mirror the chaos of complaints. Ignoring the pre-war start, and seeing that the path to creation was blocked by a century of masterpieces, great and small, post-war artists have taken apart or parodied the materials of that century. They have ridiculed its contents and dismantled its syntax. Or else they have overleaped it altogether and proclaimed themselves long-distance disciples of Dante, Dryden, or Bach, half sensing and half blinding themselves to the truth that their models were not classicists in despair and impotence, but determined utopians, encouraged by a past uncompleted or a vision ahead.

Compared with any historic expansion or contraction, our modern movements seem too timid, too scholarly, too backward-looking to succeed. The demand for "realism" and the accusations of "escape" suggest fear of the future rather than determination to create it, that is, to make a new reality in place of the hated present. Similarly, our democratic dalliance and delay in politics argued the same lack of courage and initiative until events not of our making forced the whole world to put its mind on new freedoms, new obligations, and new devices of government. As happened before the French Revolution, the twentieth century made a fresh beginning which foundered in twenty years of violence and confusion. The obvious question now is whether the world is slowly twisting its way out of the chaos and into a new classical order. Will the alternation of phases hitherto discernible in Western history prolong itself into the future which is our own?

IX

Epilogue: Romanticism in 1960

I

When the concluding words of the previous chapter were written, more than nineteen years ago, little or no evidence was at hand to suggest that Romanticism had anything more to give. After the thorough debunking of the entire nineteenth century which we owed to the decades between world wars, it seemed reasonable to expect the end of Romantic diversification, to see emerging the outlines of a cultural consolidation akin in spirit to earlier classicisms.

But the second world war and its aftermath showed that Romanticism had still one more charge in its belly. The events and implications of armed conflict reawakened the deep and vivid emotions that a time of peace, wit, and satire tends to repress. The ideas attached to this rebirth of feeling naturally bore upon the fate of the individual and took the familiar form of a feud against society. Young and vigorous artists, with their clients and interpreters, quickly established as the mark of the sensitive a creed of total rebellion against Western culture. The abstract, artificial hatred which was felt in war, and which soon becomes real cruelty, informed these attacks on bourgeois life. One heard again the tones of romanticist anger, the scorn of Stendhal, Büchner, and Gautier; one was reminded of Julien Sorel, *Woyzeck*, and the Preface to *Mademoiselle de Maupin*.

At the same time the welfare state which arose out of the war brought into social existence still another wave of consumers desiring art—large numbers of people unfamiliar with the rebel tradition. Far from weary of the pleasures just brought within their reach, they were concerned chiefly to learn and to enjoy. For their sake mass journalism and public institutions turned cultural and educative. And inevitably, in this endless task of introducing and commenting on the classics, any genuine cultural change was again postponed.

Yet the tendency of these two side effects of war, the individualistic and the socialized, has proved to be not contradictory but harmonious and single: between them, unless I am much mistaken, it is ensuring the elimination not alone of Romanticist art and its sequels, but of all the high art of the last five centuries. The Romantic purpose, in other words, has come by the severest logic to end what it began, destroying in its last effort all the romantic and classical forms that took their rise in the Renaissance.

This final Romantic purpose I speak of has as yet no official name, though it is not entirely new. Trying to describe its beginnings in my book *The Energies of Art* (1956), I ventured to call it Abolitionism, to suggest its radical character: the revolutionary intention is no longer merely to shelve the past but to erase it, and by doing this to produce in man a wholly new consciousness—not a new outlook upon the old makings of life, but a life made of a new substance.

To effect the first part of this purpose, by declaring the past to be as wrong and absurd as the conventional present, the target of the latest critical theory is Art with a capital *A*. Art as such is to be destroyed. The abolitionist temper makes no distinction between, on the one hand, its hostility to past great works, and on the other its disgust with the uses to which all Art is being put in feeding the curiosity of the emancipated masses—through the incessant propaganda of museums and libraries, of mass journalism and the cultural industries that produce discs and reproduce paintings, and of the educational institutions, naïve or fraudulent, that market the virtues of these commodities.

The most lucid interpreter of this abolitionist philosophy is Mr. Harold Rosenberg, the art critic and champion of the so-called Action Painters. In their work Mr. Rosenberg sees the definitive break with tradition which earlier men fumbled, half achieved, or retreated from. The step forward consists in replacing the old artistic intention by an act—the act of painting without preconception or intent. What results is a simple meeting between the materials and the painter's "biography," thus abolishing the very idea of the "work of art." This act, substituted for Art, takes away from painting its esthetic properties, the last remaining bit of meaning after earlier revolutionists had removed moral properties and intellectual properties. Our critic says: "The big moment came when it was decided to paint . . . just TO PAINT. The gesture on the canvas was a gesture of liberation, from Value—political, esthetic, moral."[1]

Mr. Rosenberg rejoices in this quietus of Art and in this he is backed by the arti—that is, by the actioneers themselves. One stumbles over their proper title, but with respect. For their words and attitudes are not singular or whimsical, and in any case not negligible. One need not be a practitioner to see that "Artists" have painted themselves into a corner. There is nothing left for them to "say" in any manner that relies on mind. Every conceivable stance, all imaginable devices have been tried, combined, and parodied. The heedless prolongations into our century of the several Romantic styles, their dilution, overdevelopment, or self-conscious avoidance, have driven our most gifted men literally out of their minds and into the realm of gesture, where the most random is the truest.

Nor is this situation confined to the plastic arts. An experienced critic of new music, who is also a composer and a musicologist, Mr. Richard Franko Goldman, supplies apropos of Stravinsky's latest work a confirmation of the view that the arts have come to rest in a Grand Central Terminal. Speaking of Stravinsky's long search through the past for musical substance that might still be fertile, Mr. Goldman concedes "the inevitability, in our anxious and history-conscious age, of the artistic ransacking of the past in search of a companionship that Mozart and Beethoven no longer provide. They are not only too big for us, on a different scale, but represent a different relation to civilization." And he considers the likelihood that "harmony is dead, that the composers of the eighteenth and nineteenth centuries have explored all the possibilities of what we have come to call traditional harmony, and that the

[1] Rosenberg, *The Tradition of the New*, New York, 1959, p. 30.

composer today can add nothing to what they have left us."
This relation of past to present, taken together with the enor-
mous verbalism that goes with the slightest of new works, leads
the critic to conclude: "I fear that [like Webern who 'so analyzed music that only style remains'] enough like-minded activists on the periphery of art will succeed in analyzing music
out of existence."[2]

Mr. Goldman mentions in passing that Stravinsky may wind
up exploring electronic music. The remark is a clue to the
logical course dictated by the exhaustion of the past. It tells
us of the abolitionists' second purpose, which is to develop a
new consciousness, pure and unheard of. So far, the sounds
of electronic music are meaningless, like the drippings and
droppings of the abstract expressionist and action painters, like
the words and images that the beat poets seek to capture with
a tape recorder during their mind-less monologues or in the
trances of drug taking. The search is for materials absolutely
disinfected from Art and ideas. Each kind of artist wants to
come upon, overhear, or summon forth something that shall
in no way be remembered literature, music, or painting. The
suspension of intent is to preclude in the "act" any habitual
choosing of the material or censoring of the sensibility. The
aim is to flee from the previously actualized and also from
the prescient foreshadowing. It is a sacrificial effort, a true
antimental education.

The social and political image of this program is obvious.
It is the dream of total revolution: to start with a fresh slate,
to discard even the ghost of an echo of the past. Undoubtedly
the temper, if not the doctrine, of Marxist Leninism lies behind much of this energy to achieve a liberating blankness;
and in this, too, one can see the ultimate intensification of the
original Romanticist idea: Marx's abolitionism, based on Romantic premises,[3] leads logically to destroying the contents
of any institution connected with the past. We thus arrive at
the esthetics of annihilation, which best suit a century exasperated by two world wars and twenty abortive revolutions.

[2] *Musical Quarterly,* April 1960 (xlvi No. 2), pp. 262–64.
[3] For the historical sequences supporting this view, see my *Darwin, Marx, Wagner,* 2nd ed., Anchor Books, New York, 1958.

Yet precisely because this exasperation is now magnified by the awareness of recurrent disaster, a distinction has to be made between the first Romantics' revolutionary animus and ours. Exasperation can be of the mind or of the senses or of both. The Romantics got rid of the burden of old art and old periwigs with senses fresh and eager for a world of experience which they knew existed just beyond the arbitrary barriers of classicism—physical nature, remote lands, barbaric centuries, the vocabulary of common words and feelings, the truths of private thought, the abysses of love, religion, and despair—in short, the varieties of experience as against the proprieties of reason and social life.

Some romanticists did go on to explore the self with the aid of drugs, trances, and dreams, and they all systematically "worked" the materials and techniques of their arts. But by and large they enjoyed for their artistic purposes free access to great abundance. Their heroism lay in the struggle with society and with the riddle of the universe. But they did not have to strain for subject matter, forms, or doctrines. They did not need to contrive a painting machine to produce unexpected designs, like our contemporary Jean Tinguely; or to record factory noises as the makings of music, like the composers of *musique concrète*. Nor did they feel impelled to rely on chance motions, scattered points, or number systems as a means of avoiding the *déjà vu*, as do some of our poets and painters and serial composers. On the contrary, the first Romantics found a vast realm of sensation and imagination which the neglect or prohibitions of their predecessors had kept untouched—the realm which artists now agree is used up.

The Romantics, moreover, went forth on their adventures with an expressive purpose that was by turns or together moral, social, political, psychological, or esthetic. They were working, for the sake of new institutions, at an improved definition of Man. For we must not forget the most important fact about the nineteenth century, which is that it immediately followed the eighteenth. That is to say, the Romantics were brought up in the Age of Reason and carried its faith and intellect forward. Our latest romantics are of necessity in a different case. They want to carry nothing forward, but to get rid of all their inherited esthetic and intellectual lumber; they have no public hope, for they feel soiled and guilty from contact with any part of existing society. They want to strip bare and dig down to a hoped-for bedrock showing no trace of an earlier passage of man. This is what Mr. Allen Ginsberg means when he says that man himself is obsolete;[4] this is what Samuel Beckett and others are trying to show us on a stage where no responses are predictable or congenial; this is what Mr. Henry Miller is explaining at length in works where visions of love and feasts of sexuality outrank and displace all other concerns; this is what Mr. Norman O. Brown theorizes about in *Life Against Death*, which pronounces the doom of mankind unless we return to the indiscriminate self-gratification of the infant: Man is played out, an orgiastic mysticism is in the air, expressive of the search for a total renovation.

To such sensibilities, it is clear, the old high Art since Petrarch and Giotto is a horror of childish contrivance and intellectual ax-grinding. The only acceptable art is the art of Unconsciousness, of Accident, of No-meaning. And hence in the majority of artists an obsessive preoccupation with those parts of experience that are forever neutral in themselves and that mean only what the intellect attaches to them by an act of will—sexuality, narcotic visions, or the bare sequences in a stream of images.

As I said a moment ago, the germs of this near-nihilism existed before the present generation of beat poets and of painters calling themselves Obsessionists or makers of *"art brut."* We find those germs in late French Symbolism (Ducasse, Laforgue, Jarry), in Marinetti's Futurism, in the German Expressionists, in the Surrealists, in Kafka who wanted his works destroyed, and in Paul Klee, who said: "I want to be as though newborn, knowing nothing, absolutely nothing of Europe." In practice, the first collage was the first denial of art. Yet here again one feels the difference between words and attitudes directed in the old way, as a criticism of life and a preparation for a new Art (of which these same critics were to be the makers), and the present mode of denunciation which is a calculated, intrepid striving for purposelessness.

[4] Private communication (July 1960).

At this point the disturbing thought occurs that these artist enemies of Art are moved not alone by nausea at the idea of the past, and not alone by fear and hatred of a society in the grip of science and machinery, but irresistibly also by the model of science itself. Proclaiming a universal purposelessness and seeking by experiment an unknown substratum which shall prove bedrock reality is the paradigm of science. It seems a further contradiction that men who vilify the age of machine industry conduct so many of their trials toward the new non-Art with devices born of that industry. The drugs of their trances (heroin, lysergic acid), the tools of their search (tape recorders, electronic synthesizers), the forms of their rationalization (number, algebraic logic) as well as their critical and advertising vocabulary[5] are none of them products of art or nature, all smell of the factory or the lab. And in this, I think, we must see not a concession or a convenience but a reenforcement of the desperate hostility to Art.

II

The specter of our industrial world brings us to the second great influence tending toward the same Carthaginian end. On first considering the situation of our most advanced artists and their small numbers, it might be thought that their fury of destruction would be checked and reversed by the tremendous surge of desire for the arts which has agitated the societies of western Europe since 1945. Surely, in an age of such intense dissemination of "our priceless heritage," multiplied as it effectively is by mechanical means, it cannot perish at the hands of a few men, however exasperated. The people, considered by Romanticism the true seedbed of culture, seem to have regained their rights of possession; they will not soon let go this high art from which they were excluded until, precisely, the Romantics rediscovered their role as culture makers and en-

---

[5] By way of example, the composer John Cage, who uses random points on paper to assure his music the desired "indeterminacy," calls the resulting text not a score but a "graph." In this kind of pseudo-scientific usage he is at one with the majority of twentieth-century artists.

joyers. Can we not trust their developing taste? Is it not, in any case, a noble extension of popular rights when the modern state gives its citizenry free access to the arts and encourages their study or practice? This, this at last, is sharing the wealth! Presumably, not only the Romanticists of the 1800s but also the Rationalists of the 1700s would approve, seeing in this diffusion the spread of light and the blessed outcome of the free popular education which they struggled to establish.

All this is true. Something like a cultural revolution has occurred in the West during the past thirty years, especially in the United States, where it seems a natural accompaniment of industrial democracy.[6] Anywhere, it is as fully a consequence of the Romantic Revolution as the nihilism just described. And to the extent that this dalliance with art brings our increasingly leisured working population pleasure or even simple distraction from care and boredom, the change is matter for rejoicing.

But there is another aspect to these same facts. That most artists and our best critics express indifference or scorn at sight of the popularizing of Art cannot be attributed entirely to professional envy or habitual discontent. The most radical naturally resent the confusion delaying the advent of non-art. But when those who are not abolitionists also distrust the cultural boom, we ask why. The answer is simple: feeling the old attachment to high Art, they see in the very abundance and availability of the democratized arts the causes of a prompt dissolution.

And they are right. The powerful devices of mechanical reproduction and high-pressure distribution to which we owe the cultural "awakening" necessarily distort and thus destroy. All the new media make arbitrary demands on the materials fed through them. And because the public to be served is large and failure costly, it is important that the product suit— hence the endless cutting and adapting, reworking and dilut-

[6] On this development, see my essays: *Music in American Life,* New York, 1956; "America's Passion for Culture," *Harper's,* March 1954; "The New Man in the Arts," *American Scholar,* Autumn 1956; and "Centering the Arts," *Columbia University Forum,* Winter 1960.

ing, which end in travesty.[7] The films of *Hamlet, Wuthering Heights,* or *David Copperfield* are obvious examples of one kind of demolition. There are subtler ones. To see the works of the Impressionists twisted into backgrounds for advertising perfume; to hear the melodies of Bach, Mozart, Berlioz, and Chopin rehandled by Tin Pan Alley; to listen to absent-minded hacks giving the lowdown on high art, not solely in blurbs for books and discs, in mass media, or over the air, but also on the walls of museums and in the glass cases of propagandistic libraries—all this is destructive in the same measure that it is communicative.

The very bulk of the output kills appetite. Symphonies in bars and cabs, classical drama on television any day of the week, highbrow paperbacks in mountainous profusion (easier to buy than to read), "art seminars in the home," capsule operas, "Chopin by Starlight," "The Sound of Wagner," the Best of World Literature: this cornucopia thrust at the inexperienced and pouring out its contents over us all deadens attention and keeps taste stillborn, like any form of gross feeding. Too much art in too many places means art robbed of its right associations, its exact forms, its concentrated power. We are grateful for the comprehensive repertoire which modern industry for the first time puts within our reach, but we turn sick at the aggressive temptation, like the novice in the sweetshop.

Even the otherwise commendable Do-it-yourself movement, represented by the Sunday painter and the Friday-evening singer or player, contributes to the dissipation of the artistic tradition: high art was not made for these uses. In its own time, its receivers fed on a scarcer diet, and their sense of style was adjusted to their sense of scale, as measured by the drawing room, the theatre, the market place. Now that a whisper can resound mechanically over a multitude and a string quartet

---

[7] A crude understanding of the greatest good of the greatest number haunts all the purveyors of these expensive cultural goods. We have recently had the spectacle of a well-endowed and well-patronized museum of twentieth-century art which so bedeviled its director with anxieties about the public "approval" of the collection that he gave up his job. He resigned on finding that the trustees had hired a polling agency to ascertain whether the unabating flood of visitors "really liked" what they saw.

fill a stadium, forms and ideas are reduced to indistinctness. Any given art tends to become a homogeneous substance, its great works losing in their repetition the character of events.

One observes this not as an occasion for reproach, but simply as a reminder that the masterpieces of high art since the Renaissance possess three characteristics that nothing in modern life or in the education of the new consumers prepares them to receive and cherish. The art with a capital A which is being repudiated, as well as popularized, is an art of discourse, that is, full of ideas; it embodies and evokes the strongest emotions rather than purveys immediate pleasure; and it is highly organized esthetically. Now what characterizes the contemporary taste in art, whether Classic, Romantic, or Modern? It is the dislike and distrust of ideas, the substitution of sensation for strong emotion, and the taking refuge from esthetic understanding in the intricacies of technique. Hence the inevitable distortion of what the larger public assimilates.

These preferences of today are of course legitimate. They explain why for thirty years the smaller public, knowing or naïve, has swallowed without resistance every innovation of contemporary art. The former philistines have learned their lesson well and managed to see in the new whatever seemed congenial to the yearning for privacy. And the New has branches to suit all tastes: there is the plain New for the brisk vanguardians, the Near-New for the faltering, the Old-New for the laggards. A little ahead and in a seasonable haze stands the New-New, from which at times, by a tremendous effort, particles of the New-New-New detach themselves, like a helium nucleus out of radioactive material. In all these can be enjoyed the absence of articulate thought, of high passion, and of the specific artistry of the last half millennium. But when these self-protective tendencies, bred in the best minds and soon unconsciously acquired by others, go to work upon the art of another time, they automatically twist it out of shape, suppress its meaning, reduce it to fragments, and finally eliminate what has been absorbed till no one is left who instinctively knows what the whole is all about.

If one adds to this the recent and infinitely depressing *po-*

litical use of art by foreign offices and departments of State,[8] and goes on to note the growing demand for government support of contemporary art in countries that had so far escaped that burden, one is ready to conclude that the Western world faces a period of permeation by broken-down, low-calorie art that can only range all sensible people in the anti-Art party. The Romantic worship of art, having lost its purpose, heads toward self-extinction. The nations of the West now resemble those tribes that eat their gods to get the good there is in them.

If this is so, we are at one of those turning points that are so difficult to believe in, because on the surface many continuities seem to assure the future of the tradition. Underneath there is emptiness—what Blake saw and said at the end of the eighteenth century,

> The sound is forced, the notes are few.

There can be a great deal of sound and but few notes.

III

To say this is not to condemn the age, but to discern its fate. There are moments in history, as Burke late in life observed of the French Revolution, when the tide sets so universally in one direction that the spectacle is like the hand of Providence at work. A man—or even mind itself—would be time's fool to say anything but that the outcome bears the seal of necessity. And just as intellect should refrain from passing judgment, so should the moral sense and the intimate emotions. There is nothing to reprove and nothing to bewail. One might prefer to have been born in an age when creation was abundant and its enthusiasm contagious. It is a flattering self-indulgence to wish so. But one should always doubt whether at the time one would have found that creation genuine and that enthusiasm healthy. One might, with many others, have regarded the new work as the end of all agreeableness and reason; and what is even harder to concede and yet is true,

[8] As late as 1937 this abuse was confined to the dictatorships. See my notes on the Paris Fair of that year in *Of Human Freedom*, New York and Boston, 1939, Chapter III.

one might have been right as far as the available evidence
went. An age is always too crowded for seeing in it the few
things that are by definition unique. One sees chiefly the cloud
of dust around them, or one does not know where to look for
them, or one sees them in a denaturing light which later, suddenly and mysteriously, will go out. The Gettysburgs and
Waterloos are but a vast confusion; it is largely accident when
to any apt witness the field of carnage appears as the park
commissioner will preserve it for posterity.

An example of the difficulty in its various stages is the curious uncertainty of the present time about the cultural work
done in the first decade and a half of this century—fifty years
ago. One of the men close to that work, Blaise Cendrars, says
"Cubism has disintegrated." Denying this categorically, a more
recent observer, Mr. John Golding, calls Cubism "the most
complete and radical artistic revolution since the Renaissance."[9] This and the proposition that Cubism was not a fan-
tasy but a new and exact realism still seem paradoxes; yet having thought much on the subject and tested my reflections in
numerous ways, I find myself in agreement with Mr. Golding.
I go further and think it demonstrable that Cubism and its
allies in the other arts represent the sought-for break with Romanticism. On this account, Cubism (using the term inclusively and not just for painting) is still the most important and
productive, as it is certainly the purest and strongest, of all the
movements of this century.

Cubism broke with the Romantic tradition by breaking with
the method of Symbolism and Impressionism, which were then
the latest, and seemed the last, flowering of the old tree. Cubism changed the direction of thought and emotion by subor-
dinating what is individual and subtle to a new desire for
structure and solids. Concerned with space and time, Cubism
caught and fixed the new perceptions arising from changes in
man's command over space and time. And these perceptions
it managed not merely to render but to organize.

Intellectually, the new art was not regressive but contemporary; it was in tune—knowingly or not—with the characteristic data of the turn of the century: the work of Planck and

[9] *Cubism*, New York, 1959, p. 15.

Einstein, the Eiffel Tower and the *Galerie des Machines,* motion pictures and Blériot flying the English Channel, the rehabilitation of the Will by DeVries and Nietzsche, Bergson and William James—the will which vindicated the artist by brushing aside determinism and supplying a principle of control in the complexity of altered sensations. Independently, the arts responded to the vision of a vast simultaneity of elements— ideas, sights, feelings, memories, colors, planes of existence— which it was obviously the business of the artist to reduce to memorable order.

Logically, architecture was the first to succeed in this task; its materials and specifications were so clearly *given,* and its function, as always, fitted it best to express the social as against the individual reality. Railroad architecture had begun to show what could be done in the mode of simplicity to accommodate the emergent masses in their anonymous blurring of individual outlines. In keeping with this model, Cubism was abstract and dense and (it was the vogue word) dynamic. It was an art of masses in the technical sense, that is, of objects, and of mind working upon objects. By 1912 the vagrant line and vaporous air of Impressionism and Symbolism—Verlaine's beloved "nuance"—were finally The Past. The new exploration was no longer of the self, its dreams or its drugged senses, but of the world and the fresh sense of its multiplying parts. The vulgarity of the world when taken analytically had alienated the Symbolists and had turned them inward upon themselves; but this vulgarity disappeared when the shape of the world was abstracted from the particulars: it makes no difference in the *Nude Descending the Staircase* whether the "person" in it is beautiful or ugly, moral or immoral, illiterate or learned, male or female. The painting itself, the art which it exemplifies, makes beauty and truth out of all possible cases or guesses at the actual fact by a synthesis which is the collective reality.

This is so radically at odds with the "art of comment" which returned to favor, for emotionally understandable reasons, after the massacre of 1914–18, that Cubism has not yet made its full revelation. Yet many have felt unease at our inability to give up the Symbolist art of analysis and nuance. This was certainly in Gide's mind when he wrote in 1943: "I cannot believe that the art of the future will delight in affectation, subtlety, and complication." More recently a number of books on the Cubist period have tried, with an envious kind of wonder, to discover what impulse moved the strange decade before 1914. No one so far has plucked the secret. This may come when the contemporaries are gone, together with the deserters, exploiters, and muddlers.

Meantime we remain face to face with our heroic activists, who are trying to break the spell, to finish with Romanticism by a last romantic act. Goethe's Faust perceived that to make a world "In the beginning was the deed." The deed is no less necessary to make an end, especially in an age like ours, in which naïveté combined with power would go on forever finding new layers of population to instruct in the meaning of Mona Lisa's smile, while out of every million a few discovered and refined on Rimbaud and Mallarmé. The various "deeds" of our Obsessionist painters, sinister playwrights, and electronic musicians are at least interrupting that daisy chain. We see in the growing response to their work how right they are. The pleasure they give goes much deeper than that of being shocked, puzzled, and a little insulted. Rather, what the public is responding to is the promise of liberation, it is the idea of "Enough! Good-bye to all that." The *duty* towards art—to love it and understand it, to be independent, to side with the best, to catch allusions, to interpret myths, to remember names, titles, influences, versions, and principles, to refute error, to draw distinctions, to stay sensitive, to know it all, but also to be fine and avoid all that needs avoiding: the vulgar, the middle brow, the highbrow, and sometimes the avant garde—these infernal commandments of our religion of art become dead letters the moment there is no art to behold, no ideas, words, purposes, or principles to follow, but simply an event in somebody else's life, of which no special cognizance need be taken. To know this is like experiencing the relief that Henry James found even in the death of those best loved; it is the license to practice a serene and silent atheism.

Outside the feelings, in the seamless fabric of history which suffers no discontinuity, the condition of our cultural affairs necessarily shows a different aspect. And the student of history, though unable to prophesy, is prompted by all he knows to believe that the most violent of endings have sequels. No Protestant Reformation, no French Revolution, endures as a pure thought or a live act for very long, and cultural acts and thoughts are liable to even more rapid mutation. What may we expect of the artistic abolitionism which has been gathering strength for a hundred years and has come forth as the indispensable act of the present moment? Quite apart from the transiency of all things, it seems to me a state of mind especially difficult to sustain. Assuming as I do that its heroes will not retreat, I see a peculiar difficulty in the scope of its denials. Their work is all denial. This is indeed the ground of the heroism and of our gratitude. But action that is wholly against must lead to inaction as soon as it is successful. Success means: to create a blank, a void, an absence of oppressive things and intolerable memories. Suppose them abolished, what then? The void is not in itself a danger, for by the time it is reached life has changed, the new mind is taking shape and the open space inspires it like a fresh page. But to the makers of the void, who being men cannot help being purposive, the prospect of success must inevitably seem, if not a dead end, at least the outer edge of the known world.

Our realization of this only heightens our respect and our confidence. The total repudiation of Art by our leading men coincides with the frittering away of high art through vulgarization. What can this convergence mean except that the act of abolition will not be nullified by the persistence of old objects in the common memory? And if we are assured of this, then we may suppose the birth of a new consciousness neither far off nor unwelcome. Whatever the time, we have every reason now for believing our artists when they tell us that Art is dead. They are, as always, the best witnesses to our present position; we must echo them and defend them, just as we must second and encourage the acculturation of the eager newcomers to Art. We repeat after each, but not inconsistently: "Art is dead, long live the arts!"

X

"Romantic"—A Sampling of Modern Usage

I.   Assorted Meanings

ATTRACTIVE:
"Tiny glints of gold make dull hair romantic."—Advertisement,
1938

UNSELFISH:
"[In Soviet Russia] if one factory has beaten another factory
in the race for increased production, it is in honor bound to
send its best men . . . to bring the other factory up to the level
of production. This sounds romantic . . . but it is in the
interest of each plant to increase the productivity of every
other plant."—Beatrice Webb, *What I Believe*, 416

EXUBERANT:
". . . all round him seethed and bubbled the heady wine of
the new Romanticism. Chateaubriand and Victor Hugo, with
their titanic tragedies, their unbridled imaginations, their pur-
ple passages, were the acknowledged literary demigods of the
period."— G. W. Pierson, *Tocqueville and Beaumont in America*, 743

ORNAMENTAL:
"A new shop . . . on the third floor . . . specializes in women's
clothes that are romantic and utilitarian at the same time."—
New Yorker, April 20, 1940, 70

UNREAL:
"For the purposes of this Exhibition, Romanticism was an attempt to substitute purely emotional values for realities through (1) a sentimental interpretation of contemporary life, and (2) a retreat to distant times and places."—*A Souvenir of Romanticism in America*, Baltimore Museum of Art, May–June 1940, Introduction

REALISTIC:
"And they are romantic [the workings of a large department store] not because he is bedazzled by them, but because his shrewd provincial eyes are fresh and strong enough to see them in their quiddity. . . ."—Dixon Scott, "Arnold Bennett," *Men of Letters*, 121

IRRATIONAL AND MATERIALISTIC:
"Nazism looks for support in the German philosophy and literary movement of Romanticism and accepts the philosophical theses of irrationalism, intuitivism and the so-called German *Lebensphilosophie*, which is either similar or on many points identical with evolutionism, utilitarianism, vitalism, and also in some respects with the Darwinian materialist conceptions of the development of life. . . ."—Eduard Beneš, *Democracy Today and Tomorrow*, 158

FUTILE:
"This explains why, for example, so frequently good writers suffer shipwreck in politics . . . why people otherwise talented conduct a romantic policy, which shows a lack of practical psychology. . . ."—E. Beneš, *op. cit.*, 207

HEROIC:
"On the attacking side that literature is courageous and romantic like the *Communist Manifesto* of Karl Marx."—Thurman Arnold, *University of Chicago Law Review*, April 1938, 357

MYSTERIOUS? SOULFUL?:
"Miss Margaretta Scott has a dark romantic beauty and great intelligence, but she never surprised us, never made us catch our breath. . . ."—James Agate, "Romeo and Juliet," *Daily Express*, August 12, 1934

NOTEWORTHY:
"The pipe-line, which began at Rhayader, already made ro-
mantic by Shelley's honeymoon with Harriet, skirted Radnor
Forest, crossed Severn above Bewdley, and discharged its flow
into the new reservoir, on the northern side of the Clent Hills."
—Francis Brett Young, *The Black Diamond*, Prefatory Note

CONSERVATIVE:
"There is, secondly, among the ideological factors, the conser-
vative heritage of German political thought, whether Lutheran
Protestantism, Hegelianism, or romanticism."—Carl Mayer,
"On the Intellectual Origin of National Socialism," *Social Re-
search*, May 1942, 246

REVOLUTIONARY:
"But romanticism looked toward the future also; . . . it fostered sympathy for the oppressed . . . and looked forward to
a new social system, a Utopia. It thus connected itself with
the revolutionary tendency. . . ."—W. V. Moody and R. M.
Lovett, *A History of English Literature*, 237

BOMBASTIC:
"His style also is frequently unfortunate. Mr. [Harold] Fisher
is at heart a romantic, and there are moments in this exposition of the behavior of money when he ceases to be clinical
and becomes religious."—Harold Nicolson, *Daily Telegraph*
(reprinted in *Living Age*, November 1934, 263)

PICTURESQUE:
"But Pope, chief exponent of classicism in poetry, showed romantic tastes by making fun of regularity in gardens . . . and
introduced into his garden at Twickenham a romantic grotto."
—G. F. Reynolds, *English Literature in Fact and Story*, 150

NORDIC:
"The difference in the handling of these few bars [of Mozart's
Magic Flute] . . . one may almost say is the difference between the German and the Italian view, or more generally between the Romantic and the Classic."—Unsigned review, *London Times*, August 14, 1934

FORMLESS:

"But beyond these limits he is wanting in architectonic power —the power of duly proportioning a great whole—and sprawls about in as purely romantic fashion as Spenser."—Havelock Ellis, "Walter Savage Landor," Introduction to *Imaginary Conversations,* Everyman ed., xxiv

FORMALISTIC:

"Now is it not the characteristic of romanticism that the form takes precedence over the subject and that once . . . found, it is clung to and insistently repeated . . . ?"—A. Jullien, *Hector Berlioz,* 1888, 319

EMOTIONAL ON PRINCIPLE:

"Being 'romantic' means obedience to the commandment 'I ought to feel deeply.' Being classical means obedience to: 'I ought to feel deeply about art.'"—Stephen Potter, *D. H. Lawrence,* 145

FANCIFUL:

"I have conceived a romantic idea of educating and adopting her; as we descend into the vale of years our infirmities require some domestic female society."—Edward Gibbon, Letter to Lord Sheffield, August 1789. *Autobiography,* Oxford, 238

STUPID:

"Delacroix is one of those complex artists whom it is impossible not to admire, yet each of his admirers finds a different reason for doing so. During his lifetime he was thought of, in France, as the leader of the Romantic movement. . . . That is, of course, an oversimplification, for . . . Delacroix was intelligent as well as passionate. . . ."—Eric Newton, *The Arts of Man,* 1960, 206

ROMANTIC BUT NOT ROMANTIC:

"Romantic attitudes and impulses are conspicuous in Mazzini's biography down to his very last years; though perhaps one should not overstress their importance, since they are just the outer covering, so to say, of a deeper literary, ethical and religious romanticism which was Mazzini's great glory and his great fight. . . ."—Ignazio Silone, "Presenting Mazzini," *Living Thoughts Library,* 9–10

II.   Contrasting Uses

ABOUT LOVE:

"Having once begun to think consciously about sex, we can never again treat it with the unashamed innocence of the ape; we can only exalt it into romantic love, in the Western-Mediterranean-Christian way, or debase it into bestiality, which is something no beast knows."—Dorothy Sayers, *Begin Here*, 111

Professor [E. K.] Kirk himself writes about marriage and suggests three possible solutions to the sex problem: Realism, which stands for the Christian idea of monogamy; Pessimism, which regards the relations of man and woman as a desperate mess . . . and Romanticism, which allows young people a considerable degree of liberty in sexual experimentation. Though Professor Kirk gives the Devil Romanticism his due, he believes that Realism gives better results."—*The Living Age*, 1934, 173

ABOUT MUSIC:

"Perhaps one of the main reasons for the ever-increasing popularity of the music of Johann Sebastian Bach lies in an intuitive feeling on the part of the listener that, despite its technical complexities, the music is fundamentally that of a Romantic."—David Hall, *The Record Book*, 1940, 223

"[Rachmaninoff's] treatment of the Marche Funèbre in Chopin's B flat minor sonata is a glaring example of how the romantic school of thought would allow the total disregard of dynamic markings in the score, for the sake of a more 'personal' interpretation."—David Hall, *op. cit.*, 221

"But a truce to consistency or logic where our 'romantic' is concerned. Berlioz sings as he will and we listen and glory in the color and poignancy of his art."—Olin Downes, New York *Times*, December 11, 1942

"Possibly . . . [Mr. Mitropoulos] would argue that the Third Symphony is highly 'romantic' as the much-abused word is construed today, and therefore that the Brahms tradition

should not exclude variety and subjectivity in expression."—
Olin Downes, *ibid.*, December 25, 1942

ABOUT NATIONALITY:
"The idea of nationality in its modern European sense was the
noble flower of individualism and romanticism, and grew out
of the enlightenment and the French Revolution."—Eduard
Beneš, *op. cit.*, 10

"The idea of the 'Volkstum' is again only a nebulous, vague,
romantic myth, similar to those adopted sometimes by very
primitive nations, who formed their different myths either from
nature or from their past life and history. But this myth of
'Volkstum' today plays a great part in practical German politics."—E. Beneš, *op. cit.*, 163

ABOUT ART AND LITERATURE:
"Romantic Art, in short, almost invariably fixates at the erotic,
falling-in-love stage."—Harry Overstreet, *About Ourselves*, 41

"True romantic art . . . does not refuse the most pedestrian
realism. *Robinson Crusoe* is as realistic as it is romantic: both
qualities are pushed to an extreme, and neither suffers."—
Robert Louis Stevenson, "A Gossip on Romance," *Memories
and Portraits*, Biographical ed., 244–245

"*David Copperfield* is not only both realistic and romantic; it
is realistic because it is romantic."—G. K. Chesterton, *Charles
Dickens*, 1906 (1942 ed., 140)

"Most of us get our ideas of India . . . from a living English
romanticist, Rudyard Kipling. Kipling shows the usual romantic interest in the primitive and the subrational."—Irving Babbitt, *On Being Creative*, 1932, 245

"He is a romantic, whereas I rather incline to the primitive
state."—Gauguin on Van Gogh, *Lettres de Van Gogh à Emile
Bernard*, 1911, 17

"[Dekker's] . . . 'Gentle Craft' is one of his brightest and most
coherent pieces of work, graceful and lively throughout, if
rather thin-spun and slight of structure: but the more serious
and romantic part of the action is more lightly handled than

the broad and light comedy of the mad and merry Lord Mayor. . . ."—Swinburne, *The Age of Shakespeare*, 1908, 64

"[The Romantics] all wrote dramatic poems; and all for the same reason, which may be summed up in one word—Shakespeare. . . . Sir Henry Taylor's adoption of the Elizabethan method of drama was purely romantic, that is to say, he adopted it without really understanding it."—Lascelles Abercrombie in *The Eighteen Sixties*, 6

ABOUT CHRISTIANITY:
"I found this objective Christianity in Ruskin, in the great Romantics, particularly in Hugo, above all in Tolstoy."—H. J. Massingham, "The religion of a journalist," *H. W. M.*, 274

". . . the romantic humaneness of Jesus' sayings answered their need for order and gentleness and thrift in the savage and already obsolete world of swordsmen and hangmen and torture and filth and agony and waste all about them."—John Dos Passos, *The Ground We Stand On*, 26–27

". . . the mean of reason, the christian ethic, the scientific spirit, and human worth [are] all alien to the German outlook . . . to effect a national regeneration it was necessary to cast back to the irrational springs of the true German spirit. Thus did the postwar years witness the rise of a new romanticism in Germany."—Rohan D'O. Butler, *The Roots of National Socialism*, 297, 232

ABOUT SENSUALITY AND MORALS:
"One might apply to the whole [romantic] school the term paroxyst . . . The Rousseauist is in general loath to . . . impair the zest with which he responds to the solicitations of sense. . . ."—Irving Babbitt, *Rousseau and Romanticism*, 216

"But being exaggerated and ascetic, it is definitely romantic." —Thomas Mann, "Presenting Schopenhauer," *Living Thoughts Library*, 27

"For he uses the language of moral judgment in his book, and when not in the mood of hard-boiled romanticism would probably admit that a 'frame-up' is a moral crime."—Sidney Hook, *Reason, Social Myths, and Democracy,* 60

"In common especially with the transcendentalists, as well as with many other 'moral' and 'romantic' philosophers, he [Thoreau] can be said to share these two beliefs, (1) that solitary contemplation of nature brought a harmony with the spiritual force which created the world, and (2) that what is right is so by reference to intuition. . . . [In this] Thoreau resembles . . . Buddha, Jesus, and Lao Tze."—Theodore Dreiser, "Presenting Thoreau," *Living Thoughts Library,* 8

ABOUT THE INDIVIDUAL AND THE GROUP:
"Disillusioned and bored, his philosophy is half Eliot's despair, half Cummings's mockery. Fitts is a romantic, though he would probably deny it, and this world, uncongenial as it is to individualism, apparently does not please him."—Eda Lou Walton, *The Nation,* July 17, 1939

"National Socialism has shaken off sobriety and piety in the willing acceptance of the tribal self-adulation of romanticism." —Hans Kohn, *The Nation,* November 22, 1941

ABOUT THE REAL AND THE RATIONAL:
". . . in the confused controversy of a century ago, in Germany, England, and France, between the 'classicists' and the Romanticists, the words Imagination and Reason were used to mean an opposition between two mutually exclusive processes . . ."—Graham Wallas, *The Art of Thought,* 125–126

"It is not a romantic conception, but a classic conception of good citizenship, which we are striving to realize. . . . Democratic citizenship is not merely a matter of information and reason; it implies active participation, and is a matter of feeling, self-discipline and imagination, which can be developed through experience in the arts as well as the sciences. . . . The predominantly rationalistic temper of our times has almost lost sight of this fact."—President Lewis W. Jones, "Liberal Education and the War," Bennington College, September 13, 1942

"[Rousseau's] view of man in society was realistic where the rationalist Enlighteners had been hopelessly and pathetically romantic."—Peter F. Drucker, *The Future of Industrial Man*, 203

". . . in the obscure detail which that [classical] taste is too abstract to include . . . [romanticism] finds fresh sources of inspiration."—Geoffrey Scott, *The Architecture of Humanism*, 39

"Today . . . we can at least meet events with our minds cleared of some of the romantic garbage that kept us from doing clear work then."—John Dos Passos, Preface to *Three Soldiers*, Modern Library ed., ix

ABOUT HISTORY:
"The romanticists turned in upon themselves . . . [and] 'created an east impossibly oriental . . . forests impossibly primeval, and periods impossibly medieval.' "—F. B. Artz, quoted in John B. Wolf, *France*, 146

"The great antiquarian and novelist [Sir Walter Scott] showed historians that history must be living, many-coloured, and romantic if it is to be a true mirror of the past. . . . His Scotch novels are his best. They are the real truth about the land which 'the Shirra' knew so well. . . ."—G. M. Trevelyan, *Clio, a Muse and other Essays*, 39 and *n*.

ABOUT WORDS:
"Notice the amount of 'romantic' words, now well-known hacks, 'solstice, languorous, eternal, frail, diaphanous, tremulous,' which help to date the passage. . . . For Mandarin prose is romantic prose and realism is the doctrine of the vernacular opposed to it."—Cyril Connolly, *Enemies of Promise*, 24, 63

"Now consider the difference between a *vindictive prosecution* and a *vengeful pursuit*. Obviously the first phrase is the more rigid, technical, and prosaic, the second is the more vivid, romantic, and poetical. . . ."—Henry Bett, *Some Secrets of Style*, 1932, 27

ABOUT CHARACTER:

"In short, he has a romantic temper, open to all the caprices, the fragile ecstasies, the elegiac melancholies, the plaintive moodiness and the chronic low spirits that were so characteristic of the romanticists of his day."—W. F. Giese, *Sainte-Beuve*, 1931, 14

"Action is left to come, when it comes, from an impulse of sensibility seeming very like caprice, because Sainte-Beuve's sensibility is feminine and mobile and lacks the torrential power of romantic passion. His nature is not romantic. . . ." —*Ibid.*, 55–56

"He [Havelock Ellis] was a romantic rationalist . . . an idealogue on a heroic scale, a yearner and a throbber in terms of the highest intelligence."—Bernard DeVoto, *Saturday Review of Literature*, November 4, 1939, 10–11

"His [W. B. Yeats's] romantic life and thought are here recorded as faithfully as . . . long personal knowledge of the poet and . . . familiarity with his work make it possible. . . ." —Ernest Boyd, "Romantic Ireland's Dead and Gone," *New Leader*, March 6, 1943

"Poland . . . has the highest traffic accident rate in the world. . . . Every day the press printed articles pleading, scolding and wheedling drivers and pedestrians to look where they were going. This precaution is disdainfully disregarded. . . . To heed it may be construed as a bit of cowardice unbecoming to Polish romanticism." New York *Times*, September 19, 1958

ABOUT SYSTEMS:

"When I was young, I was infatuated with that pessimistic and romantic conception of the universe which set off against each other life and spirit, sensuality and redemption, and from which art derived some most compelling effects. . . ." —Thomas Mann, *What I Believe*, 193

"The Romantic Movement represents an attempt to achieve the perfect consciousness of reconciled instinct and reason in creative intelligence or imagination."—Hugh I'Anson Fausset, *The Proving of Psyche*, 27–28

"Romanticism [was] a liberation of the less conscious levels of the mind [from] . . . the rigid censorship exerted by our sense of what is fact and our sense of what is fitting."—F. L. Lucas, *Decline and Fall of the Romantic Ideal*, 277

"Romanticism devoted to social problems and ethical problems as well as the problem of knowledge the widest possible effort."—Oscar Ewald, *Romantik und Gegenwart*, 25

ABOUT SCIENCE:

"At the same time, in the unromantic sphere of science, the development of biological and genetic psychology brought man within the system of nature."—R. B. Perry, *Shall Not Perish From the Earth*, 76

"And the same thing is going on all round us today. Modernist movements against the tyranny of dogma, romantic movements in literature, in art, in theology, and now, even a touch of romanticism in science."—L. P. Jacks, *The Revolt Against Mechanism*, 1934, 71

ABOUT NEO-CLASSICISM:

"More's main object, presumably, is to destroy romanticism . . . , but in practice More's deification of the inner check leads merely to another kind of romantic nostalgia."—H. B. Parkes, *The Pragmatic Test*, 68

"The passage, we need have no doubt, is an excellent portrait of Mr. More. He is an incurable romantic, trying to extract more out of a definite thing than that thing has to give, and he betrays this by his continual forcing of the note."—Bonamy Dobree, *Modern Prose Style*, 71

"Pastiche or neo-classicism, being a dissatisfaction with the present and a nostalgic idealization of the past, is, of course, a romantic escape."—Henry Boys, "Stravinsky," *Monthly Musical Record*, December 1934

"Babbitt was in love with order; he had a positively romantic lack of moderation in his insistence upon it."—Alfred Kazin, *On Native Grounds*, 297

III.   Historical Uses and Variants

F. GREVIL (1628):
"Does not his Arcadian Romantics live after him?"—*Life of Sidney*, publ. 1652, 13

ANTHONY A WOOD (1659):
"[George Herbert] . . . was born in the sometimes most pleasant and romancy place in Wales called Mountgomery Castle."
—*Athenae Oxonienses*, London, 1817, 5 vols., III, 239

PEPYS (1667):
"These things are almost romantique and yet true."—*Diary*, March 10, 1667

SWIFT (1712):
"Fifteen of our Society dined together under a canopy in an arbour at Parson's Green last Thursday; I never saw any thing so fine and romantic."—*Journal to Stella*, May 31, 1712

POPE (1735):
> "Whether the charmer sinner it or saint it,
> If folly grow romantic, I must paint it."
>   —*Moral Essays*, Ep. 2, 15–16

BOSWELL (1763):
"He took delight in hearing my description of the romantic seat of my ancestors."—*Life of Johnson*, Oxford, 1904, I, 309

SCOTT (1829):
"It was a step in my advance towards romantic composition."
—*Waverley*, General Preface, Centenary Edition, Edinburgh, 1871, I, 10

MACAULAY (1849):
"To unhappy allies . . . he extended his protection with a romantic disinterestedness."—*History of England*, II, i, 199

DAVID LIVINGSTONE (1865):
"Marvels equal to the most romancing tales of ancient travelers."—*Zambesi*, xix, 389

THOMAS SECCOMBE (1910):
"It is here that he is a true romancist, not for boys only, but also for men."—"Charles Lever," *Encyclopaedia Britannica*, 11th ed., XVI, 509b

T. S. WOTTON (1934):
"Some of the confusion has arisen from our employment of the same term to express two dissimilar French words—'romantique' and 'romanesque.' The former word is confined to an artistic movement. . . . For this movement English writers would be advised to employ the term romanticist, both as substantive and adjective. . . . 'Romanesque' is the equivalent of our 'romantic' in common usage, and has nothing to do with art."—*Monthly Musical Record*, December 1934, 220

IV. Useful Reminders

"Romanticism will exist in human nature as long as human nature itself exists. The point is (in imaginative literature) to adopt that form of romanticism which is the mood of the age." —Thomas Hardy, Journal, November 1880. *The Early Life of Thomas Hardy*, 189

"We hear the history of art speak of folk art and civilized art, of renaissance and the baroque, of classicism and romanticism, of idealism and realism, through all times and among all peoples. . . . There is need for a rigorous and correct definition of 'romantic,' 'classic' and similar terms in the history of art, just as for . . . 'absolutism,' 'democracy' . . . in political and civil life."—Benedetto Croce, *History*, 1941, 266, 135

"If there is anyone who lightly says that classicism is all for form and romanticism all for content and spirit, he may be lightly ignored. For he is holding something which is obviously false."—L. Arnaud Reid, *A Study in Aesthetics*, 1931, 367

"The most that the realist can do is to select the character and situations that seem to him to serve best as types of men and life; and his selection differs only in degree, as a rule, from the romanticist's choice of material. . . . At best, then, our terms 'romantic' and 'realistic' can only be vague, because they will always be relative."—H. R. Steeves, *Literary Aims and Art*, 11

"Just as critics, during the last thirty years, have often used the word 'romantic' as if it were a synonym for 'sentimental' or 'absurd,' so have some living writers confused style with affectation and preciosity."—Clifford Bax, "On style in some of the older writers," *Yale Review*, 1941, 734

"The pioneer has usually been looked upon as a typical product of the American environment; but the truth is that he existed in the European mind before he made his appearance here. Pioneering may in part be described as the Romantic Movement in action."—Lewis Mumford, *The Golden Day*, 1926, 47

"[Then] . . . commenced the great Literary Revolution of Europe—by teaching to each nation that the true classical spirit for each, must be found in the genius of its own Romance."—Edward Bulwer Lytton, "Life of Schiller" in *Poems and Ballads of Schiller*, 1844 (1890, xiii)

"What romanticism gave the world was new life and new order. The formulas of some of its proponents . . . were of no lasting satisfaction. But no formulas have been . . . Order in itself has never been productive of aesthetic satisfaction. . . . The probability is that the order of the classicist is the order of mechanical balance; that of the romanticist the order of life. A living being has a kind of order which is spread out in time and to which no one was sensible before the nineteenth century."—George Boas, "In Defence of Romanticism," *The Symposium*, July 1931, 382–383

"A romanticism which includes the classical virtues is more necessary to the salvation of the modern Western world than a classicism which opposes romantic vices."—Hugh l'Anson Fausset, *The Proving of Psyche*, 317

Notes and References

[These notes are cast in such a way that they can be read consecutively as a review of, and running commentary on, the main text.]

I

Page xi. WOODROW WILSON. The quotation, slightly rearranged, comes from his address, "The Variety and Unity of History," delivered at the International Congress of Arts and Sciences, 1904 (St. Louis, 1906, II, 17).

Page 4. Critics who maintain that BYRON's crying to the thunderstorm, "A sharer in thy fierce delight, etc. . . ." is "all very well for a solitary poet on Lake Geneva," but leads to barbaric imperialism when it becomes the mood of a whole nation (Herbert Agar, *A Time for Greatness,* 65 ff.) forget that the memorable expression of an emotion is not always its cause. What Byron felt has often been experienced by others. For example, an American scholar such as John W. Burgess, who is hardly to be suspected of jingoism, writes in his memoirs: "I [have] trod the deck of an ocean greyhound in the midst of the dread cyclone and . . . felt that, in some sense or other, by being there, I was master of the tempest and of the dark waters lashed by it into harmless fury at my feet." (*Reminiscences,* N. Y., 1934, 196) Yet historic imperialism—that of Athens and Rome and Charles V—did not need Byron's nature poems as encouragement or explanation.

Page 7. The parallel between ROMANTICISM AND RENAISSANCE is more than casually relevant. Both were periods of expansion and discovery, and being alike periods of high individual achievements, they have been difficult to define, date, and keep within the limits of an abstraction. In the preface to his interesting monograph on *The Renaissance*, Wallace K. Ferguson calls his subject "the most intractable problem child of historiography" and he goes on to review the treatments it has received since Burckhardt. Whoever believes that ROMANTICISM is the only unclassifiable mess in history should read Professor Ferguson as well as those he cites.

Page 8. A few names of distinguished men alive during the Romantic Period but who are not fully of its spirit may be mentioned: Cobbett, Ingres, Horne Tooke, Sidney Smith, Sainte-Beuve after his "conversion," Thomas Love Peacock, the Younger Pitt, Malthus. It is sometimes believed that GUIZOT was by temperament and conviction an anti-romanticist. A glance at his life and work shows the contrary. Not only was he a student of Shakespeare and an historian who felt that Scott and Cooper had invented the proper way to write history, but as a man of sentiment (see the account of his courtship) and as a conservative liberal who wanted to consolidate the gains of the revolution while preventing its recurrence, he is a highly representative romanticist. His extraordinary powers of work are also characteristic, and if he appears in history as a cool and reserved, rather than a flamboyant figure, it is only another proof that romanticists are not all cast in one mold.

Page 11. *Enchanted Wanderer, The Life of* CARL MARIA VON WEBER, by Lucy and Richard Poate Stebbins, N. Y., 1940. The quotations come from pp. 102–103, 14, 106, 87, 66, 41, 34, 106, and 39.

Page 15. ESCAPE AND CREATION. The biographers of Weber are right to make the essence of romanticism mean "standing on the intolerable reality" and saying, "I re-create." Those who term "escapist" the artist who battles reality seem not to see that accepting only past reality means "whatever is, is right." Whereat the critic cries "conformist!"

Page 16. GREATNESS AND MISERY OF MAN. This is the theme

of Article II of Pascal's *Pensées* (Brunschvicg ed., nos. 60–183). The most obviously relevant passages, both from this section and from succeeding ones, are as follows: "Who will not wonder that our body, which a moment ago was hardly visible in the universe, infinitesimal in the midst of the whole, should now be a colossus, a world, or rather a whole with respect to the Nothingness which man can never probe . . . ? For what is man in Nature? A nothing with respect to the infinite, a whole with respect to Nothingness, a mid-point between all things and none. . . . Man is naturally credulous, incredulous, timid, daring . . . bored, unhappy. . . . [Yet] our whole dignity consists in thinking. Thinking makes man great. Man is but a reed, the weakest in nature; but he is a thinking reed. The universe need not take arms to crush him; a whiff of air, a drop of water, suffices to destroy him. But even though the universe destroy him, man is still nobler than that which kills him, because he knows he is being killed, and the superiority which the universe has over him the universe never knows." (Nos. 72, 125, 139, and 347)

The romanticists' sense of contradiction finds utterance in a manner so similar to Pascal's that one could believe in direct derivation if chronology did not establish that the romanticists read Pascal late, as a confirmation of their own views and not as a source of them. Here are a few romantic statements antedating Cousin's famous *Report on Pascal* of 1842:—

ROUSSEAU: "When I consider my state, it is with a kind of shudder that I find myself thrown, lost in this vast universe, and as if drowned in the infinity of beings. [Yet] possessing intelligence, I alone can survey the whole . . . I can contemplate the universe, lift myself up to the hand that governs it; I can love the good and perform it. And I used to liken myself to the animals! . . . But looking then for my individual place within my species . . . what do I find? . . . confusion, disorder. The animals of the field are alone happy, their lord alone is wretched. . . . Man is not one: I will and I will not; I feel both free and slave; I see the good and do evil."—"The Faith of the Savoyard Vicar," *Emile*, ed. Garnier, 317–324

SCHILLER: "All things in heaven and earth have no value, no

estimation, except that which my reason grants them. . . . But, unlucky contradiction of nature, this free and soaring spirit is joined to the rigid mechanical clockwork of a mortal body, bound up with its little necessities, yoked to its miserable fate—this God is banished into a world of worms. . . . Wherever I look . . . how limited man appears! How great the distance between his aims and their fulfillment!—*Philosophical Letters*, Bohn ed., 378

CHATEAUBRIAND: "Man, feeble in the means to hand, as well as in his genius, does but endlessly repeat himself."—*Essay on Revolutions*, quoted in Maurois, *Chateaubriand*, Paris, 1938, 103

DE QUINCEY: "Our revolutionary age would have unsettled his brain [Goldsmith's]. The colossal movements of nations, from within and from without; the sorrow of the times, which searches so deeply; the grandeur of the times, which aspires so loftily—these forces, acting for the last fifty years by secret sympathy upon all fountains of thinking and impassioned speculation, have raised them from depths never visited by our fathers, into altitudes too dizzy for their contemplating. . . ."—*Life and Writings*, by H. A. Page, N. Y., 1877, II, 284

BYRON: "—The dead,/ The immortal, the unbounded, the omnipotent,/ The overpowering mysteries of space—/ . . . have made me/ Unfit for mortal converse . . ./ Is spirit like to flesh? can it fall out?/ Infinity with Immortality/ Jarring and turning space to misery . . ."—*Cain, A mystery, passim*

C. M. VON WEBER: "Misery is the lot of man; never attaining to perfection, always discontented, at war with himself . . . unstable yet advancing."—*Rêverie*, quoted by Stebbins, *op. cit.*, 76

MICKIEWICZ: "Conrad Wallenrod [typifies] also the man of genius, the creator of a real world, and thus akin to God. [But] gifted with powers, he feels this world a land of misery."—*Polish Romantic Literature*, by Julian Krzyzanowski, London, 1930, 77

CARLYLE: "*Ach Gott*, when I gazed into these stars, have they not looked down on me as if with pity, from their serene spaces; like Eyes glistening with heavenly tears over the little lot of man! . . . What art thou that sittest whining there? Thou art still Nothing, Nobody: true; but who, then, is Something, Somebody?—*Sartor Resartus*, Everyman ed., 137

BURKE: "Why do I feel so differently from the Reverend Dr. Price . . . ? For this plain reason—because it is *natural* I should; because we are so made, as to be affected . . . with melancholy sentiments upon the unstable condition of mortal prosperity, and the tremendous uncertainty of human greatness; because in those natural feelings we learn great lessons; because in events like these our passions instruct our reason. . . ."—*Reflections on the Revolution in France*, Everyman ed., 77

GOETHE: "Then he [J. J. Ampère] has spoken no less perceptively of my *Faust*, in representing not merely the gloomy, dissatisfied striving of the protagonist, but likewise the scorn and bitter irony of Mephistopheles as parts of my own nature. . . ."—*Conversations with Eckermann*, May 3, 1827

SCHLEIERMACHER: "What I aspire to know and make my own is infinite, and only in an infinite series of attempts can I completely fashion my own being. . . . It is man's peculiar pride to know that his goal is infinite, and yet never to halt on his way, to know that at some point on his journey he will be engulfed, and yet when he sees that point . . . [not] in any wise to slacken his pace."—*Soliloquies*, Open Court ed., 96–97

II

Page 19. Among the few reliable volumes on ROUSSEAU I should place first: *The Meaning of Rousseau* by E. H. Wright; *Jean-Jacques Rousseau, Moralist* by C. W. Hendel; *J. J. Rousseaus ethisches Ideal* by I. Benrubi; *Rousseau and Burke* by A. M. Osborn; and the special study by Albert Jansen, *Rousseau als Musiker*. On the interpretation of Rousseau's political theory it is important to read T. H. Green's *Principles of Political Obligation*, the essay by G. D. H. Cole prefixed to the

Everyman edition of *The Social Contract*, and the relevant pages of G. H. Sabine's *History of Political Thought*.

The notion of ROUSSEAU'S POSTHUMOUS "ENEMIES" is not a fancy drawn from that author's autobiography. As early as 1814, the year of the Bourbon restoration in France, Benjamin Constant reports: "I am far from joining the detractors of Rousseau; they are only too numerous in our day. A mob of underlings, who hope to earn fame and favor by questioning all courageous truths, busy themselves in an attempt to tarnish Rousseau's glory. That is but one reason the more for being cautious in blaming him. He was the first to make popular the sentiment of our rights. Generous hearts and independent souls awoke at his voice. But," adds Constant with a disparaging simile that has since turned into praise, "what Rousseau felt strongly he did not always define clearly; many chapters of the *Social Contract* are worthy of the scholastic writers of the fifteenth century."—*De l'Esprit de Conquête*, Paris, 1814, 109 *n.*

The influence of ROUSSEAU on ROBESPIERRE brings up the small but significant matter of the worship of Reason during the French Revolution. Peter Drucker (*op. cit.*, 191) makes the common enough mistake of ascribing this cult to Robespierre, who was presumably following Rousseau's ideas. The facts are: both Robespierre and Rousseau were theists, who would have thought the worship of Reason a form of atheism. It was precisely Robespierre who *abolished* the Cult of Reason (May 7, 1794) and replaced it by the worship of the Supreme Being. It was Pierre Chaumette—a Cordelier, not a Jacobin; a student of medicine, not of Rousseau's philosophy; a friend of Hébert, not of Robespierre—who supported the earlier creed and brought the Goddess Reason to the Convention in the shape of an actress.

Page 20. ROUSSEAU'S REMAINING "OUTSIDE" his society, his "primitivism"—in the sense of imagining other possible human relations than those embodied in current conventions—is the fruit of a long tradition. It goes back at least as far as Montaigne, takes in Pascal, and emerges in the eighteenth century as the so-called "Noble Savage" idea. Rousseau's political and social theories are thus not to be "explained" by a pathological childhood. (Cf. Hendel, *op. cit.* viii.) More important still, Rousseau's use of primitive man is slight and casual compared to that made by his predecessors and contemporaries. The most cursory reading of Aphra Behn (*Oroonoco*), Lahontan (*Dialogues Curieux*), Montesquieu ("Histoire des Troglodytes," *Persian Letters*, XI–XIV), Voltaire (*El Dorado, L'Ingénu*), Diderot (*Voyage de Bougainville*) shows that a simple-minded belief in the moral perfection of primitive peoples long antedates Rousseau. After his first essay, Rousseau's judgment of "artificial" society rested on what he knew to be a hypothesis, not an historical or anthropological fact. It is an effect of reason, not of travel to the south seas. In the form Rousseau gave to it, the idea of natural society is divorced from the example of savagery and it becomes—say in Carlyle—the work of "Pure Reason"—"A naked World possible, nay actually exists, under the clothed one. . . . The beginning of all Wisdom to look fixedly on clothes till they become transparent."—*Sartor Resartus*, Ch. X (cf. Swift's *Tale of a Tub*, Sec. II: "If certain ermines and furs be placed in a certain position, we style them a Judge; and so an apt conjunction of lawn and black satin we entitle a Bishop.")

Voltaire may have been angry at what he affected to think was Rousseau's assault on civilization, but he was no less convinced than his opponent that reform or revolution was imperative. He even borrowed a little of Rousseau's faith in Nature when in *The Man with Forty Shillings* (1767) he advocated making the air of Paris purer, urged men to eat less and exercise more, and advised women to nurse their children.—*Romans*, Garnier ed., 240

Page 21. ROUSSEAU'S VIEW OF MAN as primarily a feeling and acting creature, a view correctly interpreted as "realistic" by Mr. Drucker (*The Future of Industrial Man*, 203), is also that of Cardinal Newman: "After all, man is not a reasoning animal, he is a seeing, feeling, contemplating, and acting animal." (Quoted by A. Birrell, *Obiter Dicta*, 192.) Not only is this compatible with the Christian view, but it does not run counter to the famous proposition, imputed as a monstrous error to Rousseau, that man is naturally good. From Augustine to Aquinas, orthodoxy maintains the "natural" goodness of man, without denying the fact of evil or the need of grace. It is only with the doctrines of predestination that man is found evil "by nature" and Sin is viewed as a cause, standing as it were *behind* sinful acts.

As for ascribing badness to man's institutions, it is no paradox but an everyday experience that the force of custom can corrupt good motives and pervert its own original intent. The failure of the social order to reform itself, just because it is an established order; the powerlessness of "reform candidates" to lead old and complacent corporate bodies; the folly, in short, of decanting new wine into old bottles, is the perception Rousseau put into his so-called paradoxes. It is only when one makes rigid abstractions of Man and Goodness and Evil that Rousseau's position presents difficulties. And it is only by ignoring both empirical and textual evidence that criticism can say: "There were a number of important differences between Rousseau and Voltaire in their attitude toward history and social problems. In the first place, Voltaire was purely intellectual and critical and little moved by sentiment; Rousseau was almost pathologically emotional, sympathetic and sentimental. In the second place, Voltaire was realistic and practical; Rousseau was idealistic and Utopian."—H. E. Barnes, *A History of Historical Writing*, Univ. Oklahoma Press, 1937, 168

Page 23. Though the SOCIAL CONTRACT is a hypothesis, the condition of being bereft of the contractual state is not unknown to mankind. To say nothing of the Pilgrim Fathers and the Mayflower Compact, the so-called "Great Fear" lasting from April to July during the first year of the French Revolution was a collective paralysis, more or less intense, resulting from the feeling that an old contract had run out and a new one had not yet been concluded. Tacitus records a similar instance, which produced unaccountable madness and violence. —*History*, Everyman ed., II, lxiii, 50. (For putting the date of the "Great Fear" as early as April 1789, see Madelin, *French Revolution*, 69)

Page 23. In trying to harmonize the claims of the individual with those of the group, Rousseau prophetically set the political problem in the form in which the Revolution bequeathed it to the nineteenth century. Coleridge, following Burke, but allowing for greater forward movement, saw the two principles conditioning progress as the historical force of group persistence and the individualist tendency to adapt forms to changing needs. Carlyle asks a question having the same purport: "How, in conjunction with inevitable Democracy, indispensable sovereignty is to exist: certainly it is the hugest question ever heretofore propounded to Mankind! The solution of which is work for long years and centuries."—*Past and Present*, London, 1888, 215

By the side of this formulation, Aristotle's deductive "classical" view asserts the priority of the state, clearly seeing the democratic consequence if this axiom is denied: "in the order of nature, the state is prior to the family or the individual; for the whole must necessarily be prior to the parts . . . for if this is not so, then each individual, being complete in himself, will be in the same position as the others with respect to the whole."—*Politics*, Bk. I, Ch. II (Bohn ed., 7)

Page 26. MR. COLE's remark on Rousseau's use of human freedom comes from his Introduction to *The Social Contract*, Everyman ed., xviii. It is interesting that in these days when the nature of freedom and of obligation is once again being discussed under the shadow of crossed swords, Rousseau's endeavor to "make chains legitimate" should recur as a solution to these questions. Guglielmo Ferrero reintroduced the notion of legitimacy in his last work, *The Principles of Power*, feeling that the post-Napoleonic era of reconstruction offered valuable precedents for our use. Publicists like Walter Lippmann (*N. Y. Herald Tribune*, May 2 and 5, 1942), Peter Drucker, *op. cit.*, and Gaetano Salvemini (*passim*) have dealt with the same difficulty, but without discovering any firm footing outside Rousseau's combination of historic habit with popular consent.

Page 29. BURKE. In her valuable *Rousseau and Burke*, London and N. Y., 1940, Miss Osborn leaves no doubt about the kinship of the two men's philosophies: ". . . in spite of Burke's scathing denunciations of Rousseau . . . there was no important divergence of opinion on the question of fundamental principles. Indeed, when on occasion Burke presents a statement of abstract principle, he gives the best possible phrasing of Rousseau's doctrine." (vii)

In Burke, Rousseau's two basic principles, "self-love" and "sympathy" (i.e. the social sense), appear as "self-preservation" and "society." (*On the Sublime and Beautiful,* Sec. vi) Burke's later works, culminating in his masterpiece, *The Reflections,* express ever more vividly the romanticist sense of life as drama, as contradiction unplumbed by easy rationalism: "The nature of man is intricate; the objects of society are of the greatest possible complexity: and therefore no simple disposition or direction of power can be suitable either to man's nature, or to the quality of his affairs." (*Reflections,* Everyman ed., 59) And again: "We do not draw the lessons we might from history." (*Ibid.,* 137) "It appears to me as if I were in a great crisis, not of the affairs of France alone, but of all Europe, perhaps of more than Europe. . . . Everything seems out of nature in this strange chaos of levity and ferocity. . . . In viewing this monstrous tragicomic scene, the most opposite passions necessarily succeed, and sometimes mix with each other in the mind. . . ." (*Ibid.,* 8)

Burke, like the romanticists, complains of the growing materialism which is a reduction of experience to "substance and quantity" (*Ibid.,* 181), and he asserts with them that Man is a "wonderful structure . . . whose prerogative it is, to be in a great degree a creature of his own making; and who, when made as he ought to be made, is destined to hold no trivial place in the creation." (*Ibid.,* 89) Like Rousseau whom he calls an "acute though eccentric observer," he fears the dissociation of religion from society, for in setting some men over others, a common bond must exist to prevent a reckless exploitation of the ruled by the rulers. (*Ibid.*) Change, which Burke does not exclude, must be by evolution, for "the subject of our demolition and construction is not brick and timber, but sentient beings, by the sudden alteration of whose state, con-

dition, and habits, multitudes may be rendered miserable."
(*Ibid.*, 165)

Page 29. ROUSSEAU's remarks on the need for a lawgiver, his
imputing revolutionary outbreaks to the blindness of kings,
and his lively sense of national tradition in forming individual
character and re-forming institutions, are all to be found in his
Social Contract, Everyman ed., pp. 34 and 40. In his *Considerations on the Government of Poland* (1772) his awareness of nationality and his rejection of *a priori* planning are as
conspicuous as his modesty in offering general suggestions and
his prophetic anticipations of nineteenth-century European
developments—e.g. his warnings against government by finance (Burke says the same thing, *Reflections*, 191 ff.); his
recommendations to open careers to talent, to tax incomes,
and to muster a citizen army; his recognition of the worthless-
ness of treaties of guarantee and of the disintegrating effect
of a rootless cosmopolitanism. He ends with a virtual forecast
of Sieyès's appeal to the French bourgeoisie in 1788: ". . . the
Polish nation is composed of three orders—the nobles who are
everything; the bourgeois who are nothing; and the peasants
who are less than nothing."—*Oeuvres de Rousseau*, Geneva,
1782, II, 269

Page 30. HEGEL. The best short account of German political
theory is an essay by G. P. Gooch written in 1915 and reprinted in his *Studies in Modern History*, N. Y., 1931, 208–
232. It provides a first inoculation against the recurrent epi-
demics of anti-Hegelism, though one must fortify the dose with
a reading or re-reading of *The Philosophy of Right* and even
The Phenomenology of Mind. In their light, the often-cited
Philosophy of History, which is a difficult set of posthumous
lecture notes, takes on a clearer and sounder meaning. A comprehensive view destroys the commonplace interpretation of
Hegel as a Prussianizer *à outrance*. Having myself been guilty
of repeating this vulgar error in a previous book, I am glad of
the opportunity to rectify it with apologies, and to thank Professor Walter Dorn for the gentle reproof which led me to
reconsider not only Hegel but the whole German school. It is
worth noting that while American critics continue to write,

"Thus an intellectual madman such as Hegel, whose system of thought led a nation to the assumptions of *Mein Kampf*, etc., etc. . . ." (New York *Times*, December 29, 1942) the British, despite their limited paper supply, are bringing out a new translation of *The Philosophy of Right* and announcing it as "particularly important today in view of the part Hegel's ideas are *supposed* to have played in the development of German totalitarian theory."—Blackwell's *Forthcoming Publications*, Oxford, Winter 1942

Page 31. A good test of the PUBLIC'S ATTITUDE toward Hegel in the middle of the last century, before imperialist policies had twisted a part of his doctrine to new uses, is the embarrassed admission of his interpreters that "no doubt, Hegel's philosophy is liberal and progressive," as if that were a blemish to be overlooked for the sake of the rest.—A. Vera, *Introduction à la Philosophie de Hegel*, Paris, 1855, 17. (See also Caird in *The Progress of the Century*, 1901, 157: "Hegel's principle is as hostile to reaction as to revolution, and as hostile to an authoritative system . . . as to mere individualism.")

Page 31. NAPOLEON as despot. Since he has been baptized "a child of the revolution," Napoleon's actual tyranny has been minimized, if not forgotten. But though this may be a proper enough perspective for a later age, the facts looked very different to contemporaries. Twenty years after Waterloo, Alphonse Karr could still define Napoleon as "a Corsican word meaning 'invasion'" and as early as 1818 a by no means unpatriotic Frenchman, once a counselor of the Emperor's, had to admit that "since 1793, France must have seemed a reservoir of barbarians who rushed out periodically to pillage and enslave Europe."—Jean Fiévée in anon. *Lettre à Fiévée sur l'honneur du nom de Français*, Paris, 1818, 6

Earlier still, Wordsworth had written: "It is, I allow, a frightful spectacle—to see the prime of a vast nation propelled out of their territory with the rapid sweep of a horde of Tartars; moving from the impulse of like savage instincts; and furnished at the same time, with those implements of physical destruction which have been produced by science and civilization. Such are the motions of the French armies; unchecked by any thought which philosophy and the spirit of society, progressively humanizing, have called forth. . . . These revolutionary impulses and these appetites of barbarous (nay, what is far worse, of barbarized) men are embodied in a new frame of polity which possesses the consistency of an ancient government without its embarrassments and weaknesses. And at the head of all is the mind of one man who acts avowedly upon the principle that every thing which can be done safely, by the supreme power of a state, may be done . . . and who has, at his command, the greatest part of the continent of Europe. . . ."—*Convention of Cintra* (1809) Oxford, 1908, 178

Modern comparisons between Napoleon and Hitler have favored the former because he is supposed to have carried equality and fraternity in his train (see D. E. Lee, *The World on the Way to War,* Boston, 1942) but Napoleon's victims saw on the contrary a combination of revolution and aggression made into a "new polity." In the same way we tend to assume that National Socialism is more than a dictatorship with imperialistic motives, and more than a wartime extension of planned economy. Careful scholars point out, however, that Nazidom has properly speaking no theory of state, and an attentive reader of *Mein Kampf* is surprised to find there the rights of men held superior to the state, and the state itself called a means and not an end. This does not prevent the German dictator from scorning democracy as a talking shop and a decaying corpse—much in the manner of Napoleon. If style and coherence in demagogy have gone down one notch since the latter's day, it is due rather to the difference in the public now aimed at than to any intrinsic lowering of theorizing power: Napoleon's "ideas" were no more free of self-seeking and national egotism than those of twentieth-century tyrants. (See *Behemoth: The Structure and Practice of National Socialism* by Franz Neumann, N. Y., 1942.)

Page 32. FICHTE'S ULTIMATE GOAL for mankind is conveniently expressed in his most popular work, *The Vocation of Man,* Open Court ed., 120–125. In his patriotic addresses, Fichte did utter occasional extravagances about the superior merit of the Germans, their unique fitness as civilizers, and so on.

These statements have a particularly ugly sound after the mass persecutions of our century. But they are far from being peculiar to Fichte or to German writers generally. Each remark could be matched with comparable ones made by the French about themselves almost at any time between the age of Louis XIV and the world war. Before the French, it was the Italians and the Spaniards who had the unpleasant habit of considering every other people barbarous, nor is it so long ago that an identical Anglo-Saxonism was rampant in English-speaking countries. What encouraged both this last movement and the earlier Germanism of Fichte was the generally held theory—accepted even in France by Montesquieu, Guizot, and many others—that it was the German peoples who had brought the idea of freedom to European civilization. (Hence Hegel's calling the modern period of general freedom "Germanic.") Without this purely Germanic strain of liberty-loving individualism, it was felt, Europe would have been forever crushed under Roman and Catholic imperial might. Was it not Germany that made the Reformation, another outburst of free individualism? And did not Tacitus (whose *Germania* we now scan for testimony about German ferocity) stress the free temper and institutions of the ancient Germanic tribes?

This current of opinion, which lasted until well past the middle of the nineteenth century, shows how difficult it is to interpret national egotism such as Fichte's, and how dangerous it is to assign a permanent "nature" or train of thought to a national group. To do so is in fact nothing else than retorting the race fallacy of the pan-Germanists upon themselves, and with about the same chance of having it true to fact.

Page 34. ADAM MÜLLER has been drawn out of his obscurity because of his contribution to the theory of the corporate state. In his own day, however, he made a relatively superficial impression. (Silz, *Early German Romanticism*, Harvard University Press, 1929, 89) It is rather the new protectionism of our own epoch that has turned attention, not merely upon Müller, but upon List, Fichte, Carlyle, and others, who during the romantic period protested against those patent evils of unchecked competition which might be called economic libertinism.

One interesting feature of these nineteenth-century speculations is their express admiration for Louis XIV's minister, Colbert. But the context shows that political romanticism had made an advance over seventeenth-century mercantilist sovereignty, thanks to Burke's and Rousseau's ideas. In a very good treatment of the economic point, Professor G. A. Briefs concludes that "political Romanticism was prosecuting its war on a double front"—against the Revolution and against "the all-pervading bureaucracy of the absolute state and . . . the mercantile policy of that state."—*Journal of the History of Ideas*, June 1941, 296 (See also Ewald, *Romantik und Gegenwart*, Berlin, 1904, Part I—"Friedrich Gentz.")

III

Page 40. PASCAL undermines the CLASSIC IDEAL: I say this on the strength of the Thoughts contained in Article I (Brunschvicg ed. nos. 15–59). When he defines eloquence as a correspondence which the orator tries to establish between the head and the heart; when he says it is not enough that a thing be beautiful, it must be appropriate; when he praises his own reflections for their closeness to the ordinary matter of life; when he condemns as jargon all the "poetical beauties" and prefers to find a man in a book instead of an author—he is a romanticist in letters. When he dwells on particulars in his analysis of government and society (Article V), he is a romanticist in political theory. When he urges the necessity of faith, the "wager" or risk involved in true belief (Article III), he is a romanticist in religion. I shall give further citations in the order in which they fit the text of my book. Meanwhile, I subjoin two secondary proofs of his intrinsic romanticism. The late Abbé Brémond wrote: "Romanticism, then, would not mean only Shakespeare or Victor Hugo; it would also mean Pascal." (*Pour le Romantisme*, viii) This is confirmed by the frequency with which Pascal is called a "sickly romantic" and "a strange philosopher" in French anti-romantic criticism—e.g. Baron Ernest Seillière, *passim*; René Lote, *Les relations franco-allemandes,* Paris, 1921, 159; Valéry, *Introduction à la Méthode de Leonard de Vinci, passim.*

Page 41. HERRICK's couplet comes from the *Hesperides,* no. 991.

Page 42. The objections and exceptions to the CLASSIC ORDER were not slow to appear, and a list of them would make a long book. Those who are interested in the subject may consult Emile Deschanel's four volumes, *Le Romantisme des Classiques,* Paris, 1887–1891; the excellent life of La Fontaine by E. Pilon and F. Dauphin, prefixed to their edition of the *Fables,* Garnier ed.; *L'Envers du Grand Siècle* by Félix Gaiffe; Koppel Pinson's *Pietism as a Factor in the Rise of German Nationalism;* and generally the scholarly work of the present century upon almost any of the great seventeenth-century figures—Newton, Fénelon, Leibniz, etc.

By way of sample, I bring together a few remarks about two writers who are usually taken as representative of the "cold," classical, social-minded rationalism of the Great Century: "Molière . . . [was] . . . sensitive, indulgent, and tormented." Critics of his own day "charged him with anarchism, atheism, and impiety . . . to them he was a splendid or infamous revolutionary . . . [his] sense of the unlimited energy and possibilities of life . . . [of the] human spirit too various to be limited by a formula . . . his disposition, grave and melancholy, contemplative and given to fits of abstraction . . . exposed [him] to criticism and calumny such as few men have had to sustain."—John Palmer, *Molière: His Life and Works,* London, 1930, 199, 413 ff.

Of PIERRE BAYLE, the author of the famous *Historical and Critical Dictionary* that furnished so many telling arguments to the eighteenth-century philosophes, a student of his letters says that he was "out of sympathy with the classic ideal" and she quotes his opinion of the contemporary dramatist and satirical writer, Cyrano de Bergerac: "I love to see him take the bit in his teeth in a book and run without let or hindrance over hill and dale." (Letter to Minutoli, February 10, 1674, in Ruth Cowdrick, *The Early Reading of Bayle,* Scottdale, Pennsylvania, 1939, 28 *n.,* 29) Bayle naturally took the side of the "mod-

erns" in the famous quarrel which rent the republic of letters
and finally broke the dictatorship of the Academies. On the
history of this confused debate (Bayle said of it, "no one answers Perrault [the modernist], they declaim at him") the
standard work is by Hubert Gillot, *La Querelle des Anciens et
des Modernes en France*, Paris, 1914. Gillot makes the interesting point that those whom we call the great classicists—
Molière, Racine, La Fontaine, La Bruyère—used the authority
of the ancients to defend themselves and their *innovations*
against unceasing attacks from two opposite quarters: the objectors to their "roughness and irregularity" and the objectors
to their "smoothness and gallantry." As Mr. Palmer finds himself doing with Molière, M. Gillot speaks of them as "the revolutionary minority of the great classics." (*Op. cit.*, 369)

Page 42. LA FONTAINE'S LOVE OF NATURE is not only recorded
in his biography and in the careless way he discharged his
office of forester, but it creeps out in his verse, with not unexpected associations:—

> *J'aime le jeu, l'amour, les livres, la musique,*
> *La ville et la campagne, enfin tout; il n'est rien*
> *Qui ne me soit souverain bien,*
> *Jusqu'au sombre plaisir d'un cœur mélancolique.*
>
> —*Psyché* (1669)

While on the subject of seventeenth-century pleasures, it may
be apt to refer once again to Pascal's judgment: "The king is
surrounded by men whose only thought is to entertain him
and keep him from thinking about himself. . . . This is all that
men have been able to invent in order to be happy, and those
who affect to be philosophical on the subject and who think it
unreasonable to spend the day running after a hare which no
one would even buy, are hardly acquainted with human nature. The hare could not keep away from us the sight of death
and misery, but hunting takes our mind off it and does keep
it away." (No. 139)

Page 43. In addition to Boileau's Prefaces, one could cite as
moderately egotistical his several addresses to the King in the
form of Satires or Epistles, of which the theme is:

Va, la foudre à la main, rétablir l'équité,
. . . Moi, la plume à la main, je gourmande les vices.

                                    —Discours au Roi (1665)

Elsewhere, despite the formal imitation of Horace and the suggestion that Louis is Augustus, Boileau declares that he is striding forward boldly, guided only by himself.

The truth is that the artistic temperament has a certain constancy of pride and self-assertiveness throughout the ages, which the conditions of classicism only obscured. These conditions, in turn, are closer than we think to those we have been familiar with since the control of culture by totalitarian governments. In seventeenth-century France the dictatorial spirit emanated from Colbert, who held the purse-strings. One must read the *Conférences de l'Académie Royale* (ed. A. Félibien, London, 1705; A. Fontaine, Paris, 1903) and the history of the French Academy both at Paris and at Rome (H. Lapauze, Paris, 1924; and A. Montaiglon, *Mémoires . . . , Procès-Verbaux . . .* and *Correspondance des Directeurs . . .* Paris, 1853 ff.) to become aware of the unflagging and ruthless zeal with which the state used its power to produce—what? The dullest school of French painting and the most sterile debates on style. The efforts of the plastic artists to prove to one another that their work conformed to the ideas of Vitruvius and the practice of the ancients—none of whose works were extant —were equally pathetic and futile. Meantime they neglected their duties as teachers of the young to such a degree that the students organized a revolt, charging the Academy with inefficiency and lack of practicality. The leaders of the insurgent youths were exiled, their followers given an opportunity to recant, and the academicians effected a few reforms. (Montaiglon, *Procès-Verbaux,* I, 197–203)

But until the end of the reign the heavy hand of LEBRUN controlled the subject matter, execution, and reward of all the work done at the capital. Outside his pleasure there was only exile or voluntary obscurity. Within it, there was the orthodox "manner," which thought it had freed art from "gothic barbarism." *La bonne manière* consisted in exalting "line," scorning color as "impure," and cramming canvases with "strictly correct" historical figures, whose poses were based on an official psycho-physical guide to the emotions prepared by Lebrun himself. Only after his death did the growing band of "moderns," proclaiming Rubens as their master, make enough headway to vindicate color and show its organic relation to drawing. By then taste in subject matter had also changed and the Regency had given vogue to the *mondain* style we associate with the eighteenth century.

Page 45. PENSION SYSTEM. The Abbé Huet's remarks, taken from his *Discours de réception à l'Académie,* are quoted in J. F. Thénard, *Les Maximes de la Rochefoucauld,* Introd., 26. On the whole national system, of which the control of art was an important division, one should read C. W. Cole, *Colbert and a Century of French Mercantilism,* N. Y., 1939, 2 vols.

Page 47. In addition to the LONG NOVELS like *The Great Cyrus,* which, incidentally, was read by both Bayle and Pascal, there developed a bourgeois school of fiction, unfashionable and somewhat dull, and as a further offshoot a sort of naturalistic school, known as the *"genre poissard,"* with a special vocabulary, setting, and morality. Its native grossness appealed by contrast to the refined eighteenth-century taste, at the very time when overdelicate criticism was finding Molière too coarse in his buffoonery.—A. Chevalier, *Molière et la comédie de caractère,* 6

Page 47. DR. JOHNSON's misfortunes are so described by Augustine Birrell, by no means a hostile critic, in *Obiter Dicta,* 120–121. He exemplifies on the contrary the very qualities for which he so fittingly praises Johnson: "his equable knowledge of human infirmities, at which he neither storms, sneers, nor chuckles as he records them." (*Ibid.*)

Page 48. CLASSICISM AND RENAISSANCE. The break which the classicists were proud of making with the past took them back to the mood of the Renaissance humanists. For instance, Raphael was praised for "having cured our minds of the disease found in the gothic and barbarous style of art, a style which before Raphael had held sway for over a thousand years, from the time when the fine arts were buried under the ruins of the

Roman Empire." (Fontaine, *Conférences inédites de l'Acadé-mie*, 93) This skipping over the centuries is hardly being "tra-ditional" in any tolerable sense. Indeed, the saving virtue of both the Renaissance and the later Classicism was that they were quite incapable of recovering the antique manner with literalness. The Renaissance turned out to be a romantic move-ment full of individual diversity, and Classicism an equally original movement of reaction aiming at uniformity. (Hauser et Renaudet, *Les débuts de l'âge moderne*, 1; F. P. Chambers, *Cycles of Taste*, 116–117)

When the facts are studied, it becomes apparent that there is no such thing as an esthetic of classicism. There is instead a well-defined attitude, a language—I would even say a pose, taking the word in a neutral sense and implying no disapproval. Whether one turns to Boileau's *Art Poétique* and commentary on Longinus, or to Dryden's prefaces, Roscommon's *Horace*, or Addison's *Account of the Greatest English Poets*[1] (1694), one finds the same respect for the same generalities, but little more than commonplaces. All these writers speak of the "improve-ment and refinement" of their speech over that of the previous age, of "harmonious numbers," of "art calling imagination to the aid of reason," of "charm and correctness." They all praise living authors by comparing them with Pindar or Vergil, but there is nothing so direct as even the simple romantic formula of "uniting the sublime and the grotesque."

Apart from the meters chosen for the several genres on the basis of vague similarity with ancient usage, the classic tech-nique consists entirely in the so-called Aristotelian unities of the drama and the practice of abstraction and generality. By this I mean what Pope did in transcribing Chaucer (whom Addison had called "rusty"). Where Chaucer writes, "the gar-den," Pope has "this charming place"; "the well": "a crystal fountain"; "a laurel always green": "verdant laurels." There is nothing wrong with Pope's words except the fact that he would have used them for any garden, well, or fountain. Similarly Racine and his contemporaries called a woman's beauty

---

[1] In these few hundred lines Shakespeare is not mentioned. Cow-ley is called "a mighty genius," and Spenser, who "amused a bar-barous age . . . can charm an understanding age no more."

"*l'attrait de ses charmes,*" which made her automatically become to the lover "*l'objet de ses feux.*"

The broad, directing principles—or perhaps the critics who administered them—were frequently inconsistent. Sometimes they followed Longinus in preferring sublime unevenness to mediocre perfection; at other times, perfection and proportion were put above "wild genius marred by unevenness." Often the critic assures us that native gifts and inspiration are needed for the highest poetry; at other times he guarantees the efficacy of the rules and utters enormities like these: "Godeau to my mind excels in saying well the trivial things [*les petites choses*] and that is how he comes closest to the ancients, whom I admire especially in this regard." (Boileau, quoted by Brémond, *op. cit.,* 23)

One need hardly add that men such as Molière and La Fontaine always insisted on the priority of meaning over rules. In an argument with Racine, Molière is reported to have said: "Regularity must always be sacrificed to expressive truth; art itself must teach us to free ourselves from the rules of art." (Taschereau, *Histoire de Molière,* 127) Boileau reworded this precept in feebler fashion in his *Art Poétique* (Bk. IV) but he was not really in sympathy with Molière, whom he criticized in the same work for having been "too much a friend of the people" and having neglected "the agreeable and the refined" in favor of "grimaces and slapstick." It is accordingly a fiction of French neo-classic criticism that Molière, La Fontaine, and Racine only produced their best work under the control of Boileau's classic ideal and personal advice.

Page 49. The cost of AUTHORITARIANISM. Gillot, tracing the development of academic control over French art, says: "Let us not forget the make-believe in this grandiose unity which was accomplished by the will of the ruling power; nor the servitude, the constraint, the sacrifices, by means of which the subordination of the individual to authority was purchased. . . . Behind the imposing order of the façade raged dissension and schism." (*Op. cit.,* 203, 366) And P. W. Wilson, summarizing one part of Professor Cole's work on Colbert, says: "No Hitler and no Mussolini has begun as yet to improvise a system of authoritarian control so absolute and so inclusive as the majestic regime into which every activity of a highly civilized France was absorbed. . . ."—N. Y. *Times Book Review,* September 17, 1939, 9

Page 50. The CHARIOTEER myth occurs in the *Phaedrus,* 54, which has other interesting connections with the classicist outlook: the definability of essences, the discrediting of poetry in comparison with science, and Socrates' conviction that "fields and trees teach me nothing; men in the city do." This does not mean that Plato's idea of man was confined to this formula. He wrote more than one dialogue and invented more than one myth.

Page 50. SPINOZA's view of the emotions is set forth in the fourth book of his *Ethics.* Proposition VII states: "An emotion can neither be hindered nor removed save by a contrary emotion and one stronger in checking emotion." His basic definition is: "An emotion, insofar as it has reference to the mind, is an idea wherewith the mind affirms a greater or less force of existing of its body than before." Hence the mind is subject to passions in the degree to which its ideas are inadequate. But there is no doubt about the place of desire or love among the passions: it is the very essence of man. In saying that Spinoza was neglected by the classicists, I should except La Fontaine, who vainly tried to thrust the *Ethics* upon his own friends with the famous question, *"Avez-vous lu Baruch?"*

Others than Spinoza, of course, opposed the prevailing theory of Reason Dominant. Swift was one. (R. Quintana, *Mind and Art of Swift,* 51) Another seventeenth-century writer, quoted but unnamed by Sir Henry Newbolt, asked: "Who has taught you to cast away Passion, an't please you, like the Bran, and work up Reason as pure as the Flower of your Cake?" (*Studies Green and Gray,* 1926, 119) By Pope's time, a halfway theory of the relation between feeling and reason had become current. It supposed, first, that each human temperament is the product of one "master passion," and second, that in some indirect way, evil motives produce socially acceptable virtues, "As fruits, ungrateful to the planter's care/ On savage stocks inserted, learn to bear."—Pope, *Essay on Man,* II, 181 ff.

Page 51. BLAKE's sentences about energy, soul, and body come from "The Marriage of Heaven and Hell," *Poetry and Prose*, Keynes ed., 191; PASCAL's about the dignity of man consisting in Thought are in Article II, *op. cit.*, no. 146. A further comment of his on the "classic" idea of emotional serenity is in point here: "To tell a man that he must live in repose is to tell him that he must be happy; it is to counsel him to adopt an altogether happy condition, which he can then consider at his leisure and find in nowise distressing . . . : it is to understand nothing of man's nature."—*Ibid.*, no. 139

Page 53. DESCARTES' *Treatise on the Passions* concludes: "And now we see that they are all good by nature and that we have nothing to avoid save their misuse or their excess, against which the remedies I have explained will suffice for anyone who takes care to apply them . . . practicing the separation, within himself, of the motions of the blood and animal spirits, from the ideas to which they are in the habit of being joined." (*Oeuvres Choisies*, Garnier ed., II, 110)

With these words compare Rousseau's "romantic" conclusions: "It is an error to distinguish between allowable passions and forbidden passions, with a view to giving oneself up to the former and denying oneself to the latter. All are good when one is master of them; all are bad when one is enslaved by them. . . ." (*Oeuvres Complètes*, 1793, Vol. 36, 113) Rousseau goes on in a vein reminiscent of Pascal and Spinoza and suggestive of Burke: "The human understanding owes much to the passions, and they, as everyone admits, also owe much to it; it is through the activity of the passions that our reason perfects itself; we seek to know only because we desire to enjoy. . . . But how is it possible to repress a passion, even the feeblest, when it has nothing to counteract it? . . . The only check on the passions lies in other passions. . . . Only fiery souls know how to strive and conquer; all great effort, all sublime deeds are their work. Cold reason has never done anything illustrious, and triumph over passion comes only from opposing one to another. . . . The true philosopher is not less subject to his feelings than another, but he knows how to conquer them, just as a pilot sails with a contrary wind." (*Ibid.*, 115)

So much has been made of Rousseau's statement that "the man who thinks is a depraved animal," that its meaning in context must be made clear. What it contrasts is the animal (whose acts are neither moral nor immoral) with man, who loses this innocence as soon as he thinks. More abstractly: when reflection succeeds to instinct, the animal's non-moral conduct is replaced by the human being's power for evil. Far from being an enemy of thought, Rousseau says: "All other things equal, he who thinks best is most nearly happy. Thinking means discovering the true relations among things and drawing from them a knowledge of the truth. . . . Thus the art of thought is the art of becoming as happy as lies in our power; and this depends upon ourselves in far greater degree than is usually believed." (*Traité élémentaire de Sphère, Oeuvres Inédites*, 1861, I, 192)

Finally, here is Rousseau's criticism of rationalist ethics: "It is imagined that the first law is the desire to be happy; this is a mistake. The idea of happiness is very complex . . . for our passions arise from momentary feelings quite independently of our reason. They are developed with the aid of reason, but the wish exists before reason—according to what principle? I repeat: the law of survival. Whatever seems to extend or strengthen our existence pleases us; whatever seems to destroy or diminish it afflicts us. The great error . . . has always been to mistake man for an essentially reasonable creature, when he is only a feeling creature who follows his passions in order to act, and uses his reason only to palliate the follies that they make him commit." *Pensées détachées, Oeuvres Inédites*, 1861, II, 356–357

Page 53. By DIDEROT's time, the analysis of feeling had once again become a subject for subtlety. It was the century of Richardson (whom Diderot eulogizes as a "great poet of the human heart"), of Marivaux, Sterne, the Abbé Prévost, and the "sensitive" poets, Gray, Collins, and Cowper. Diderot distinguished in excellent pre-romantic fashion: "Being sensitive is one thing, being able to feel is another. The one is a matter of soul, the second is a matter of judgment. The former takes in, but is incapable of rendering." (*Paradoxe sur le Comédien*, [1773–1778, published 1830], *Oeuvres Choisies*, Garnier ed., II, 313) It is this "rendering" that marks the difference between Diderot's century and the next.

Even during the first flush of classical power, a hundred years before Diderot, poets had not been wanting who disputed Boileau's dictum about clear thought producing clear words. These men had been forced to express genuine but indefinite feelings by the phrase *"je ne sais quoi."* It served to describe love, melancholy, religious emotion, and even the charm of natural scenes. By 1749, Voltaire himself had not greatly improved on this strangled utterance. In his pleasant comedy, *Nanine*, the hero, Comte d'Olban, is a "natural" man, simple and independent in his ways, who is also described as having *"l'air sombre, embarrassé, rêveur."* When reproved for his lack of display, he says: *"L'éclat vous plaît; vous mettez la grandeur/dans les blasons; je la veux dans le cœur. . . . L'usage est fait pour le mépris du sage/ Je me conforme à ses ordres gênants/ Pour mes habits, non pour mes sentiments./ Il faut être homme et d'une âme sensée/ Avoir à soi ses goûts et sa pensée."* (III, 6; I, 1) The practical Voltaire—cynical in the eyes of some—is here shown on the side of Molière's Alceste or nearly; for to declare that custom can be despised by the philosopher, who must conform as to clothes but not as to his thoughts and his "heart," is to flout society if not common reason. Yet the guaranty *d'une âme sensée* makes sure that no real revolution in manners shall occur.

This conflict between the old and the new in the second half of the eighteenth century took many forms. Diderot expressed its artistic meaning very prettily in a dialogue in which the Cuckoo and the Nightingale represent Method and Genius respectively. The Ass is brought in to judge and he finds the nightingale "bizarre, incoherent, and confused," the cuckoo far more melodic, because, as that bird says of himself, he utters "few things, but they are things of weight and order, and people retain them." We shall follow the symbolic nightingale through its triumph in romanticism ("daring modulations . . . fresh and most delicate melodies . . . tender, glad, brilliant, pathetic," says Diderot) to its use in the twentieth century as the sign of beauty crushed by reality (T. S. Eliot, *Sweeney among the Nightingales;* Auric on Satie's *Parade:* see below, p. 224).

The same indecision of the pre-romantics is reflected even more directly in Sir Joshua Reynolds's *Fifteen Discourses on Art.* These have for us the advantage of having been delivered quasi-annually before the Royal Academy from 1769 to 1790, so that the reader can trace the gradual change of the artist's principles from faith in academic Reason to an almost embarrassing uncertainty. Like the French classicists, his beginning is in Raphael, but he wants the last name uttered by him in public to be Michelangelo's. At first he thinks art can be taught; later there are no rules. "Practice will be rewarded" he promises at the start; at the end he speaks of meeting a student long ago at the French Academy at Rome, who had acquired every quality, but who had "a narrow idea of nature" and did not suffer "his taste and feelings, and I may add even his prejudices to have fair play." (Everyman ed., 249) Such were the unhappy contradictions that Blake could not understand and hence excoriated in his famous Marginalia.

Page 54. The BIOLOGICAL REVOLUTION was prepared by the explorations of the seventeenth- and eighteenth-century travelers, Galland, Chardin, Cook, Bougainville, La Pérouse, and others, from whom not only men of science but men of letters derived the knowledge which changed the outlook of Europe in the next century. A writer to whom Diderot, Goethe, and the two Darwins (grandfather and grandson) were indebted—Buffon—was himself dependent upon the reports of travelers for the materials of his great work, as influential as the Encyclopaedia —the *Natural History.* But it was to his genius alone that he owed the sense of what the new facts portended. "The true mainspring of our existence," he wrote in 1749, "lies not in those muscles, veins, and arteries and nerves, which have been described with so much minuteness; it is to be found in the more hidden forces which are not bounden by the gross mechanical laws which we would fain set over them." (*Histoire Naturelle,* II, 486)

This vitalist note sounded again in his remarks upon the literary art, where his canons are almost those of the next age: "Style is the man himself," he says, and he defines it as not merely order but *movement* in one's ideas. It is true he put prose higher than poetry, but the judgment was a sound one in an age when prose possessed all the vitality that had gone out of poetry. (See Vte d'Haussonville, *Le Salon de Mme. Necker*, I, 321–322)

Page 54. On LESSING AND SPINOZA see in addition to Jacobi's Works, K. Rehorn, *Lessings Stellung zur Philosophie des Spinozas*, Frankfurt a. M., 1877, pp. 50 ff. and H. Gonzebach, *Lessings Gottesbegriff*, Leipzig, 1940, pp. 23–24

Page 56. PASCAL's "You are embarked" is in the midst of his argument proving the necessity of the wager. (*Thoughts*, no. 233) It should be unnecessary to repeat that Pascal's way of resolving his own dilemmas does not affect their validity apart from that resolution. An ascetic and a mystic has the right to record his observations and to have them tested by the same standards as if he were a sceptical epicurean. It seems, moreover, that Pascal's alienation from worldly concerns has been somewhat exaggerated. As late as the year before his death he was having scientific conversations with Huygens. In any event, the "wager" is capable of a secular meaning, which indeed many unorthodox romanticists gave it when they spoke of the infinite task that man must face with finite powers. Pascal says: "We know there is an infinite but are ignorant of its nature." (*Ibid.*) It would be too much to say that he himself foresaw the possibility that man's merit lies more in the search than in reaching the goal, yet that is a tenable secondary meaning of the "wager." For Lessing and many romantics such as Goethe it became the primary meaning because God was pantheistically distributed throughout life.

An important question regarding the change from a universe with fixed spiritual orbits to one characterized by novelty and unpredictable movement is raised by Pascal's denouncing Descartes somewhat as Kant later denounced Leibniz. For on reading the two discarded philosophers, one finds their views of will, energy, and movement far less "rationalistic" than appears compatible with their doctrine as commonly understood. What we call their doctrine is no doubt a biased selection from the whole. Thanks to the disciples, Cartesianism and the Wolfian interpretation of Leibniz are closer to the classical spirit than Descartes and Leibniz themselves. The former's dualism, for instance, was originally bridged by his doctrine of the will, through which—he maintained—body and soul are felt as one. (*Letters to the Princess Elizabeth*) Similarly, the atomism and mechanism of Leibniz are given a very different complexion when his ethics—almost Rousseauist and Nietzschean in implication—is harmonized with his metaphysics. If this is true, one would be led still closer to the generality that the classic ideal is found at its purest in mediocrity, whether literary, philosophical, or artistic.

Page 56. RACINE's song is the third of his *Cantiques Spirituels*. The note referring to the King and Mme. de Maintenon is given by P. Crouzet, *Théâtre Choisi de Racine*, 1061 *n*. We know that the reawakening of Racine's religious emotions and his scruples about following the life of the court came in middle life, after unsuccessful battle with his enemies. Boileau's more mundane disenchantment with classic reason came later. It was near the end of his days that he is reported to have said, "Descartes's philosophy has cut the throat of poetry." (P. Stapfer, *Racine et Victor Hugo*, 59)

IV

Page 58. ROMANTICISM IS REALISM. A student of English literature, speaking of the ninth century, makes the same point: "The note of this Romance literature is that it was actual, modern, realistic, at a time when classical literature had become a remote convention of bookish culture." (Sir W. Raleigh, *Romance*, 25) Another scholar, speaking of ROUSSEAU's alleged unreality, suggests an even more important truth: "In a sense, therefore, even the Vicaire Savoyard was right when he tried to prove the existence of God by pointing to sublime mountain scenery; certainly as right as one who points to sublime tradition, to the order of seventeenth-century France, to the discipline of the thirteenth century. . . . As a matter of cold fact, the Vicar was perhaps a bit more realistic than his twentieth-century critics. For he had at least his mountain valley before him; they have merely their fanciful reconstruction of the past." (George Boas, "In Defence of Romanticism," *Symposium*, 1931, 376)

Two critical statements must serve to introduce the further evidence: One is Blake's reiterated statement that "to Generalize is to be an Idiot. To Particularize is the Alone Distinction of Merit." (*Op. cit.*, 977) Blake's tone of invective should not detract from the applicability of his esthetic proposition. At the opposite intellectual pole, we find the nineteenth-century academic historian, Auguste Trognon, saying of his own period: "We have come to feel extreme distaste for systems and a lively affection for facts. . . . Local color serves not only to arouse dramatic interest but to make intelligible the bearing of facts." (*Etudes sur l'Histoire de France*, 1822, 6, 9)

Page 59. In describing the "ROMANTIC REVOLT" it is usual to name authors exemplifying the previous, decadent classicism and to animadvert against their emptiness; it is less usual to quote them. Yet I think a few examples might give an appropriate "realistic" concreteness to the propositions advanced in the text. Here are two Frenchmen dealing with Shakespeare: "Writers have been mentioned who are supposed to have been successful without knowing or observing the rules of the art, such as Dante, Shakespeare, Milton, and others. To say this is to express oneself very incorrectly. Dante and Milton knew the ancients, and if they have acquired a reputation with monstrous works, it is because there are in these monsters a few beautiful parts executed according to the right principles. They lacked a general conception of the whole; but their genius supplied some details in which the sense of beauty is present; and the rules are nothing but this sense reduced to a method." (La Harpe, *Lycée*, 1799, § 1)

Now for verse from the most famous French poet between Voltaire and the romantics:—

> *Quels que soient les excès de leurs divisions*
> *Le talent réunit toutes les nations;*
> *En vain Londre et Paris, orgueilleuses rivales*
> *Prolongent sur les mers leurs discordes fatales:*
> *Je ne t'oublierai point, toi, dont le noir pinceau*
> *Traça des grands malheurs le terrible tableau,*
> *Qui de sombres couleurs rembrunissant la scène,*
> *D'une robe sanglante habillas Melpomène.* . . .
> *Ton sceptre est un poignard, un cyprès ta couronne,*
> *La nature pour toi n'est qu'un vaste cercueil*
> *Que parcourent l'effroi, la douleur et le deuil.*
> —Delille, *L'Imagination, Poème en 8 Chants*, V,
> *Oeuvres*, IX, 22

The "thou" with a "black brush" to whom "all nature is a coffin" is none other than Shakespeare. But about this time Shakespeare's scepter (which Delille likens to a dagger) had been handed down to a laureate named Pye. This is the opening of his *Alfred, an Epic Poem in Six Books*:—

> *While, with unequal verse, I venturous sing*
> *The toils and perils of a patriot King;*
> *Struggling through war, and adverse fate, to place*
> *Britannia's throne on Virtue's solid base:*
> *Guardian and glory of the British Isles,*
> *Immortal Freedom! give thy favoring smiles.* . . .
> *So, on my ruder lays, auspicious shine,*
> *And make immortal, verse as mean as mine.*

At a comparable time, Gottsched ruled the German literary world with his satires and critiques imitated from the French. He was so faithful an imitator that Voltaire acknowledged "Monsieur Gottsched" as the only German wit, and so fanatical a classicist that he fought for the rules "even at the expense of contents."

Page 59. The effectiveness of the new realism practised by the romantics can be gauged from the objections they encountered. Gifford called Hazlitt's wonderfully flexible and colloquial prose "broken English"; Fenimore Cooper wrote to Scott, "One frothy gentleman (French) denounced you in my presence as

having a low, vulgar style, very much such an one as characterized the pen of Shakespeare!" (Scott's *Journal*, II, 109 *n*.)
Balzac, Hugo, Burns, Wordsworth, were similarly accused of
making use of bad language and worse subjects, while young
Landor retorted on his accusers by saying that the new generation was sweeping into the lumber room "the frippery of
Gibbon" and the "inflexible plush that overloaded the distorted
muscles of Johnson." (O. Heseltine, *Conversation*, 129) This
was bravado, but it took courage and persistence to rehabili-
tate the common words which classicism had outlawed. The
need for them was real. An admirer of Thomas Jefferson and
the Declaration of Independence points out that in the last
paragraph of the original draft, Jefferson denounced slavery,
but that the eighteenth-century style that had perfectly answered in the earlier portions dealing with abstract rights fails
at the end. This is because "we do not see George III repealing
a statute of South Carolina in order that Sambo may be sold
at the port of Charleston. No, the Christian King wages 'cruel
war against human nature' . . ."—Carl Becker, *Declaration of
Independence*, 214–215

Page 59. The question of the ROMANTICS' ATTITUDE TO GREECE
deserves a whole book based on the excellent monographs already extant. (B. H. Stern, Harry Levin, Stephen Larrabee)
It is not enough to say that Greece was remade according to a
new fancy. The Greece of the romantics was *used*, often quite
consciously, for purposes of their own; it was a treasury of vivid
and varied history and art, and no longer a set of uniform per-
fections. For one thing, Winckelmann and others had studied
anew the documents and remains; for another, many of the
romantics went to the Near East and saw its shape and color
with their own eyes. It is therefore not true to say that their
Grecian dream was baseless, particularly when we compare it
with what had preceded it in the European imagination. See
for example—in addition to romantic painting—Goethe's use of
a new side of Greek mythology in *Faust II* and Hugo's description of "Thessaly in the time of Aeschylus" in the Preface
to *Les Burgraves*.

Page 60. HUME's observations upon art come from his essay

on "Simplicity and Refinement in Writing," Green and Grose
ed., I, 240, 241

Page 61. SCOTT. It may re-enforce his case to quote what Leslie
Stephen, always suspicious of romanticism, says of him: ". . .
though called a romantic, [he] is as much a naturalist in his
descriptions of Dandie Dinmont or Edie Ochiltree as George
Eliot in her Adam Bede or Tulliver." (*George Eliot*, 110) As
for the mood of knighthood, hear the master himself: "Ballan-
tyne blames the Ossianic monotony of my principal characters.
Now they are not Ossianic. The language of the Ossianic poetry is highly figurative; that of the knights of chivalry may
be monotonous and probably is. . . . Sooth to say, this species
of romance of chivalry is an exhaustible subject. It affords materials for splendid description for once or twice, but they are
too unnatural and formal to bear repetition."—*Journal*, II,
122–123

Page 62. Lionel Trilling's words on SHELLEY come from the
New Republic, May 5, 1941, 637. Dowden's notion that Shelley could not think for himself is repeated in *The French Revolution and English Literature*, 1897, 50; and the still more
common belief that Shelley had no sense of fact reappears,
with less excuse, throughout Lascelles Abercrombie's *Romanticism*, London, 1926.

Page 63. FORM IN ROMANTIC ART. Two contradictory clichés
are current about romanticism and form. One is that the art
of the period is formless; the other is that it is nothing but
form. L. A. Reid, quoted above, p. 167, makes short shrift of
the former idea; F. P. Chambers, in his valuable but incomplete *History of Taste*, 1932, 178–180, shows the metaphysical
sense in which romantic art is "the discovery of pure form." On
the plane of craftsmanship, both extreme positions are untrue,
but their currency can be explained by the fact that to this day
no satisfactory account of what artistic form really is has been
given. As Pascal said of poetic beauty, "*on ne sait pas ce que
c'est.*" Goethe's remark that "form is something mobile, something becoming, something passing" applies to natural objects,
particularly to plants, whose metamorphosis he is describing

in a scientific work of that name: the words are not to be taken as showing the romantics' contempt for order in art. The most direct refutation of the "formlessness" charge would be simply to count the easily recognizable forms revived or invented by the romantics. The statistics (which should include Victor Hugo's example of the Malayan pantoum in the *Orientales,* Notes, [1829]) would be convincing for literature. For the other arts, one would have to consult the most recent scholarship on the romantics, that is, the earliest books written in the belief that form is indeed to be found in their works, albeit of a different sort from the classical (e.g. T. S. Wotton's *Berlioz* or Sackville-West's *De Quincey*).

This leaves one further belief to be disposed of, namely, that when classic forms were in vogue the *average* of style was high. "The worst scribblers of the seventeenth century, the very chambermaids, have a certain air and touch of style . . . all they had to do was to pick up the current common manner, which was excellent, limpid, and healthy." (G. Bertrand, *Revue Germanique,* 1863, 8) A study of the materials gives a different result: ". . . If I compare the best French written in the eighteenth century, that of Voltaire, or rather of Montesquieu, with the best written in the nineteenth, that of Nodier, Hugo, Anatole France, I confess I prefer the latter, for it is at once less dry and more exact (*rigoureuse*). (J. Boulenger and A. Thérive, *Soirées du Grammaire-Club,* Paris, 1924, 130)

Page 65. WORDSWORTH's lines occur in *The Prelude,* II, 214–215; III, 59–63

Page 65. SCIENCE. On the error of taking Keats for an enemy of science, see C. D. Thorpe, Introd. to *Complete Poems and Selected Letters of Keats,* Odyssey ed., N. Y., 1935, xlii–xliii. On Wordsworth in the same connection, see Wm. Knight, *Wordsworthiana,* 1889, 199–217. The biographical detail about Faraday is from Tyndall's Introduction to the *Experimental Researches in Electricity,* Everyman ed., xviii. And in an excellent summary applying to the German philosophers in particular, Professor James Gutmann concludes: "There was among the romanticists not a rejection of science, though there was constant criticism of the mechanistic theories of the 18th century. There was certainly no general protest against Reason, though there was criticism of rationalistic dogmas in religion, for example, or ethics. To oppose Rationalism is, however, hardly the same as to reject Reason. To deny mechanism is not equivalent to denying the importance of science."—Introd. to Schelling, *Of Human Freedom*, Open Court ed., xxii

Page 66. FREUD, SUBJECTIVISM, EGOTISM. Confirmation of my view may be found in Matthew Josephson: "Long before Freud, the romantics intuitively and unashamedly told what they felt, even likening an adored mistress to a mother, thus associating human sentiments which, as an elder statesman like Barthou held, should not approach each other." (*Victor Hugo*, 1942, 222 n.) Parallel cases, in which the romantics speak "intuitively and unashamedly," have led to the imputation of obsession with the self; it may be we who are obsessed and project our anxiety on the romantics. See Sir Henry Taylor's *Autobiography*, I, 181, for an anecdote about Wordsworth's "egotism."

Page 70. VICTOR HUGO. The quotation comes from the Preface to *Cromwell* (1827), Nelson ed., 31. This seems a good opportunity to say a few things about Hugo as thinker and artist. Matthew Josephson's biography rehabilitated him as a character and a man of action, but the opinion still prevails that he is a loose craftsman and a pompous poet who only thought he thought. Certain critics, slowly working their way back to romanticism, prefer Vigny to Hugo as "more serious." One or two reminders of demonstrable truth may be in order here. In the first place, Hugo's artistry as a poet is supreme. This may not be apparent to English readers for whom one alexandrine is much like another because none has "real rhythm," but it is apparent to French ears, such as the sensitive ones of Paul Valéry: "Through sixty years . . . Hugo never wearied of fortifying his art and training himself to be more accomplished in it. . . . What prodigious lines, lines to which no other lines of poetry can be compared for extent, internal organization, resonance, and fullness, did he not compose in the last period of his life! In *La Corde d'Airain, Dieu,* and *La Fin*

de Satan . . . the illustrious old man attains the acme of poetical power and the highest point of the versifier's noble science."
(*Variété II*, 153)

This is far from saying that all of Hugo's tremendous output is first rate—an impossible standard for any poet to meet—but that his power is indisputable. More than power and more than bulk, however, Hugo has variety. Mr. Julian Green has noted, "I re-read Hugo's poems. What a number of lines written with a single line in view! But side by side with empty, bombastic pieces, there are some so lovely that they make my heart beat faster. [1931]" (*Personal Record*, 1933, 48) and Proust, who preferred the mood of Vigny and Nerval: "I do not think that in all the *Fleurs du Mal*, that sublime but sardonic book, one can find a poem equal to [Hugo's] *Booz endormi*. . . . Victor Hugo always does marvelously what has to be done. It is impossible to wish more precision than in the image of the crescent moon. . . ." (*Chroniques*, 1920, 242)

I have chosen on purpose three critics whose own place in French literature makes them a priori unsympathetic to romanticism, but gives them at the same time the right to speak with authority.

If one wants a short first introduction to Hugo's mind and art, written with knowledge and sufficient hardheadedness, one can do no better than read the philosopher Renouvier's *Victor Hugo: le Poète*, Paris, 1893. His chapter on Hugo as myth-maker must be supplemented by Denis Saurat's more recent work on Hugo's religion (Paris 1929), after reading which—but not before—one has the right to speak of Hugo's powers and defects as a thinker.

Page 71. IDEALIZING. The romantics themselves were so aware of the real that they often accused themselves of idealizing when they chose subjects or adopted methods other than the directly descriptive. Thus Hawthorne on *The Scarlet Letter*: "The wiser effort would have been to diffuse thought and imagination through the opaque substance of today . . . to seek resolutely the true and indestructible value that lay hidden in the petty and wearisome incidents and ordinary characters with which I was now conversant." Compare this with De

Quincey's definition of the picturesque: "It is . . . the characteristic pushed into a sensible excess. The prevailing character of any natural object, no matter how little attractive it may be for beauty, is always interesting for itself, *as* the character and hieroglyphic symbol of the purposes pursued by nature in the determination of its form. . . ." And he gives as an instance the cart horse, describing its dullness *and* interest. (*Life and Writings,* II, 287–288)

To use the real and make it serve a purpose is the common feature of romantic realism; it does not imply ignorance but subordination of reality. As Scott says: "Though an unconnected course of adventure is what most frequently occurs in nature, yet the province of the romance writer being artificial, there is more required from him than a mere compliance with the simplicity of reality." The "naturalism" of Thomas Hardy fits under this definition just as well as "idealistic" romanticism. Hardy in fact chose that passage as the motto for *Desperate Remedies.* He might have added, still from Scott: "The whole adventures of Waverley . . . suited best . . . the road I wanted to travel, and permitted me to introduce some descriptions of scenery and manners to which the reality gave an interest which the powers of the author might have otherwise failed to attain for them." (*Waverley,* General Preface, Centenary Edition, I, 11) The union of factuality and truth—truth being fact seen from a point of view—is what many other romanticists meant by Imagination (Coleridge distinguished it as the Secondary Imagination), the faculty that creates, or re-creates, reality, and to which we owe all art.

The quality of any given transformation of reality depends, of course, upon technique. Students of Turner have pointed out how, with wrong details of town or landscape, he gives the truest impression of a particular place. (Ch. Holme, ed., *The Genius of Turner,* London, 1903, v) In all romantic work the beholder must follow the flexible intention, instead of responding rigidly as if the work professed to be a direct transcript. The most reliable artist is he who modulates freely from experience to imagination, for it requires a sense of fact to depart from fact without getting lost.

Yet the critical confusion about "truth" recurs in a thousand places, for instance, in the excellent *Outlines of Russian Culture* based on Paul Milyukov's *History of Russian Civilization*. One finds the romantic poet Pushkin credited there with reintroducing life into poetry, and quoted as complaining that "all I read about romanticism is wrong." (Letter to Bestuzhev, Nov. 30, 1825) So far, so good. But this is followed by the historian's comment: "When at last he thought he had found true Romanticism in Shakespeare, it was not Romanticism but artistic realism." (*Op. cit.*, 28) One would suppose that Pushkin might be allowed to know best what romanticism was, particularly when another contemporary critic, Belinsky, had written: "The true poetry of our day is a realistic poetry, a poetry of life, a poetry of actualities." This was said about the time when Stendhal was trying to make the same feeling intelligible to Frenchmen: "*Lanfranc* is a romantic comedy because the events *resemble* those that happen daily under our very eyes." And again: "Shakespeare's *Tempest*, however mediocre it be, is none the less a romantic piece, even though the events last but a few hours and take place in and around a small island in the Mediterranean." [I.e. not the unities in themselves, but their fitness for a realistic purpose, determines romantic realism.] (*Racine et Shakespeare*, 165, 175)

The failure to keep in mind the *variety* of romantic work is part of the trouble. Mention romantic poetry and everyone thinks of *Tintern Abbey* and *Kubla Khan;* rarely will someone think of that other masterpiece, Burns's "Tam O' Shanter," which is perhaps the clearest romantic tour de force, with its combination of high and low, real and imaginary, superstition and moral force, free rhythm and perfect form. But to feel it all, at the headlong pace of a narrative which conceals its own art, one must learn to modulate in tune with the author.

Since I have mentioned Gogol in the text, I should give here the references to contradictory criticism concerning his work: W. L. Phelps, *Essays on Russian Novelists*, 48; P. Kropotkin, *Russian Literature*, 85; M. E. de Vogüé, *Russian Novelists*, 80. Milyukov, discussing the same tug-of-war between realists and idealists over Gogol, informs us that "he became the victim of conflicting opinions on this work [*Dead Souls*]" (*op. cit.*, 35) and, attempting to correct its "hideous reality," lost himself in the theoretical puzzles invented by critics who did not know how to modulate.

Page 74. THE WORD "ROMANTIC," its origin and use, are fully discussed by Alexis François in *Annales de la Société Jean-Jacques Rousseau*, V, 199 ff. and by Logan Pearsall Smith in a tract of the Society for Pure English (no. XVII). It is to the former writer that I owe the references to Rousseau and Letourneur. By François's account, the word "romantic" is of English origin and goes back to the popular romances of the seventeenth century. It is the classic age, therefore, which gives us the idea, the word, and its source—the novel of love and adventure.

Pearsall Smith adds to his own investigation of "romantic" useful comments on three other words historically associated with it: "genius," "original," and "creative." Professor Smith's tone and critical judgment are, however, not above reproach. He speaks of romanticism as "the battle cry of a school of wild poets and Catholic reactionaries," whom he further defines as "scorning and rejecting the models of the past and the received rules of composition" while priding themselves "on their freedom from law and on their own artistic spontaneity" (pp. 16–17). This hardly fits even his own apt quotation from Goethe, who states that the distinction between romantic and classical poetry came originally from Schiller and himself.

Smith's confusion gives point to Wotton's suggestion that we find a parallel for the distinction made in French between *"romantique"* and *"romanesque."* The latter—as in Rostand's play, *Les Romanesques*—would cover any element of wild fancy or improbability, while the former would keep the historic and intrinsic meanings outlined in the present book. The exact equivalence of French *romanesque* with English "romantic" in its vulgar sense can be shown by an example. In 1755, Grimm writes of Voltaire's new book: *"Charles XII avait beaucoup de romanesque dans son caractère . . . son histoire peut donc avoir cet air de roman. . . ."* (1812 ed. 16 vols., I, 348) The English translator, early in the nineteenth century, renders this as: "The character of this hero . . . is in a manner truly bold, easy, original, I might almost add, romantic."—*Memoirs of Grimm, Excerpts,* 4 vols., London, 1815, I, 69–70

Page 75. SENTIMENTALITY. Blake's strong words are as good as any: "He who desires but acts not breeds pestilence. . . . Sooner murder an infant in its cradle than nurse unacted desires." (*Op. cit.,* 193, 195) WILLIAM JAMES's recommendation to act out a feeling of benevolence by speaking genially to one's grandmother occurs in his chapter on "Habit," *Psychology,* I, 126. Under "The Emotions" he says: "The sentimentalist is so constructed that 'gushing' is his or her normal mode of expression. Putting a stopper on the 'gush' will only to a limited extent cause more 'real' activities to take its place; in the main it will simply produce listlessness." (*Op. cit.,* II, 467)

It should be added about Werther that it was not solely disappointed love but also frustrated ambition that led to his suicide. Consciously or not, Goethe gives him two extraordinarily powerful motives to arouse what a modern would call his death wish.

Page 77. MUSSET's character. Here also, it would seem, "the common belief as to Musset's habits was greatly exaggerated." (A. Houssaye quoted by W. H. Pollock, Introd. *Fantasio,* Oxford, 9). As for Burns, whose reputation is that of a poet incompetent in practical life, it turns out that he was a very efficient customs collector. (See Catherine Carswell, *The Life of Robert Burns,* N. Y., 1931, 311.)

V

Page 79. ROMANTIC BECOMES CLASSIC with time. This suggestion was first made, so far as I know, by Stendhal in his *Racine et Shakespeare.* It is incidentally surprising that this entertaining work should never have been translated into English, nor even used more widely than it is by students of English literature. In Renouvier (*op. cit.*) who cites the same two poets, we find Stendhal's idea accounting for a double movement of our sensibility: "we forgive Racine his platitudes, his dull courtier-like effusiveness, and his rhetoric, which has worn thin in many places; we forgive Shakespeare his grossness and conceits in the Italian manner: and it will come to that with the speech and rhetoric of the romantics." (*Op. cit.*, 205)

The next step is that we not only forgive, we forget. What I say of SOCRATES is also true of Dante. In the eighteenth century, the *Divine Comedy* was purely and simply a "monstrous work." By the time of Leigh Hunt, it had become great again, though with reservations about its cruelty, length, obscurity, and its author's overweening pride. (*Stories from the Italian Poets*, Vol. I, "Critical Notice on Dante.") The mention of any of these defects nowadays would brand one as a philistine. Dante has become angelic, his poem is calmness itself, and every word he wrote is in the classic tradition—except for the use of Italian. Stendhal says: "The romantic poet par excellence is Dante; he adored Vergil; and yet he wrote the Divine Comedy, with the episode of Ugolino, which is the one thing in the world least like Vergil. He wrote it because he understood his age and feared Hell." And again: "Sophocles and Euripides were eminently romantic . . . to imitate Sophocles and Euripides today—that is to be a classicist. I do not hesitate to suggest that Racine was once romantic: he gave the marquis of the court of Louis XIV a picture of passions tempered by extreme dignity, of the kind then fashionable, which was such that a duke of 1670, however fond of his son, invariably called him *Monsieur.*" . . . "The Romantics [of today] advise no one to imitate Shakespeare directly." (*Op. cit.*, 39, 33, 39)

Page 79. One example must suffice of the ROMANTIC ARTISTS' unsentimental VIEW OF NAPOLEON. On January 12, 1814, Byron writes to Lady Melbourne: "By the bye, don't you pity poor Napoleon? and are these your heroes. . . . This man's spirit seems broken; it is but a bastard devil at last, and a sad whining example to your future conquerors . . ." —*Correspondence*, 1922, I, 231

Page 80. JOUBERT'S words about Bonaparte are quoted by Maurois, *Chateaubriand*, Paris, 1938, 136.

Page 81. GOETHE'S CLASSICISM. A further word may be said on this subject to show that Goethe recognized the strength of romanticism and was acting, in middle age, as moderator of the extremism of youth. He wrote in the summer of 1813: "Instead of singing the praises of our Romanticism so exclusively and sticking to it so uncritically—our Romanticism, which need not be chidden or rejected, thus obscuring its strong, solid, practical aspect—we should rather attempt to make this great fusion between the old and the new, even though it does seem inconsistent and paradoxical; and all the more should we make the attempt because a great and unique master [Shakespeare] whom we value most highly and often without knowing why, has already most effectively accomplished this miracle." (*Goethe's Literary Essays*, ed. J. E. Spingarn, N. Y., 1921, 182)

There is hardly any need to point out that a "Back to Shakespeare" movement would not have satisfied the classicists of 1813, whether in Germany, France, or England, and that the Goethe-Schiller "fusion of romantic and classic" is but a nuance in the midst of the Romantic Movement. CARLYLE, the greatest student of German romanticism, leaves no doubt on this score: "That since the beginning of the present century, a great change has taken place in German literature, is plain enough, without commentators; but that it was effected by three young men, living in the little town of Jena is not by any means so plain. The critical principles of Tieck and the Schlegels had already been set forth, in the form of both precept and prohibition, and with all the aids of philosophic depth and epigrammatic emphasis, by the united minds of Goethe and Schiller in the *Horen* and *Xenien*. The development and practical application of the doctrine is all that pertains to these reputed founders of the sect. But neither can the change be said to have originated with Schiller and Goethe; for it is a change originating not in individuals, but in universal circumstances, and belongs, not to Germany, but to Europe." —*Critical Essays*, London 1872, I, 246 (Preface to *German Romance*, Edinburgh, 1827)

Page 81. CHATEAUBRIAND's sense of his own exuberant strength is given in Maurois, *op. cit.*, 13

Page 83. TIECK. (Ricarda Huch, *Die Romantik*, Leipzig,

1920, vol. I, 116) Even Professor Silz, it seems, has to be corrected. He limited the name "lazy romantic" to Tieck. (*Early German Romanticism*, 21) But now comes Dr. E. H. Zeydel with a massive study in his hand to tell us that Tieck was not only the most prolific of German writers, but one who "combated his own duality in a brave and constant struggle and never ceased fighting like a crusader against the sordid, the trifling, the egoistic. . . . The purity of his ethical and artistic character at least cannot be impugned."—*Ludwig Tieck, the German Romanticist*, Princeton, 1935, 337, 341

Page 83. For the pressure on GOETHE and others to conform to established models, see his *Poetry and Truth, passim*, and G. H. Lewes's great biography of the poet (Boston, 1856, 2 vols.), Vol. I, 97 ff. For French letters, see Sainte-Beuve's early writings, Hugo's and Vigny's prefaces, as well as Stendhal's *Racine et Shakespeare*. For English, Wordsworth's criticism and De Quincey's essay on Wordsworth. In the romantic period itself the literature of anti-romanticism was large. Its tenor is that in violating the rules of classic common sense romanticism is ugly, incoherent, symbolic, materialism, as well as the fit expression of bohemian art for art's sake (*sic*). The conclusion we must draw is not simple but double-barrelled: from the artist's point of view, romanticism was not a revolt, because classical ideas were dead; he did not break with tradition, tradition broke with him. But from outside, the romantic artist's fight with the academic survivors of the literary old regime amounted to a revolution and his creations marked the beginning of a new tradition.

Page 85. BIOGRAPHY. Space is wanting to set forth the canons of a proper technique for writing the lives of artists. But the negative advice, "Avoid the official style and the debunking style equally," covers the commonest faults. Shaw, who is expert at presenting and interpreting historical figures, suggests that ". . . the first question of the professed biographer is, 'What is the evidence for this?' and the cognate question of the intellectually honest judicial critic [is], 'What else could I have done had it been my own case?'" (*Postscript* to Frank Harris's *Bernard Shaw*, 420)

The allusions and quotations in the text come from: Abercrombie, *Romanticism,* London, 1926, 10 ff., 58 ff.; Sackville-West, *De Quincey,* New Haven, 1936, *passim;* Wotton, *Hector Berlioz,* London, 1935, 194; Blunden, *Leigh Hunt's 'Examiner' Examined,* London, 1928, 80; Barr, *Mazzini,* N. Y., 1935, *passim;* Trilling, *New Republic,* 1941, 637; White, *Life of Shelley,* N. Y., 1941, 2 vols.; Grabo, *The Magic Plant,* Chapel Hill, 1936; Silz, *Early German Romanticism,* Harvard Press, 1929, 11; Thorpe, *Complete Poems of Keats,* N. Y., 1935, xli; Dunning, *Truth in History,* New York, 1937, 176; Green, *Personal Record,* N. Y., 1939, 133.

Page 87. DESCARTES' *Discourse on Method* was originally to be entitled *The History of My Mind* (B. Aubé, Introd. *Discours de la Méthode,* Paris, 1894, 4). This lends force to the use I make of the discourse, while the change emphasizes the caution characteristic of Descartes. I hasten to add that the excommunicating and burning of philosophers practised in his day were good grounds for caution.

Page 89. PAUL ELMER MORE's reworking of the drunkard simile occurs in *Platonism,* Princeton, 1917, 157.

Page 90. NEW HÉLOÏSE. Rousseau knew the defects of his work as well as anybody; this does not excuse them, but it vindicates his artistic judgment no less than his modesty. He is in fact too modest when he calls himself "more zealous than enlightened in my researches, but sincere always, even against myself." As for the book, he says: "Those are fantastic loves [I depict] . . . the first two parts contain much verbal filler . . . which I could never correct. The Fourth Part is the best, and the two following may be useful. . . . My imagination is unable to embellish things; it wants to create . . . all my talent comes from the lively interest I take in things. I used to meditate in bed with my eyes closed, turning my periods over and over in my mind with the most incredible difficulties; then when I had succeeded in being satisfied with them, I committed them to memory . . . only to forget them [in the day's routine]." *Oeuvres,* 1788, IV, 242–245

Page 90. In speaking of LOVE LYRICS as appropriate to youth

and of other poetic tasks to age, I am only giving in for argument's sake to one of the critical absurdities of our time: Goethe, Landor, Peacock, Hugo in their old age are enough to disprove any general rule in the matter. Yet it is important, for the reason stated in the text, that the exclusive association between romanticism and young love be broken up. It would in fact not be very difficult to document the thesis that romantic literature dethroned Eros and made him take his place as one of many subjects. Whereas most classical novel writing deals exclusively with love, Balzac, Dumas, Scott, Dickens, Vigny, introduce all manner of hitherto untouched facts and feelings into their stories. Has it not been said that Balzac created "the metallic hero," namely, Money? And in Scott's own mind, as we saw, the knightly love intrigue was a subject soon exhausted and of always secondary interest.

Page 91. The literature of NATIONALISM is vast. The student should begin with C. J. H. Hayes's pioneering *Essays* and his indispensable *Historical Evolution of Modern Nationalism.* Professors Koppel Pinson and Eugene Anderson have made notable contributions, in book and article form, to the elucidation of German nationalism. For France I may refer to appropriate chapters in my two books, *The French Race* and *Race: A Study in Modern Superstition,* the critical bibliography in the latter volume containing many other titles.

HERDER's detestation for the words "races of men" is recorded in *Sämmtliche Werke,* Suphan ed., XIII, 257. The reader should also consult pages 155, 160, 322, 384–385 for further evidence of his anti-imperialism; and the *Briefe zu Beförderung der Humanität* in Volume XVIII, especially *Briefe* 114–124.

GOETHE's remarks to Eckermann concerning his inability to write hate songs were uttered on Sunday, March 14, 1830.

Page 93. The recognition of GREATNESS IN FAILURE is implicit in the Pascalian conception of man. The thought may have moved Hegel to point out the error of thinking like the valet in the saying that no man is a hero to his valet. For the hero worshipers like Carlyle or Emerson, the hero was not necessarily successful, not a Napoleon but a doer and leader in any field, a force *like* Napoleon. Chateaubriand wrote: "Napoleon was all the weaknesses and all the greatnesses of man." (*Mémoires d'Outre Tombe*, Nelson ed., 302) And before him, Burke had told his electors at Bristol that the goal of life was "to act with effect and energy, rather than to loiter out our days without blame and without use." Constantin prophesied: *"La grandeur se mesurera à la misère."*

Page 94. The lines from FAUST are not the last of the play, but the last that Faust speaks. (II, v, 6) The essential humanity of Faustian striving, that is, of the romantic theory of life, is perhaps best expressed by H. A. Korff, who is the greatest authority on German romanticism. Using Goethe, though not exclusively, to discover the sense of the era, Korff traces the passage from Enlightenment to Subjectivism, and shows that it is not the subjectivism of personal happiness but of self-development: man's task is to exhibit his humanity. This raises the question, "What is Man?" Eighteenth-century humanism had answered, "A reasoning being." Kant modified this answer by showing reason as a form-giving function of man's mind. The "Sturm und Drang" period went farther and showed man as a creative being. Then came Goethe and Schiller, who effected a synthesis of the two new positions, a true humanism combined with a "heroic religion." The term is Korff's and he concludes: *"Humanität und Romantik gehören also zusammen." Humanismus und Romantik*, Leipzig, 1924, 114, 128–129, 140

VI

Page 96. To the manifestations of EIGHTEENTH-CENTURY RO-MANTICISM must be added the Methodist Movement within the Anglican Church. It not only prized and encouraged genuine religious fervor—stigmatized as "enthusiasm" by its opponents—but it began to speak once again the language of simple feeling. As Henry Bett has pointed out, there is nothing between Crashaw and Coleridge that has the ring of Charles Wesley's hymn:

> I cannot see Thy face and live,
> Then let me see Thy face and die . . .

The date is 1749, the year of Goethe's birth, which disposes again of the false belief that romantic thought and expression arose in one place, Germany, and spread by contagion. A thorough canvassing of Pietism in England, France, Germany, Spain, and Italy would show that this movement (including seventeenth-century Quietism) had struck roots everywhere in western Europe; that its origins could be found in the sixteenth century; and that the classic centuries had merely concealed or contracted its significance.

Page 97. FRENCH REVOLUTION. The statement I use in several contexts to show that the revolutionary era "cleared the ground" comes from Stendhal's *De l'Amour* (1822): ". . . the generation rising among us has nothing to *continue:* it has everything to create. The great merit of Napoleon is to have cleared out the house." (Paris, 1926, II, 207) Similar declarations could be cited from De Quincey, Schlegel, Blake, Byron, Burns, and others. For particulars, one should read Crane Brinton's *Political Ideas of the English Romanticists;* Alfred Cobban's *Edmund Burke and the Revolt against the Eighteenth Century;* A. Gregory, *The French Revolution and the English Novel;* C. Cestre, *La Révolution et les Poètes anglais;* and Dowden's lectures previously cited, the last three of these books to be used with caution. One direct citation from SHELLEY will show his awareness of the political genesis of culture. Writing to Byron on September 8, 1816, he says: "[Fontainebleau] is the scene of some of the most interesting events of what may be called the master theme of the epoch in which we live—the French Revolution."—Byron, *Correspondence,* 1922, II, 15

Page 97. POLAND AND RUSSIA. The *Outlines of Russian Culture,* in three volumes, based on Milyukov's history and published by the University of Pennsylvania Press, 1942, supply a more comprehensive view of the subject than the older, purely literary histories. Under the title *Polish Romantic Literature,* Dr. Julian Krzyzanowski has published some admirable lectures (London, 1930), which are to be recommended as virtually a running confirmation of the main points of my present chapter. Note particularly the effect on Poland of the French Revolution, Napoleon, and nationalism; and the blend of realism, symbolism, and the historical sense in the great Polish romantics.

Page 101. VICTORIAN COMPROMISE. On this subject, read not only the somewhat discursive opening volume of Halévy's history, but more especially the writings of G. M. Young, including his collection of essays, *Daylight and Champaign*, London, 1937.

The "romantic aims" I refer to can be illustrated from two speeches of Victor Hugo's delivered in 1849 and 1851 respectively. "There is at the core of socialism a part of the unhappy realities of our time and of all times. There is the eternal distress of human infirmity and that aspiration to a better lot, which is no less natural. . . . There are miseries that are deep, true, pathetic—and also curable. Finally, there is . . . the new feeling given to men by our revolutions, which have put a high price on the dignity of man and the sovereignty of the people; so that the man of the people suffers today from the double and contradictory consciousness of his misery resulting from the facts and his greatness resulting from his rights." And two years later, before the same National Assembly, a speech on "True and False Questions": "The true are economic and social; the false are doctrinaire and philosophical on small matters." (*Actes et Paroles*, 1882 ed., I, 282 and 326) In this loose and rhetorical form suited to the occasion, Hugo is summing up the work of half a century of Utopian Socialism. Not all the romantics were socialists, but nearly every one was striving for an order based on justice, the right to work, and some form of equality—even the so-called reactionaries, like Scott, Balzac, Carlyle, Rodbertus, Lassalle, and Friedrich List. For the relation of Utopian Socialism to Marx and "realistic" socialism, see my *Darwin, Marx, Wagner*, Part II, and for the kindred Mazzini-Cavour relation, S. Barr, *op. cit.*, 210, 240, 244.

Page 102. One of the most lifelike accounts of oncoming "realism" in science is in a neglected but delightful book by the mathematician De Morgan, *A Budget of Paradoxes*, London, 1872, 274 ff. His account of the pre-Darwinian flurry caused by the anonymous *Vestiges of Creation* is as valuable as his criticism of pseudo-Baconian method (p. 52); and his idea of the way the future Book of Genesis would be written is not short of prophetic: "In the beginning was an imperial quart of oxygen at 60° . . . and this oxygen became God." (276) Goethe, perhaps with a like foresight, has Wagner say in the Second Part of *Faust*, "And what Nature was wont to organize, we crystallize instead." (ii, 2)

Page 103. The candid scholar is Maitland, speaking of Kemble's historical work.

Page 104. FLAUBERT. The letter quoted from was written to Mlle. Leroyer de Chantepie, November 4, 1857, *Correspondence*, Centenary ed., II, 321. J. P. BISHOP's comment is in his article on Hemingway in *After the Genteel Tradition*, 1937, 198. An interesting and little-known parallel to the hardened romanticism of men of letters such as Flaubert and A. H. Clough is that of Bismarck, whose loss of faith was not supplied by the philosophies of Feuerbach, Hegel, and David Strauss. After a period of misery and despair, Bismarck returned to a combination of toughness and traditional faith. Yet he continued to think of himself as "soft." "Most characteristic . . . was Bismarck's rupture with the ideas of the romantic politicians who had controlled affairs under Frederick William IV." Where the King and the Gerlachs had seen a conflict between monarchy and liberal ideas and a union of nations on this principle, Bismarck saw *Realpolitik* unattached to principle. (Erich Brandenburg, "Bismarck," *Encyc. Britannica*, 14th ed.; also, *Some Historians of Modern Europe*, ed. Schmitt, 295; Georg Brandes, *Ferdinand Lassalle*, 28)

The dependence of Realism upon a previous Romanticism can be strikingly shown by one of Irving Babbitt's remarks. He thinks it symbolic—and rather rejoices in the idea—that "right opposite Wordsworth's house," a stone quarry "has made a hideous gash in the hillside on the shores of Rydal." (*Rousseau and Romanticism*, 302) It is evident that Babbitt cannot know the gash is hideous unless he accepts as true Wordsworth's sense of natural beauty which he elsewhere rejects as "un-realistic."

Another American critic has a juster view. "What I really think," wrote John Jay Chapman to Henry James, "is something like this: The great romancers of the mid-century—Victor Hugo, Dickens, Balzac—clothed their extravagant romantic fictions in vivid grotesque figures and would have regarded themselves as realists—if the term had been invented. As the romantic *souffle* died out of the world, their lessons and examples as realistic writers survived—and especially the followers of Balzac continued and refined and explored and became obsessed with externals. . . ." (February 11, 1920, *Letters*, 370) Henry James was certainly ready to accept this interpretation, since he had written fifteen years before, in *The Lesson of Balzac*: "We do not, at any rate, get away from him; he is behind us, at the worst, when he is not before, and I feel that any course about the country we explore is ever best held by keeping him, through the trees of the forest, in sight. So far as we do move, we move round him; every road comes back to him." (115–116)

Page 105. FLAUBERT'S gratitude to the romantics: e.g. his life-long respect for George Sand, and such an exclamation as "What a man, old father Hugo! Thunder and damnation, what a poet! I have raced through the two volumes [of *La Légende des Siècles*] . . . I feel the need to bellow these 3000 verses such as no man has ever written."—*Correspondence*, Charpentier ed., III, 212

GISSING. Looking back, as a practitioner, on "realism in Fiction" (1895), Gissing expressed a fairly general feeling among critics: "I could wish, to begin with, that the words *realism* and *realist* might never again be used, save in their proper sense by writers on scholastic philosophy. In relation to the work of novelists they never had a satisfactory meaning, and are now become mere slang. Not long ago I read in a London newspaper, concerning some report of a miserable state of things among a certain class of work-folk, that 'this realistic description is absolutely truthful,' where by 'realistic' the writer simply meant painful or revolting, with never a thought of tautology. When a word has been so grievously mauled, it should be allowed to drop from the ranks." (*Selections from the Works of George Gissing*, N. Y., 1929, 217) Among those responsible for launching the word forty years before, were a group of second-rate French writers who in 1857 issued six numbers of a short-lived periodical called *Le Réalisme*. Champfleury, its editor, published a volume of reminiscences in 1872 which, together with the prefaces to his novels and those of Feydeau (a correspondent of Flaubert's), should be consulted by the curious.

Page 106. "OUR MUTUAL FRIEND." Originally the character of Boffin in this novel—which is perhaps Dickens's masterpiece—was to remain harsh and grasping after his corruption by money. The idea of making his wickedness a pretense ran counter to Dickens's own mood of despair at the time of writing; yet even with the change the novel was not popular. (See John Forster, *Life of Dickens*, Bk. IX, Ch. V)

Page 107. For the complex relations of WAGNER to his time and the significance of his straddling two schools, see Ernest Newman's various volumes and Part III of my *Darwin, Marx, Wagner*.

Page 107. COURBET. One further fact to complete the "interpretation" of the two portraits of Alfred Bruyas: the solid business man visualized by the house critic of the National Gallery has, in Courbet's portrait, a book under his hand. The title is: *Etudes sur l'Art Moderne*. The painting by Courbet which I call "The Naked Truth" is known in French as "L'Atelier." It depicts Courbet himself painting a standing nude, while half a dozen Realists from the ranks of literature and the arts lend their moral support to Courbet's depiction of the naked truth. The portrayal of these gentlemen in an artist's studio with an undraped female caused a scandal. On the question of realism in painting see Jacques-Emile Blanche, *Les Arts Plastiques*, 1931, 28 ff.

Page 108. TURNER, BLAKE, DELACROIX and IMPRESSIONISM. Turner said, "Indistinctness is my forte. . . . An artist ought to paint his impressions." (Quoted by Ruskin, *Modern Painters*,

IV, Part 5, Ch. XV, § 33) This view of himself must be supplemented by a later critical summary, indicative of the way
the "four phases" coexist in one man: "Turner's manners were
almost as many as his pictures, or at any rate as his *subjects*.
Of his 275 best-known canvases, the styles are not successive
but concomitant. . . . In broad lines [we distinguish] three
manners: 1. French or Wilsonian (classical) 2. English (realistic) 3. Evocational or Turnerian." These correspond to "1.
Admiration of the Masters, 2. Study of Nature, and 3. Art for
art's sake." ("The Oil Paintings of Turner" by Robert de la
Sizeraine in *The Genius of Turner*, London, 1903, i–iii)

It should be mentioned here that CONSTABLE was also a
romantic impressionist, who towards the end of his life was
practising "divisionism" and knife painting. But his influence
was slight because by the time Impressionism came into notice
he had become a mere name. The link between BLAKE and the
Pre-Raphaelites is to be found in the direct disciples that he
made during his latter years (after 1818)—Palmer, Linnell,
Finch, Varley, and others, who formed "a premature Pre-
Raphaelite Brotherhood" and thought of Blake as a primitive
master. (A. Clutton-Brock, *Blake*, N. Y., 1933, 132–133) The
quotation from Ford Madox Brown—another neglected master,
whose best works are to be seen in and around Manchester,
is in *Ruskin, Rossetti, Pre-Raphaelitism*, ed. W. M. Rossetti,
London, 1899, 47. See also Sheldon Cheney on Delacroix, *A
Primer of Modern Art*, N. Y., 1924, 76–77. The best treatment
of this period in English art is by T. Earle Welby, *The Victorian
Romantics*, 1850–1870, London, 1929.

Page 109. SYMBOLISM. One should not overlook the importance
of romantic writers like Lamb, Carlyle, and Gérard de Nerval
in showing the way to the linguistic preciosity of the nineties.
At the mid-point of the century, Browning's and Meredith's
prose, and Baudelaire's translations from Poe, the first to be
styled "prose poems," supply the necessary connection. The
movement is continuous, not disjointed.

Page 111. For further comment on the task of reshaping language see Chapter VII and consult *New Directions*, No. 1,
1937, and *Transition*, No. 27, spring 1938.

Page 112. NATURALISM. It is more usual to call Naturalism an offshoot of Realism than to class it with Symbolism as a neo-romanticism. Nevertheless, the latter is the true designation, as is proved by a mass of diverse evidence. First, naturalism existed among the romantics; we have seen Scott called a naturalist by Leslie Stephen. Analyzed instances from Byron, Goethe, Gogol, would disclose the same connection. An amusing one can be found in an early piece by Gautier, in which he is making fun of romantic naturalism at the same time as he practised it:—

> Par l'enfer! Je me sens un immense désir
> De broyer sous mes dents sa chair, et de saisir,
> Avec quelque lambeau de sa peau bleue et verte,
> Son cœur demi-pourri dans sa poitrine ouverte.
> —Daniel Jovard ou la Conversion d'un
> Classique (1832)

I leave the verses untranslated for those who read Baudelaire in the original and think he invented an entirely new *genre macabre* combining love and horror. Baudelaire's naturalism is more accurately described by Paul Valéry: "Baudelaire's problem could—must, in fact—be put in this way: 'how to be a great poet without being Lamartine or Hugo or Musset' " . . . What Baudelaire seeks is "to charm continuously." (Compare Mr. Welby's comment on the Pre-Raphaelites: "Their excessive concentration on esthetic effect is a kind of short cut to beauty." *Op. cit.*, 44) Valéry goes on: "Baudelaire, though romanticist in origin, and even romantic in his tastes, occasionally appears as a classic . . . [by] *choosing* within romanticism and . . . discerning in it a good and an evil, weaknesses and virtues. . . ." (*Variété*, II, 146, 155)

In the second place, the esthetic principles of a Zola, or, more consciously, of a Thomas Hardy, are often nothing more than reaffirmations of romantic beliefs against a constricting convention. Hardy, for example, writes: "My own interest lies largely in non-rationalistic subjects, since non-rationality seems, so far as one can perceive, to be the principle of the Universe. By which I do not mean foolishness, but rather a principle for which there is no exact name. . . . [I] prefer the large intention of an unskilful artist to the trivial intention of an accomplished one: in other words, I am more interested in the high ideas of a feeble executant than in the high execution of a feeble thinker." And again: "They forget in their insistence on life, and nothing but life, in a plain slice, that a story *must be worth the telling*. . . . The business of the poet and novelist is to show the sorriness underlying the grandest things, and the grandeur underlying the sorriest things." (*The Early Life* [and *The Later Life*] *of Thomas Hardy*, N. Y. 1929, 2 vols., II, 90–91, 158, I, 222–223. See also Carl Franke, *Emile Zola als romantischer Dichter*, Marburg, 1914)

For other proofs of the relations between the beginning of the nineteenth century and the end, consult the works of Francis Thompson, Oscar Wilde, Villiers de l'Isle Adam (who said "*A chacun son infini*"), Blasco Ibáñez (who claimed literary descent from Victor Hugo and not from Zola), the letters of Van Gogh to Emile Bernard ("Is it not rather intensity of thought, and not a calm touch, that we are groping for?" p. 42), and finally, the collection of Zola's essays called *Le Roman Expérimental*, which should be read with Léon Deffoux's *Le Naturalisme*, Paris, 1929, as a guide.

Page 113. Among the many books on late-nineteenth-century and modern music, Cecil Gray's "trilogy" (*A History of Music, A Survey of Contemporary Music*, and *Predicaments: or Music and the Future*) is indispensable. To it must be added Constant Lambert's *Music Ho!*, which assumes familiarity with names and facts. On Alfred Bruneau, the only work in English is by Arthur Hervey, London, 1907, but see also Romain Rolland, *Musicians of Today*.

Page 114. SCIENCE: its place in Naturalism and Neo-Romanticism. The quotation from Zola occurs in several places throughout his works. In the collection of essays cited above it will be found on page 111.

In closing this commentary on a tangled period still very near to us, it is necessary to point out that to the naturalists one of the objectionable things in romanticism was its rhetoric—certain words that kept recurring irritatingly. Near as we are to the naturalists, we are beginning to find *their* rhetoric detestable: "science," "the facts," "reality," "gradual evolution," "great social movements," "experimental method," are words which outside their original and strict application have no power but that of annoying. Butler, James, Nietzsche, have made us dissatisfied with them, have deflated them, as every period deflates the fighting vocabulary of its predecessor. And we understand precisely what is meant when still later critics liken Blake, Pascal, Nietzsche, and Samuel Butler to one another; when William James speaks of F. W. H. Myers as "the radical leader of the new 'romantic movement' in psychology" which Freud was to carry on; when Professor Figgis believes Nietzsche was a romantic to the end of his career; and when Mr. R. M. Wenley, putting John Davidson close to Blake and Nietzsche, concludes: "So Romanticism comes full circle." (These allusions come, in order, from Andler, *Nietzsche*, I, 45 ff.; James, *Memories and Studies*, 153; Figgis, *The Will to Freedom*, 255; Davidson, *Poems*, Modern Library ed., Introd. xxxii.)

VII

Page 116. My previous account of MODERNISM in art is in *Of Human Freedom*, Boston, 1939, Ch. 3.

One needs only to look about if one wants evidence of modern bombast, illusion, and smugness. To suggest a standard of comparison for bombast, I juxtapose without comment two modern texts, the first referring to a romanticist, the second to a modern: "Mozart's Symphony in E Flat moved the fantastical E. T. A. Hoffmann to an extraordinary rhapsody: 'Love and melancholy are breathed forth in the purest spirit tones; we feel ourselves drawn with inexpressible longing toward forms which beckon us to join them in their motion with the spheres, in the eternal circles of the solemn dance.'" (From the Program Notes of the Boston Symphony Orchestra, November 18, 1927, 412) In the same Program (pp. 416–420), Bohuslav Martinů writes: "In this symphonic rondo 2–2 I have portrayed the tension of spectators at a game of football. 'Bagarre' is properly speaking an analogous subject, but multiplied, transported to the street. It's a boulevard, a stadium, a mass, a quantity which

is in delirium, clothed as a single body. It's a chaos ruled by all
the sentiments of enthusiasm, joy, sadness, wonder. . . . It is
grandly contrapuntal. All interests, great and small, disappear
as secondary themes are fused at the same time in a new composition of movement, in a new expression of force, in a new
form of powerful, unconquerable human mass. But 'La Bagarre'
is not descriptive music. It is determined according to the laws
of composition. . . ." Upon which the commentator writes:
"He shows a leaning towards neo-classicism derived from the
modernisme of today."

Page 117. SELF-CONSCIOUSNESS. Matthew Josephson, whom I
quoted above, generalizes favorably about the "unashamed"
self-revelations of the romantics. The modern disease of wanting to reveal and hold back at the same time is related, on the
one hand, to the problem of the unconscious—known to the
romantics but made universally public since their time—and
on the other, to the fear of consequences in a world less and
less receptive to eccentricity. With Samuel Butler and Oscar
Wilde, Shaw and James, the paradoxes and inconsistencies of
private behavior and public judgment became common property. The first three of these writers turned conventions inside
out by converting platitudes. Thus Butler could say something
important and truthful by the inversion, "It's better to have
loved and lost than never to have lost at all," a trick which he
called "quoting from memory." But the trick once learned,
their juniors continued to use it, not as an attack on Victorian
morality, which was dead, but as a day-to-day defense against
life at large. It is bound to disgust as soon as routine replaces wit, e.g. this fragment from Ezra Pound's "The Social
Order":—

> This government official
> Whose wife is several years his senior
> Has such a caressing air
> When he shakes hands with young ladies.
> —*Personae*, N. Y., 1926, 115

The quotation in my text is from the same volume, 114. To
compare with E. E. Cummings's tone when bringing together

money and roses, here is the same simile handled by a romantic: "Money . . . is, in its effects and laws, as beautiful as roses." (Emerson, *Works,* Riverside ed., 1883, III, 221) Henry James must have had our contemporaries in mind as he wrote: "When they had hustled all sensibility out of their lives, they invented the fiction that they felt too much to utter." ("The Marriages," *Novels and Tales,* Vol. 23, 238)

Yet it would not be fair to suggest that no one before our day suffered from paralyzing self-consciousness and sulky despair. One can put side by side with Eliot's line (from *Ash Wednesday, XXV*) about terror and surrender, Wordsworth's line, from *Resolution and Independence,* about

> . . . the fear that kills
> And hope unwilling to be fed . . .

Page 120. THE ROMANTIC NIGHTINGALE. We saw above how Diderot, reporting Galiani, launched the nightingale as a critical symbol. Among the romanticists, Goethe gave the image its most precise significance. To him it represented the completeness of achievement through the power to transcend its own class. (*Elective Affinities,* Ch. xi) In the modern period, it has come to represent an impossible dream, a beauty that cannot survive, or which is at least spoiled—as by Sweeney—through contact with sordidness. A French musician, Auric, has described Erik Satie's score, *Parade,* as "submitting very humbly to reality, which drowns out the nightingale's song under the clanging of street-cars." Eliot used the nightingale again in *The Wasteland,* "And still she cried, and still the world pursues, 'Jug Jug' to dirty ears." (II, 102)

In this contrast are embraced the technique and the message of modernism. A French critic observes the same obsession in French poetry, and he draws an instructive parallel between the utterances of two young diplomat-poets separated by a century—Lamartine and Paul Morand. Both sang their loves on the same shores of the Bay of Naples. Lamartine finds sadness and beauty. In Morand's free verse, the hotel on the hillside comes in for a satirical description in the very terms in which it is advertised: "Large verandah, weekly dances, moderate

prices, pretty view," near the end of which the beloved breaks
in with:—

"What is really pretty is legs like mine!"
Yet already death was advancing behind us,
On rubber soles.

(Gérard Bauër, "Les Métamorphoses du romantisme," *Cahiers
de la Quinzaine*, 1928, 2nd, 8) The critic concludes, like
Constant Lambert, that anti-romanticism is a metamorphosed
negative romanticism; in short, that the wish for the nightingale is still with us.

He documents his conclusion with statements from contemporary writers, most of whom seem to agree with the theory
of contrasts which I quote from André Breton. (*Petite Antholo-
gie du Surréalisme*, ed. Geo. Hugnet, Paris, 1934, 24) For instance, Alfred Colling: "The only progress we can make from
one generation to the next is to unite in our heart more and
more contradictory and seemingly exclusive sentiments. . . ."
And Philip Datz: "My reason says: 'everything is quite useless';
My passion says: 'everything is worth undertaking' (At the
same time)." (Bauër, *op. cit.*, 53–54. See also Ramon del Valle-
Inclán's "deformed esthetic" in *Luces de Bohemia*, 1920)

Page 120. MISS RUTH BAILEY takes up the tale in her lucid argument for modern poetry, which contains (p. 88) the passage
I quote. It is representative of the current belief that romantic
poetry (a) lacked contrasts (b) dealt exclusively with "poetic
objects" (see Mr. Tate's assertion to this effect, *Reason in Madness*, 83–84) and (c) was ignorant of wit and the seventeenth-
century masters. It is worth recalling that Coleridge, for one,
acknowledged his debt to Crashaw and had a high regard for
Donne, and that it was the French romantics who vindicated
the memory of the neglected minor poets of the classic century.
The great ones, they naturally knew by heart.

As for point (b) it is enough to say that Scott and Byron
admired the verse of Swift and Crabbe; that the two former
prided themselves on the prosaic quality of their verse ("Damn
it, Tom, don't be poetical," said Byron to Moore); that a modern like Auden has acknowledged a debt to Byron for precisely

this hard, anti-poetic quality combined with movement, as in the opening lines of *The Siege of Corinth;* and that "poetic objects" do not by any means preponderate among the themes chosen by Wordsworth, Goethe, Victor Hugo, or Pushkin.

On the score of wit and contrast, I shall content myself with giving one scholarly opinion: "Flippant, cynical pieces were deliberately inserted throughout [Heine's] *Buch der Lieder* (1827) . . . praises of the joys of sensual love hard on songs breathing eternal devotion . . . Heine had his full share of Romantic irony . . . conscious of a tendency to sentimentalize [he] constantly pulls himself up with a jerk. . . ."—L. A. Willoughby, *The Romantic Movement in Germany,* Oxford, 1930, 136

Page 121. CONSTANT LAMBERT's paragraph comes from *Music Ho! A Study of Music in Decline,* London, 1934, 178–179.

Page 122. VALÉRY's metaphysics is expounded in his *Ebauche d'un Serpent* and exemplified in *Cimetière Marin.* On the importance of "smallness" in the eyes of certain moderns, it may not be unjust to refer to the "three small books" that Mr. Eliot mentions in the preface to *Essays for Launcelot Andrews,* drawing our attention to the amount of time he had planned to take in composing them. Mr. Stravinsky's judgment upon himself is quoted by Henry Boys, "Stravinsky," *Monthly Musical Record,* December 1934, 228. (See also Stravinsky's own *avertissement* of his new classicism in *The Dominant,* December 1927.)

Page 123. G. M. YOUNG's strictures on LYTTON STRACHEY occurred in a review of E. Wingfield Stratford's *Victorian Sunset* in *Life and Letters,* February 1931, 144–145. It was a thrill for the modern ego when Mr. Strachey's hints and promises of a new art were first heard: the biographer was going to use "a subtler strategy" upon "that singular epoch," the Victorian Age; "he will attack his subject in unexpected places . . . shoot a sudden revealing searchlight into obscure recesses, hitherto undivined; . . . a little bucket . . . will bring up to the light of day some characteristic specimen . . . to be examined with a careful curiosity. . . ." (*Eminent Victorians,* Preface, v)

As Strachey explicitly admitted, the sources of the "new art" were French—a combination of the short biography with Sainte-Beuve's gossipy technique. What is less generally known is that the *long* biography with malicious intent had already been practised in France, and for the same modern purpose of "debunking" romanticism. See, for instance, A. Boschot's three malevolent volumes on Berlioz (1906–1913), in which the sporting outfit of the revealing searchlight and the little bucket is already detailed. (Notes to Vol. I); or again, see Christian Maréchal's *La Jeunesse de Lamennais* using against its subject, and through him against Rousseau, the modern device of the revolving standard. I mean by this the biographer's determination to be satisfied with nothing: if Lamennais is gloomy, that is a sign of his evil; if he conquers his depression, that proves him shallow; if he admits that perfect humility is hard to attain, he is a rebel; if he thinks he is somewhat less troubled by pride, that shows his conceit: Rousseau and the romantic ego are represented as causes of these manifestations of character, never before known to man. Such lack of biographical judgment justifies A. R. Orage's deliberate use of the argument *ad personam:* "How do *you* compare with the people you write about?" (*Readers and Writers*, 64)

To see the hand of Sainte-Beuve in all this would be to adopt a conspiracy theory of modern culture. The truth is that the modern ego adopts Sainte-Beuve because he felt towards romanticism as we do. He was a disappointed romantic poet and a man with badly twisted feelings. We may forget his unamiable person, but as a fine scholar remarked in pointing out the evil effects of the doctrine: "*Il faut dire du mal de Sainte-Beuve . . .* The great critic, if we have one, will have to begin with a dissection of Sainte-Beuve, to clear the track." (Denis Saurat, *Perspectives*, Paris, 1938, 38. For the same writer's comment on the life of Rimbaud, *op. cit.*, 121)

The modern attitude toward the FRENCH SYMBOLIST POETS is an unprecedented case of critical charity. Consult Havelock Ellis's *From Rousseau to Proust* for examples, or read the surprising feat of criticism performed by Valéry on one of Baudelaire's sonnets: "Out of the fourteen lines of *Recueillement* five or six are unquestionably weak. But the first and last . . . are so magical that the middle does not reveal its ineptitude and can easily be accounted null and void. It takes a very great poet to perform such miracles." In the same miraculous vein, Mme. de Noailles called Verlaine simple, divine, and a saint.

All this goes to prove that we cannot cut loose from Symbolism; the bulk of our art still depends on it. To see the network of relations between modern culture and the first quarter of the nineteenth century, see such writers as: A. J. George (*Lamartine and Romantic Unanimism*), Rebecca West (*Ending in Earnest*), Edwin Muir (*Transition*), R. P. Blackmur (*The Double Agent*), and Cyril Connolly (*Enemies of Promise*).

Page 124. I have several times referred to French anti-romanticism as "official." I meant two things by it—one, that the majority of French writers and artists had for the past eighty years adopted a conventional anti-romantic "line," which left the students and defenders of romanticism with a misplaced burden of proof; and two, that of this majority, many were academicians. It is also true that the anti-romantics were frequently opponents of the Republican regime, so that one would have supposed actual officialdom favorable to romanticism. It did not turn out so, for complex political reasons, and for the more simple one which Proust noted down somewhere, that the "friends of the people" want to show how pure and classical their taste is, thus atoning for their democratic politics. Even among men unaffected by such motives no agreement obtains. Compare, for example, Count de Roussy de Sales's belief that romanticism in France was a transient phenomenon with the reactionary Henry Bordeaux's apprehension of "romanticism always threatening our literature from within." (*Pélerinages littéraires*, 1905, 201) An excellent survey of the whole politico-cultural question is Hugo Friedrich, *Das Antiromantische Denken im Modernen Frankreich: sein System und seine Herkunft*, Munich, 1935.

Page 126. SEX. If a date must be set for the public recognition of this new "element," let it be 1883. This was the year during which the sales of Fitzgerald's *Rubáiyát of Omar Khayyám*, which had languished since its appearance in 1859, began mysteriously to mount up, until by 1900 it was the best-selling poem since *In Memoriam* just half a century before. Previous to 1883, a good deal of underground and explosive action had taken place. No account of the rise of sexuality as against love would be complete without mention of Wagner's librettos, Baudelaire's *Fleurs du Mal*, Wilde's *Poems*, the translation of Schopenhauer, Nietzsche, and Dostoevski out of their native tongues, and the popularization of Darwinism, true and false, which stimulated three sociological and scientific efforts—birth control, sex hygiene and education, and psychiatry and psychoanalysis. (See for example the pioneer cases recorded in *The Amberley Papers*, I, 288, under date 1864; and Samuel Butler's letter concerning Dr. [later Sir Clifford] Allbutt's difficulties with the law in 1887.)

Shaw's pronouncement occurs in his "Postscript" to his biography by Frank Harris, where it is preceded by a reassertion of the belief that in sexual matters Rousseau's views were right. (242, 244) Shaw had previously written: "Sentimental controversies on the subject are endless; but they are useless, because nobody tells the truth. Rousseau did it by an extraordinary effort, aided by a superhuman faculty for human natural history, but the result was curiously disconcerting because, though the facts were so conventionally shocking that people felt they ought to matter a great deal, they actually mattered very little. And even at that everybody pretends not to believe him." (*Preface to "Overruled,"* 1912, 66)

On FREUD and the application of his ideas to literature and biography, see Lionel Trilling, "The Legacy of Sigmund Freud," *Kenyon Review*, spring 1940.

Page 128. Since modern poets have sought for a rhythm and language that might give their verse a popular use in the causes and battles of our day, I venture to remind the reader that Canto VI of Scott's *Lady of the Lake* played its part in the Peninsular War: while Sir Adam Fergusson's company was lying on the ground under artillery fire at Torres Vedras, he read them the warlike stanzas, interrupted only "by a joyous huzza whenever the French shot struck the bank close above them."—Lockhart, *Life of Scott*, London, 1914, 5 vols., II, 169.

Shelley wrote songs for the Luddite rebels and Byron for the Greeks.

Page 130. IRVING BABBITT's request for a humbling absolute has no doubt something to do with his general view of mankind. He says: "If one deals with human nature realistically, one may find here and there a person who is worthy of respect and occasionally one who is worthy of reverence." (*Democracy and Leadership*, 1924, 261) If this is the major premise of a humanist, "committed to the modern experiment," and of one, moreover, who wishes to annex Jesus as a classical type, one might well prefer to join the reactionary followers of Joseph de Maistre, whose anti-humanism had at least the true Christian grace to say, "When I look into my heart, I shudder at what a scoundrel must be." Babbitt's plea for a "realistic" reversal of popular sovereignty occupies pp. 235 ff., 264 ff., 276 ff. of the work cited. My paraphrase of Mr. Allen Tate's remarks is based on pp. 5, 7–8 of his *Reason and Madness*, N. Y., 1941.

Page 130. The worship of the GOLDEN AGE is, like any other belief, indifferent in itself. The test is, What does it produce in those who adopt it? Renaissance, Reformation, and Romanticism were in part based on illusions concerning the recapture of a better past. Among the romantics, notably Wordsworth and Goethe, illusions were quite consciously and pragmatically employed to achieve well-defined ends. The romantics "used" Greece and the Middle Ages. But the very fact that the Renaissance and Romanticism were inaccurate, mistaken, or willful in their reproduction of elements from those periods shows that they had a strong creative urge that no amount of retrospective fervor could down. It was ahead of them, and not in the past, that they saw the model society.

Nowadays, the main effort seems to be aimed at scholarliness and mutual policing rather than at work "in the spirit of" the chosen golden age. The going is heavy and solemn and pedantic, quite beyond the caricatures that Peacock drew a century ago of Mr. Chainmail and other romantic medievalists. See Stravinsky's sour castigation of everything but the well-worn. (*Poétique Musicale sous forme de Six Leçons*, Harvard Press, 1942, pp. 5, 6, 13, 14, 29, 42, 44) The "orderly progression from truth to truth" is the ideal of the neo-medieval education preached by Robert M. Hutchins. (*Higher Learning in America*, 96)

Page 131. CLASSIC REPOSE. Here are, as a last supplement on the subject, a few reminders concerning qualities we overlook in the works of the standard Greek authors: (1) In all the plays, the lyric character of the drama, its song, dance, animation, mass appeal, which differ much from the marmoreal representations we occasionally see, and also from the copies and pictures of the Greek marbles, since these were originally painted in gaudy colors, like the inside of the Gothic cathedrals in their newness. (2) In Homer, the lack of dignity, manliness, and other stoic virtues shown by Agamemnon, Achilles, Odysseus, etc. (3) In Aeschylus's *Prometheus*, the glorying of the hero in his rebellion: "Willingly, willingly I did it; never shall I deny the deed." We must take refuge in guesses about the two missing plays of the trilogy to imagine how this revolt can be turned into a portrayal of serenity. (4) In Sophocles's *Antigone*, Haemon's suicide for love; in the *Philoctetes* the querulous wails of the wounded and unprepossessing hero. (5) In Euripides, whom we are forced to call a romantic naturalist and psychologist, we try to pass off the "modernity" as that of a decadent third in the classic line of dramatists. He was in fact a contemporary of Sophocles and, far from thinking him decadent, Aristotle calls him the most tragic of the three. (6) In Aristophanes, we overlook—but for the wrong reasons—the sprawling form, the exuberance, exaggeration, lack of social responsibility, or at least of "city spirit"; and the encouragement to emotional release from the classic "inner check." None of this would need repeating were it not for what J. J. Chapman called "that conscientious and falsetto attempt to understand and appreciate Greek literature which our current teaching inculcates."—*Lucian, Plato and Greek Morals*, Boston, 1931, 171

VIII

Page 132. NAPOLEON a son of the Enlightenment. He is so interpreted in Geoffrey Bruun's *The Revolution and the*

French Imperium in the Langer Series (Harper). In many other works, particularly textbooks, Napoleon's influence on the romanticists is presented in such a way as to suggest that he was one of them. In one such book the student is told: "Then followed that vividly romantic period known as the Hundred Days."

Page 134. On the CLASSICISM of the French Revolution read first of all Harold T. Parker, *The Cult of Antiquity and the French Revolutionaries,* which contains enough references to Cato, Brutus, Plutarch, and the Spartans to convince those who have not dipped into revolutionary journalism and oratory itself. It could be argued, by the way, that the stilted, oracular element in, say, Victor Hugo's prose is a direct imitation of the revolutionary style, continued by Napoleon in his proclamations and orders to the troops.

For the relation of art to revolutionary feeling and the revolutionary authorities, see my chapter in *Of Human Freedom,* 66–95. Savary's letter to Mme. de Stael about her confiscated work is printed in her Preface; Napoleon's worry about literature is expressed in a letter to Cambacérès, 21 November 1806.

Page 135. REASON. The contemporary position I am attacking is lucidly put by W. T. Stace: "That reason is lord over will— this is the Greek theory of man's nature. That will is lord over reason, this—derived from Schopenhauer—is the Nietzschean view. These two theories of human nature flatly contradict each other. . . . There is an obvious issue here." (*The Destiny of Western Man,* N. Y., 1942, 86–87) Drawn in these terms, the issue makes it appear that Nietzsche, Samuel Butler, William James, Bernard Shaw, and Freud are "willful" and "enemies of reason." But the same contrast can be differently put, as it was by A. R. Orage: "The elemental instincts . . . cannot be permanently tyrannized over by 'reason,' nor should they be. The rule of reason should be that of a constitutional monarch under the direction of representatives, not of itself, but of the elemental instincts." (*Readers and Writers,* London, 1922, 159) Still another position, giving reason a fragment of independent originating power, is developed by Graham Wallas in *The Art of Thought.* These writers make it clear that the problem is not so clear-cut as Mr. Stace would have us think. Indeed his view belongs to that species of thinking which I have called "thinking in pairs," and it appeals to our tendency periodically to substitute soot for chalk in our diet—reason then will; materialism then idealism; absolutism then relativism; religion then science; individualism then tyranny.

To be reasonable about reason one must distinguish, as I try to do in the text, between reason as an instrument and reason as a body of accepted truths. Reason may be an instrument for will, for passion, or for "itself": this does not alter the fact that at any historic moment it may not be identical with the beliefs which it has previously produced. This is what Wilde meant when he said: "Anybody can be reasonable, but to be sane is not common." (*A Critic in Pall-Mall*, 172) Certainly an historian is bound to take the same view, however he may reword it. "Reason," Augustine Birrell reminds us, "is the philosophy which is in vogue for the moment." Hence the "Test of Reason" should be applied "cautiously and possibly humbly to the lives and creeds of our predecessors." (*More Obiter Dicta*, 1924, 69) What is good for our predecessors is equally good for our contemporaries, with this difference, that we can seldom know in the present what the "sane" but "unreasonable" attitude will yield. This follows obviously from Shaw's maxim which dates back to *Man and Superman*, 1903, 238.

Page 136. CLASSICISM IS ORTHODOXY. T. S. Eliot, whose definition of "classical" seems to me elusive and unhistorical, nevertheless admits (in *After Strange Gods: A primer of modern heresy*) that the orthodox goes with the classical and the heretical with the romantic. The terms "absorption and elimination" applied to successive epochs of history I owe to an interesting conversation with Professor La Piana of Harvard; but the notion of alternating tasks set by "history" in different centuries is of course as old as the romantic period itself. Hegel, Saint-Simon, Comte, and many others filled it with diverse contents. In form it corresponds to evolutionary theory, though without implying progress.

The DEMAND FOR DOCTRINE lends strong support to the

notion just set forth. What is curious is to see how many combinations of systems may be made in answer to this imperious urge. It is not infrequent to note a passage, actual or theoretical, from Marxism to Thomism, and sometimes a junction of the two, according to which Marx, as an atheistical materialist, is simply an incomplete prophet of the full Thomist realism. Would it be out of order to suggest that if Marx is to be unofficially canonized among the leaders of neomedievalism, he would appropriately be known as "The Choleric Doctor"?

Acknowledgments

Permission to reprint copyright matter has been courteously granted by the following:—

The Colt Press, for an excerpt from *The Pragmatic Test* by H. B. Parkes.

The John Day Company, Inc., for excerpts from *Reason, Social Myths and Democracy* by Sidney Hook and *The Future of Industrial Man* by Peter F. Drucker.

E. P. Dutton & Co., Inc., for material from their editions of Rousseau's *Social Contract* (ed. G. D. H. Cole) and Landor's *Imaginary Conversations* (ed. H. Ellis), as well as excerpts from R. D'O. Butler's *The Roots of National Socialism*.

Harcourt, Brace and Company, Inc., for an excerpt from *H.W.M.* by H. J. Massingham.

Harper & Brothers, for two selections from *Personal Record* by Julian Green.

Houghton Mifflin Company, for excerpts from *Mont Saint Michel and Chartres* by Henry Adams; *Life and Letters of John J. Chapman* by M. A. DeWolfe Howe; and *Rousseau and Romanticism, Democracy and Leadership* and *On Being Creative* by Irving Babbitt.

Longmans, Green and Co., Inc., for material from the *Living Thoughts Library* editions of Mazzini, Thoreau, and Schopenhauer.

The Macmillan Company, for excerpts from *Democracy Today and Tomorrow* by Eduard Beneš; *The Eighteen Sixties* by Lascelles Abercrombie; *A Study in Aesthetics* by L. Arnaud Reid; and *The Early Life of Thomas Hardy* and *The Later Years of Thomas Hardy* by F. E. Hardy.

W. W. Norton & Company, Inc., for excerpts from *History As the Story of Liberty* by Benedetto Croce, and the selection by J. P. Bishop from *After the Genteel Tradition* (ed. Malcolm Cowley).

The Odyssey Press, Inc., for material from *Complete Poems and Selected Letters of Keats* (ed. C. D. Thorpe).

The Oxford University Press, for excerpts from Gibbon's *Autobiography, Hector Berlioz* by T. S. Wotton, and *The Romantic Movement in Germany* by L. A. Willoughby.

G. P. Putnam's Sons for excerpts from *Enchanted Wanderer, the Life of C. M. von Weber,* by Richard and Lucy Poate Stebbins.

Reynal and Hitchcock, Inc., for material from *The Destiny of Western Man* by W. T. Stace.

Charles Scribner's Sons, for a selection from *A History of English Literature* by W. V. Moody and R. M. Lovett.

Silver Burdett Company, for material from *Literary Aims and Art* by H. R. Steeves.

Simon and Schuster, Inc., for excerpts from the selections by Thomas Mann and Beatrice Webb in *What I Believe* (ed. C. Fadiman).

The Vanguard Press, for an excerpt from *Shall Not Perish From the Earth* by Ralph Barton Perry.

Mr. John Dos Passos for an excerpt from *The Ground We Stand On.*

President Lewis W. Jones of Bennington College for an excerpt from his address, "Liberal Education and the War."

Index

Abelard, 130

Abercrombie, L., on Wordsworth, 85, 211; on romantic drama, 161; on Shelley, 200

"Abolitionism": and romantic purpose, 141; artistic, 154

Academy: French, of Letters, 42, 45; French, of Painting, 43, 59, 72, 186, 194; English, of Painting, 59, 194; ideals of, 110; dictatorship, 185, 189; bibliography, 186; Reynolds and, 194

"Action Painters," 141–42, 143

Addison: quoted by Hume on art, 60; *The Greatest English Poets*, 188 and n.; on Chaucer, 188

Aeschylus, rebel Prometheus, 231

Agar, H., 169

Agate, James, 156

Alcibiades, 79

Allbutt, C., 229

Amberley Papers, 229

America: example of usage, 4; discovery of, 53; romantics travel to, 60; land of romanticism in action, 133, 168; James the philosopher of, 133; twentieth-century, 146 ff.

Ampère, J. J., 173

Anderson, Eugene, on nationalism, 212

Andler, Charles, 222

Apollinaire, G., 118

Aquinas: *Summa Theologica*, 129, 130; on man's nature, 176. *See also* Neo-Thomism

Architecture: romantic, 70; railroad, 152. *See also* Gothic Architecture

Aristophanes, art of, 231

Aristotle: and social contract, 27; quoted, 177; paradox on poetry and history, 73; in Dante's work, 128; prohibited in 1209, 130; dramatic unities, 188; on Euripides, 231

Arnold, Matthew: influence of his criticism, 106–7; neo-classic *Merope*, 110; and modern biographers, 123

Arnold, Thurman, 156

Artz, F. B., 163

Astrea. See Romances

Auden, 225

Augustine, Saint, 176

Auric, 194, 224

Babbitt, Irving: anti-Rousseau, 18, 161; on discipline, 130; on Kipling, 160; A. Kazin on, 165; on gash in Rydal Mount, 216–17; on worth of mankind, 230

Bach, J. S., 139, 148, 159

Bailey, Ruth, 120–21, 225

Balzac, 74, 98, 199, 215; as a realist, 62, 106, 212, 217; proponent of science, 65; his prose unlike Stendhal's, 71; and Napoleon, 80; fictional heroes, 80, 212; powers of work, 80, 82;